COOL SPOTS
CÔTE D'AZUR

teNeues

Imprint

Editor: Catherine Collin

Editorial assistants: Maia Francisco, Julio Fajardo

Photography: Roger Casas

Introduction: Catherine Collin

Layout & Pre-press: Oriol Serra Juncosa, Zahira Rodríguez Mediavilla

Translations: Bridget Vranckx (English), Christian Siegmund (German), Julio Fajardo (Spanish), Barbara Burani (Italian)

Produced by Loft Publications
www.loftpublications.com

Published by teNeues Publishing Group

teNeues Verlag GmbH + Co. KG
Am Selder 37
47906 Kempen, Germany
Tel.: 0049-(0)2152-916-0
Fax: 0049-(0)2152-916-111
Press department:
arehn@teneues.de
Tel.: 0049-(0)2152-916-202

teNeues
International Sales Division
Speditionstraße 17
40221 Düsseldorf, Germany
Tel.: 0049-(0)211-994597-0
Fax: 0049-(0)211-994597-40
E-mail: books@teneues.de

teNeues Publishing Company
16 West 22nd Street
New York, NY 10010, USA
Tel.: 001-212-627-9090
Fax: 001-212-627-9511

teNeues Publishing UK Ltd.
P.O. Box 402
West Byfleet
KT14 7ZF, Great Britain
Tel.: 0044-1932-403509
Fax: 0044-1932-403514

teNeues France S.A.R.L.
93 rue Bannier
45000 Orleans, France
Tel.: 0033-2-38541071
Fax: 0033-2-38625340

www.teneues.com

ISBN-13: 978-3-8327-9154-4

© 2007 teNeues Verlag GmbH + Co. KG, Kempen

Printed in Italy

Bibliographic information published by Die Deutsche Bibliothek.
Die Deutsche Bibliothek lists this publication in the Deutsche Nationalbibliografie; detailed bibliographic data is available in the Internet at http://dnb.ddb.de.

Contents	Page

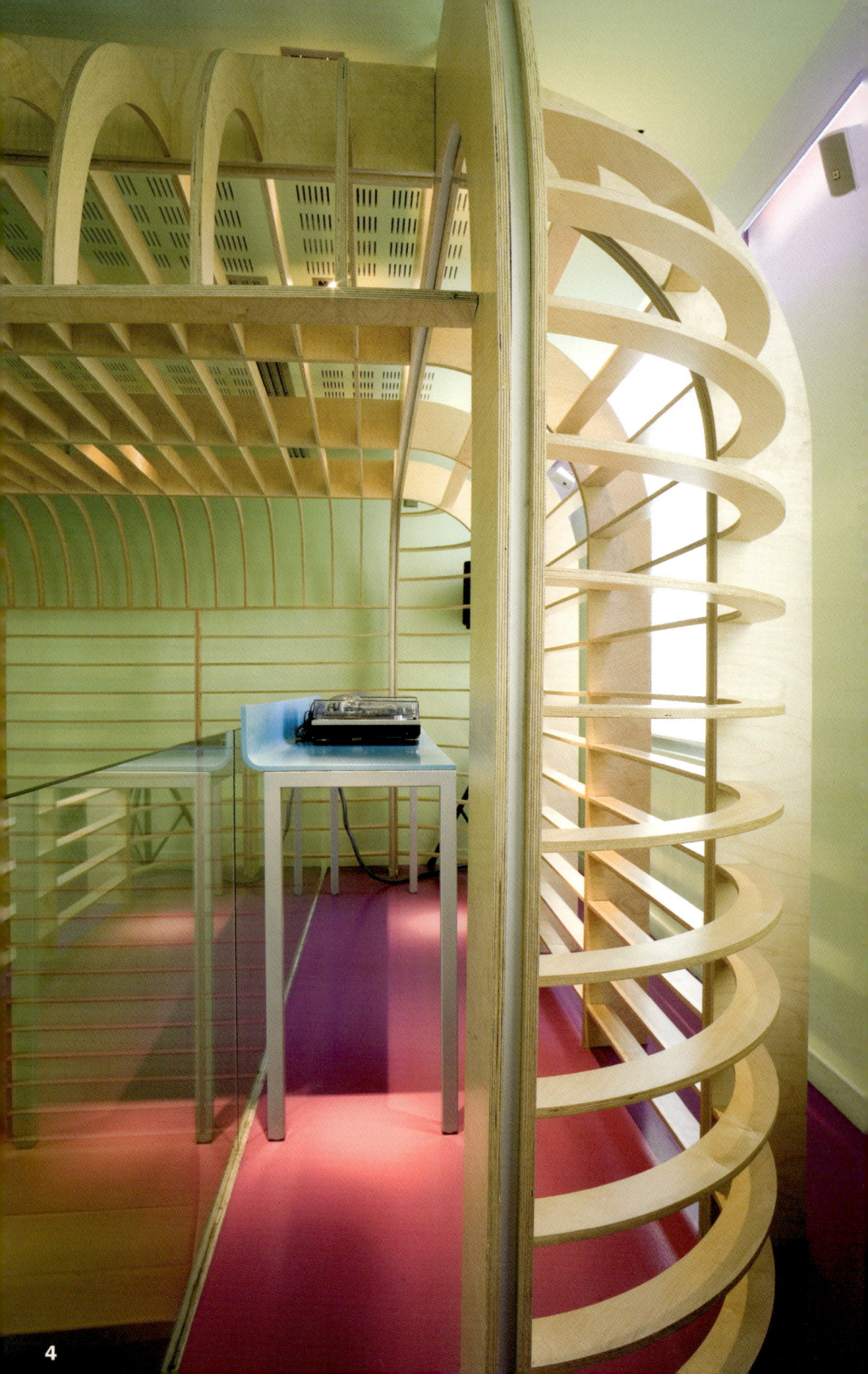

Introduction

Est-ce dû à la douceur de son climat ? A la célébrité de ses hôtes ? Aux événements médiatiques qui ponctuent son agenda ? Quelques soient les raisons qui poussent chaque année des milliers de visiteurs à sillonner les quelques 200 kilomètres de côte qui s'étendent entre Bandol jusqu' à Menton, elles représentent autant de possibilités de découvrir les petits joyaux qu'offrent la Côte d'Azur.

Dès le 18ème siècle, la Côte d'Azur est une des premières régions éluent par les précurseurs du tourisme : la noblesse britannique. Ainsi, Lady Fitzgerald s'installe à Nice dès 1755. Toute l'Europe des grandes familles bourgeoises la suit, puis les artistes tels que Cézanne, Bonnard et van Gogh. Les vacanciers de tout azimut affluent depuis sur les traces des grandes stars et des petites célébrités.

L'abondance d'un public cosmopolite et fortuné a privilégié pendant la première moitié du 20ème siècle une architecture très originale : hôtels luxueux, casinos rivalisant d'originalité, villas exubérantes, un univers très hétéroclite qui ne cesse d'étonner.

Aujourd'hui, même si les zones urbaines se sont énormément amplifiées, la côte continue à offrir une multitudes de lieux privilégiés. Que ce soit pour une escapade en amoureux ou pour des vacances en famille, un soir de libre entre deux rendez-vous ou un week-end entre amis, *Cool Spots Côte d'Azur* propose une sélection de 30 possibilités de découvrir les must de cette région et de trouver en toutes occasions ce que les autres chercheront en vain : que se soit la terrasse ombragée où boire un café, la plage idéale où oublier les rigueurs de l'hivers (et exhiber son nouveau bikini !), le club le plus en vogue où aller danser ou le restaurant novateur où déguster une gastronomie surprenante.

Une invitation au voyage et à la détente donc, dans la plus chatoyante et glamoureuse des régions françaises !

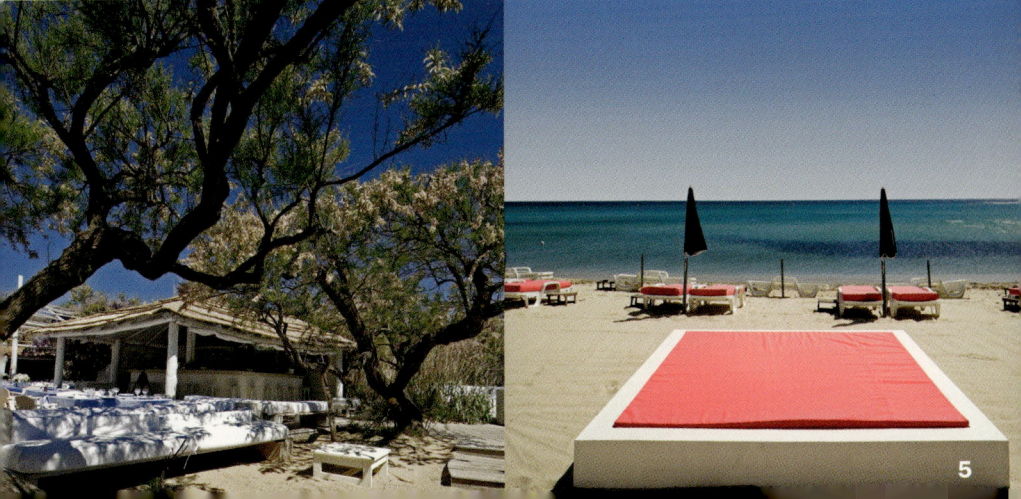

Introduction

There are many reasons people are attracted to the 200-odd kilometres of coast stretching between Bandol and Menton—its mild climate, its famous guests or year-round high-profile media events—and just as many possibilities of discovering the Côte d'Azur's little gems.

In the 18th century, the Côte d'Azur was one of the first to be chosen as a holiday destination by the vanguards of tourism, the British nobility. Thus, Lady Fitzgerald settled in Nice in 1755, closely followed by Europe's great bourgeois families and, later, artists such as Cézanne, Bonnard and van Gogh. Nowadays, the seacost is flooded with holidaymakers from all over following in the footsteps of great stars and small celebrities.

Thanks to an affluent stream of cosmopolitan and wealthy visitors throughout the first half of the 20th century, the region now boasts some very original architecture leaving a very heterogeneous world that never ceases to amaze, including luxurious hotels, casinos vying for first place in originality and exuberant villas.

Even though the urban areas have grown immensely, the coast continues to offer many privileged places. Be it a lover's get-away or a family holiday, a free night in-between meetings or a weekend away with friends, *Cool Spots Côte d'Azur* offers a selection of 30 possibilities to discover this region's musts and helps find something for every occasion while others search in vain—a shaded terrace to have a coffee, the ideal beach to forget about the hard winter (and flaunt your new bikini!), the trendiest clubs to show off your dance moves or an innovative restaurant to taste some surprising cuisine.

So, accept our invitation to travel to and relax in France's most sparkling and glamorous region.

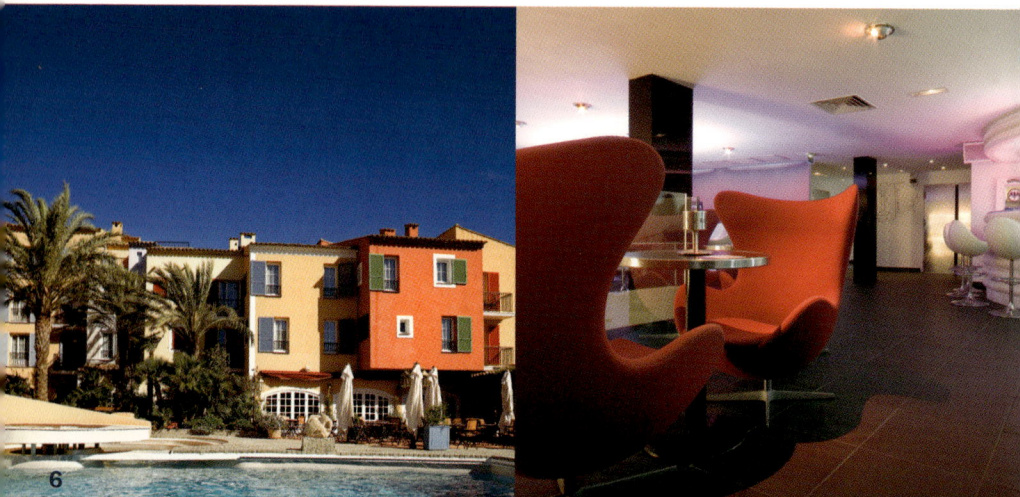

Einleitung

Liegt es am milden Klima? An der Berühmtheit ihrer Gäste? Oder ist es die Fülle medienwirksamer Ereignisse, die jahrein jahraus ihren Kalender füllen? Was auch immer die Gründe sind, die jedes Jahr tausende Besucher dazu bewegen, diesen etwa 200 Kilometer langen Küstenstrich zu bereisen, der sich von Bandol nach Menton erstreckt – sie stehen für eine Vielzahl an Möglichkeiten, die kleinen Schätze zu entdecken, die die Côte d'Azur zu bieten hat.

Schon seit dem 18. Jahrhundert gehört die Côte d'Azur zu den Regionen, die von dem britischen Adel, den Tourismuspionieren, als Ziel ihrer Sommerfrische auserkoren wurden. So kam Lady Fitzgerald bereits 1755 nach Nizza, gefolgt von großbürgerlichen europäischen Familien und schließlich auch bekannten Künstlern wie Cézanne, Bonnard und van Gogh. Inzwischen strömen die Urlauber von überall her an den Küstenstrich, um auf den Spuren der großen Stars und kleinen Berühmtheiten zu wandeln.

Das zahlreiche kosmopolitische und vermögende Publikum der ersten Hälfte des 20. Jahrhunderts hat maßgeblich zur Originalität der Architektur beigetragen. Es entstanden allenthalben luxuriöse Hotels, um Einfallsreichtum wetteifernde Spielkasinos und überschwängliche Villen, kurzum: eine äußerst abwechslungsreiche und unablässig beeindruckende Welt.

Heutzutage bietet die Côte d'Azur trotz der enormen Ausdehnung ihrer urbanen Zentren eine Vielzahl außergewöhnlicher und einzigartiger Winkel und Fleckchen. Sei es für ein amouröses Abenteuer oder den Familienurlaub, einen freien Abend zwischen zwei Rendez-vous oder für ein Wochenende mit Freunden: *Cool Spots Côte d'Azur* bietet eine Auswahl von 30 Möglichkeiten, um die Highlights dieser Region zu entdecken und das zu finden, was andere vergeblich suchen. Etwa eine schattige Terrasse, um einen Kaffee zu trinken, oder den idealen Strand, um den Winterfrust zu vergessen (und den nagelneuen Bikini zur Schau zu tragen!), den angesagtesten Tanzklub oder ein ausgefallenes Restaurant mit überraschender Gastronomie.

Dies ist eine Einladung zum Reisen oder einfach zum Entspannen – in einer der schillerndsten und glamourösesten Regionen Frankreichs.

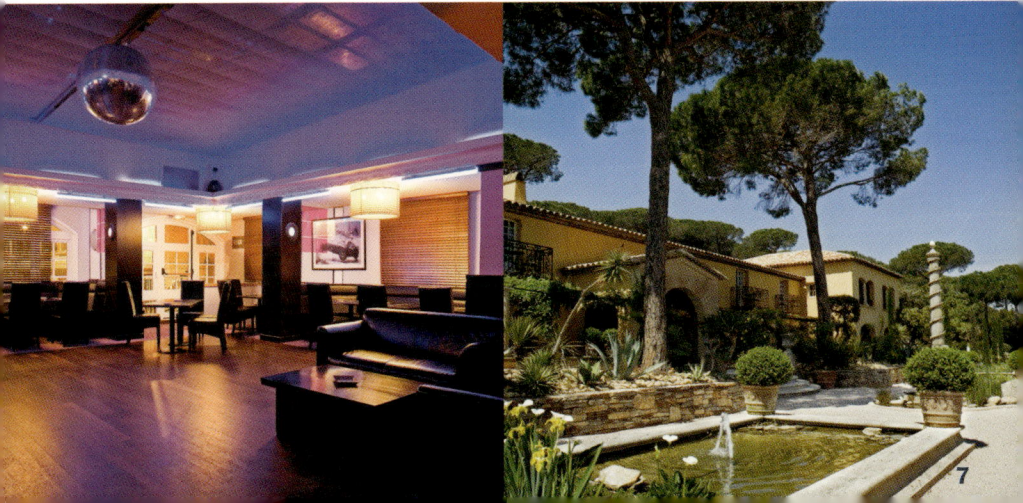

Introducción

¿Será la dulzura de su clima? ¿La fama de sus visitantes? ¿Serán los actos mediáticos que colman su agenda? Son muchas las razones que llevan a miles de visitantes a surcar cada año los más de 200 kilómetros de costa entre Bandol y Menton. Cada una de ellas representa una posibilidad de descubrir las pequeñas joyas que ofrece la Costa Azul.

En el siglo XVIII, la Costa Azul fue uno de los primeros destinos de veraneo elegidos por los pioneros del turismo: la nobleza británica. Así, Lady Fitzgerald se instaló en Niza en 1755 y todas las grandes familias de la burguesía europea siguieron su ejemplo. Más tarde llegaron artistas como Cézanne, Bonnard o van Gogh. Hoy en día, los veraneantes de todas partes del mundo siguen los pasos de grandes estrellas y pequeñas celebridades.

La afluencia de un público cosmopolita y adinerado privilegió durante la primera mitad del siglo XX una arquitectura tremendamente original: hoteles lujosos, casinos que rivalizan en originalidad, exuberantes villas, un universo realmente variopinto que no deja de asombrar al visitante.

Aunque las zonas urbanas se hayan expandido enormemente, la costa sigue ofreciendo multitud de lugares con encanto. Ya sea como destino de una escapada de enamorados o para pasar las vacaciones en familia, una cita para una tarde libre o un fin de semana entre amigos, *Cool Spots Côte d'Azur* propone una selección de 30 posibilidades para descubrir los establecimientos de visita obligatoria de la zona y encontrar fácilmente lo que los demás buscarán en vano: ya sea una terraza perfectamente sombreada o el lugar idóneo para tomar un café, la playa ideal en la que olvidarse de las inclemencias del invierno (¡y mostrar el nuevo bikini!), el club de moda para bailar o el restaurante más innovador donde disfrutar de la asombrosa gastronomía.

¡Una invitación al viaje y al descanso en la más soleada y glamourosa de las regiones francesas!

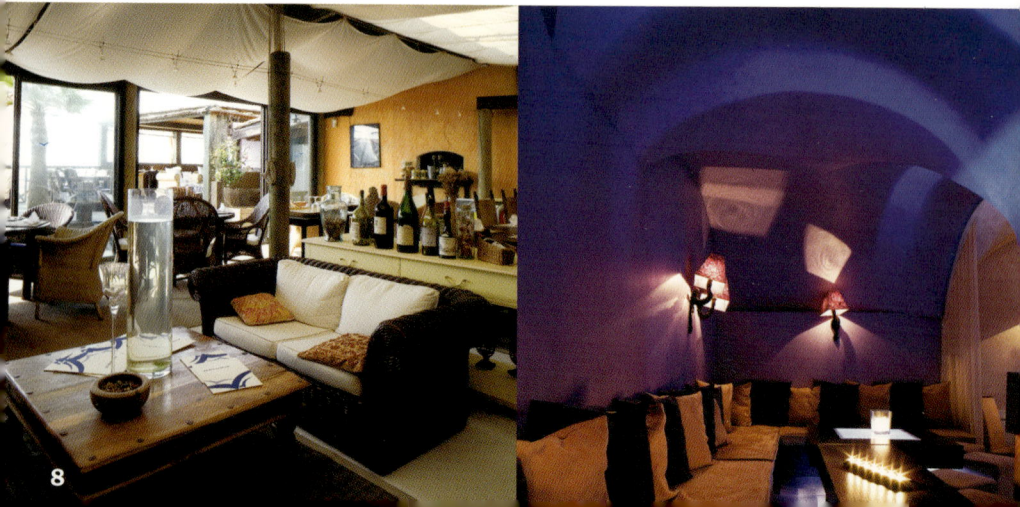

Introduzione

Sarà per la mitezza del suo clima? Per le celebrità che la frequentano? Per la sua fitta agenda di appuntamenti mondani? Qualunque siano le ragioni che spingono ogni anno migliaia di visitatori a percorrere i circa 200 chilometri delle sue coste, tra Bandol fino a Mentone, esse rappresentano altrettante possibilità di scoprire i piccoli gioielli che offre la Costa Azzurra.
Già nel XVIII secolo, la Costa Azzurra era il luogo di villeggiatura scelto dai precursori del turismo: i nobili britannici. Lady Fitzgerald si trasferisce a Nizza dal 1755 in poi, seguita dai maggiori esponenti della grande borghesia europea e da artisti del calibro di Cézanne, Bonnard e van Gogh. Oggi i vacanzieri delle più diverse provenienze affluiscono sul posto, richiamati dalla presenza di grandi star e piccole celebrità.
La presenza maggioritaria di un pubblico cosmopolita e abbiente, ha propiziato, durante la prima metà del XX secolo, l'insorgere di una architettura molto particolare: lussuosi hotel, casinò tra i più originali e spettacolari ville formano un universo molto eterogeneo che non smette mai di sorprendere.
Oggi, nonostante le aree urbanizzate si siano enormemente estese, la costa continua ad offrire un gran numero di luoghi privilegiati. Che sia per una gita romantica, per trascorrere le vacanze in famiglia, per una serata libera tra due riunioni o un week-end tra amici, *Cool Spots Côte d'Azur* propone una rassegna di 30 possibilità per scoprire i must assoluti di questa regione e per trovare, in ogni occasione, quello che gli altri cercheranno in vano: un'ombreggiata terrazza dove bere un buon caffè, la spiaggia ideale in cui dimenticare i rigori dell'inverno (e mettere in mostra il nostro nuovo bikini!), il club all'ultimo grido dove andare a ballare o il ristorante del momento in cui gustare una gastronomia sorprendente.
Insomma, un invito a viaggiare e a trattenersi nella regione più effervescente e glamourosa di Francia!

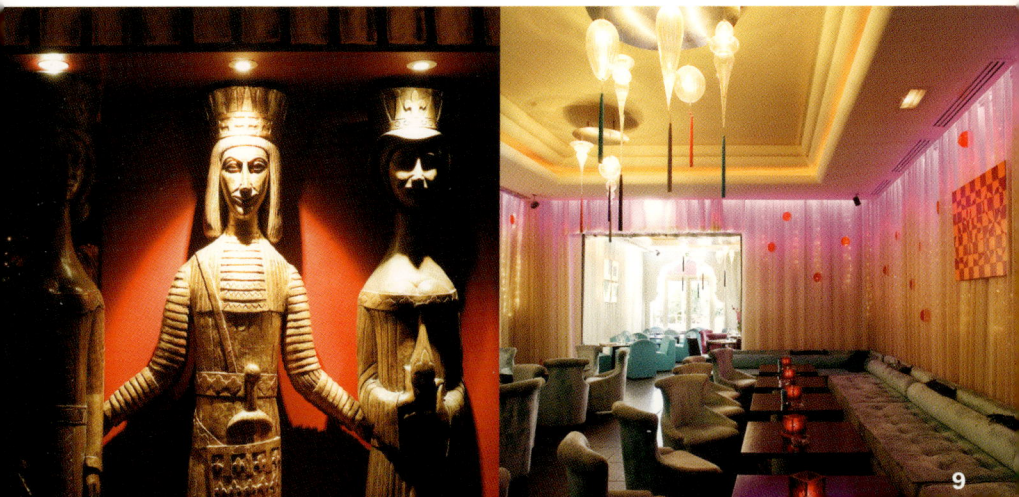

Avenue Princesse Grace | 98000 Monte-Carlo
Phone: +377 98 06 71 71
Opening hours: From 8 pm to 1 am
Special features: Created by Alain Ducasse, Bar & Boeuf is an original restaurant concept in which all dishes are based on two products: sea bass and beef

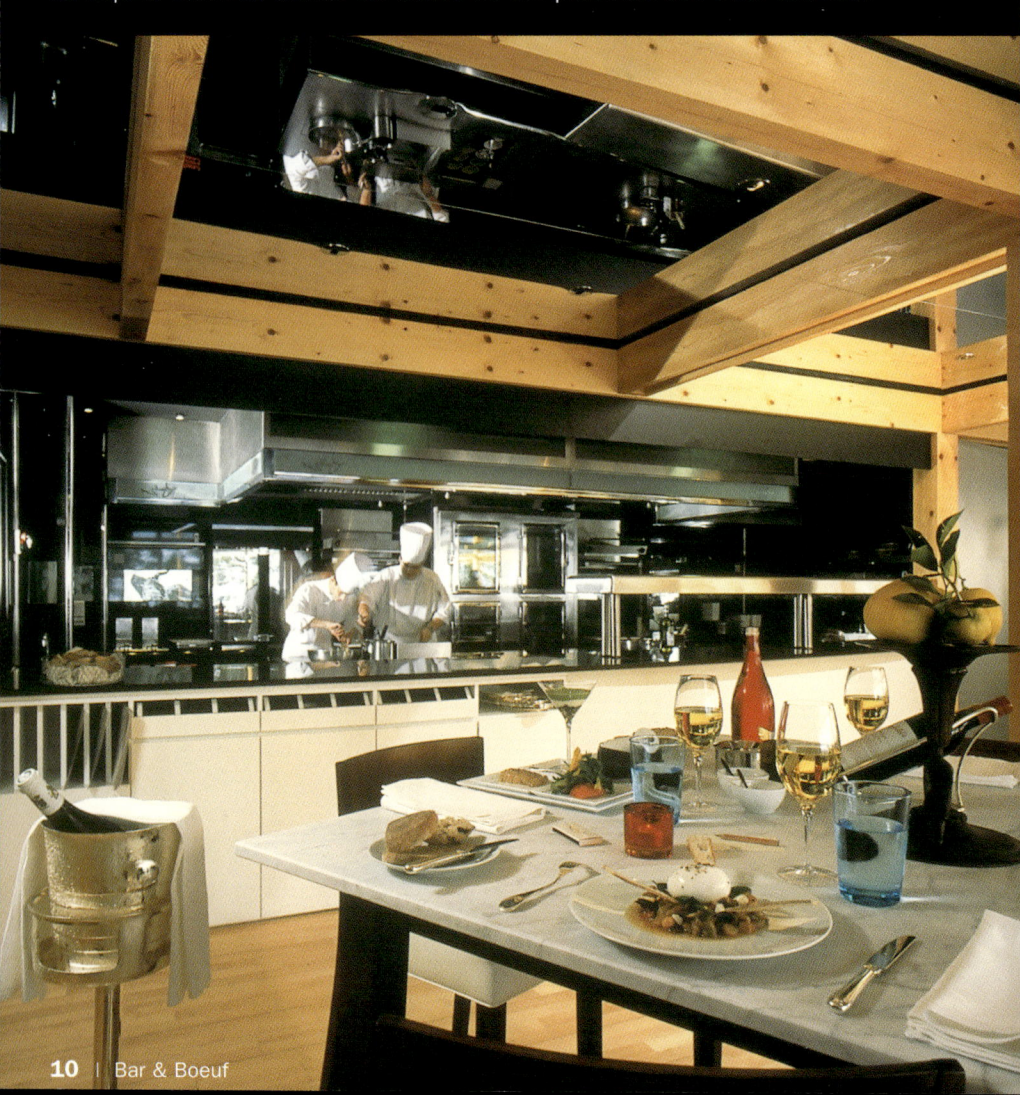

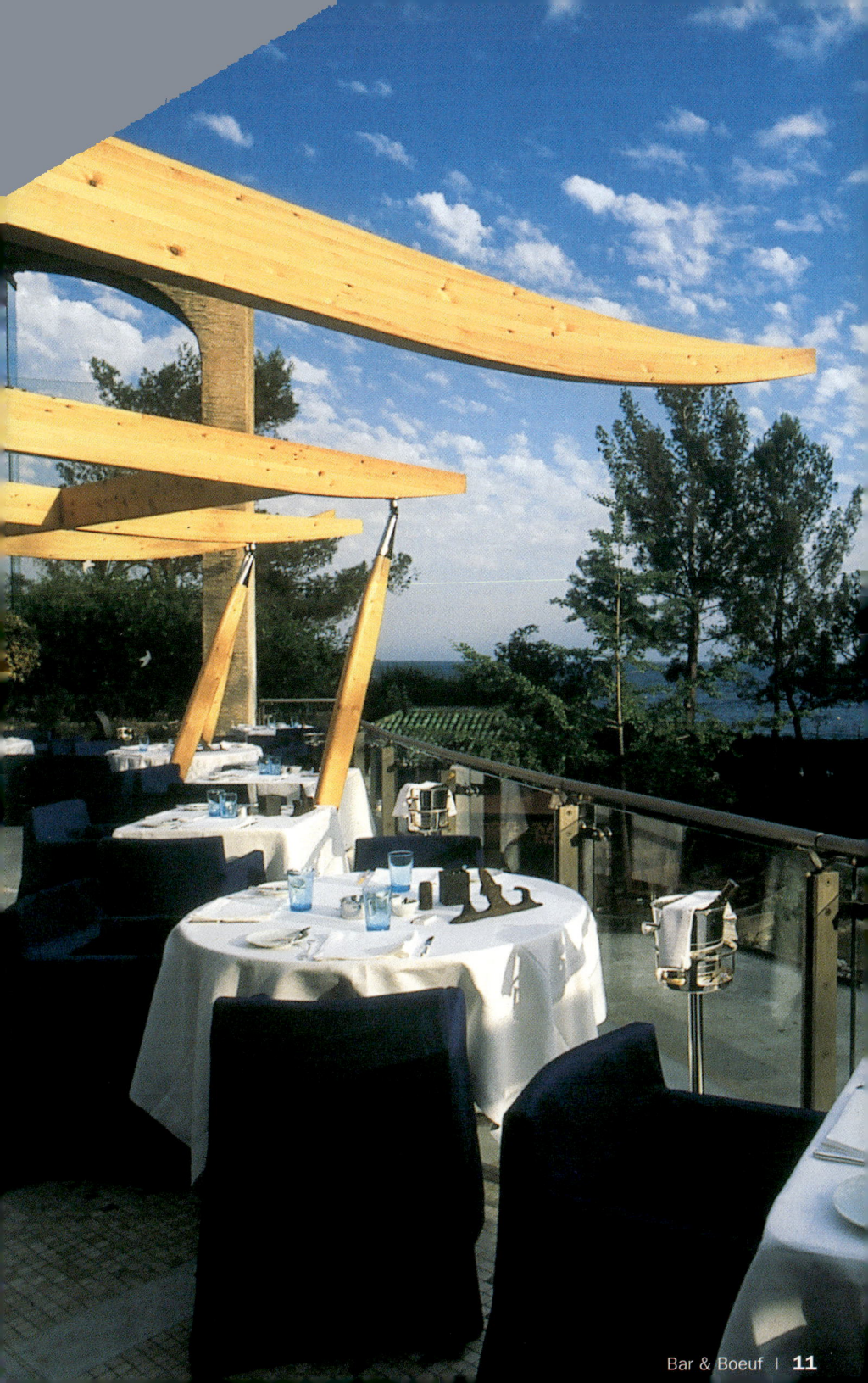

Beefbar & Co

Design: Emile Humbert

42 Quai Jean-Charles Rey | 98000 Monte-Carlo
Phone: +377 97 77 09 29
www.beefbar.com
Opening hours: Every day, from 12 am to 2:30 pm and from 8 pm to midnight
Special features: An elegant restaurant decorated in different atmospheres in
Monaco's famous Port de Fontvieille

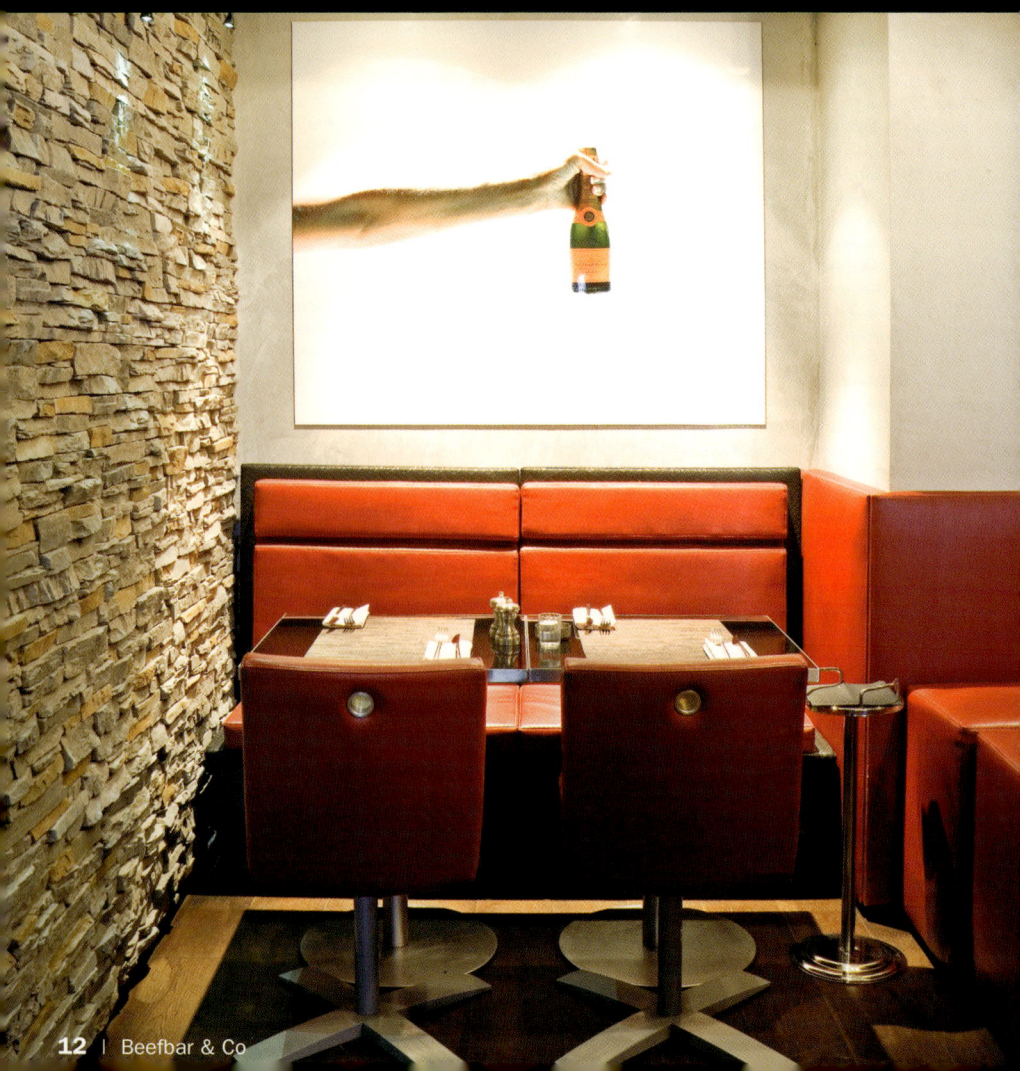

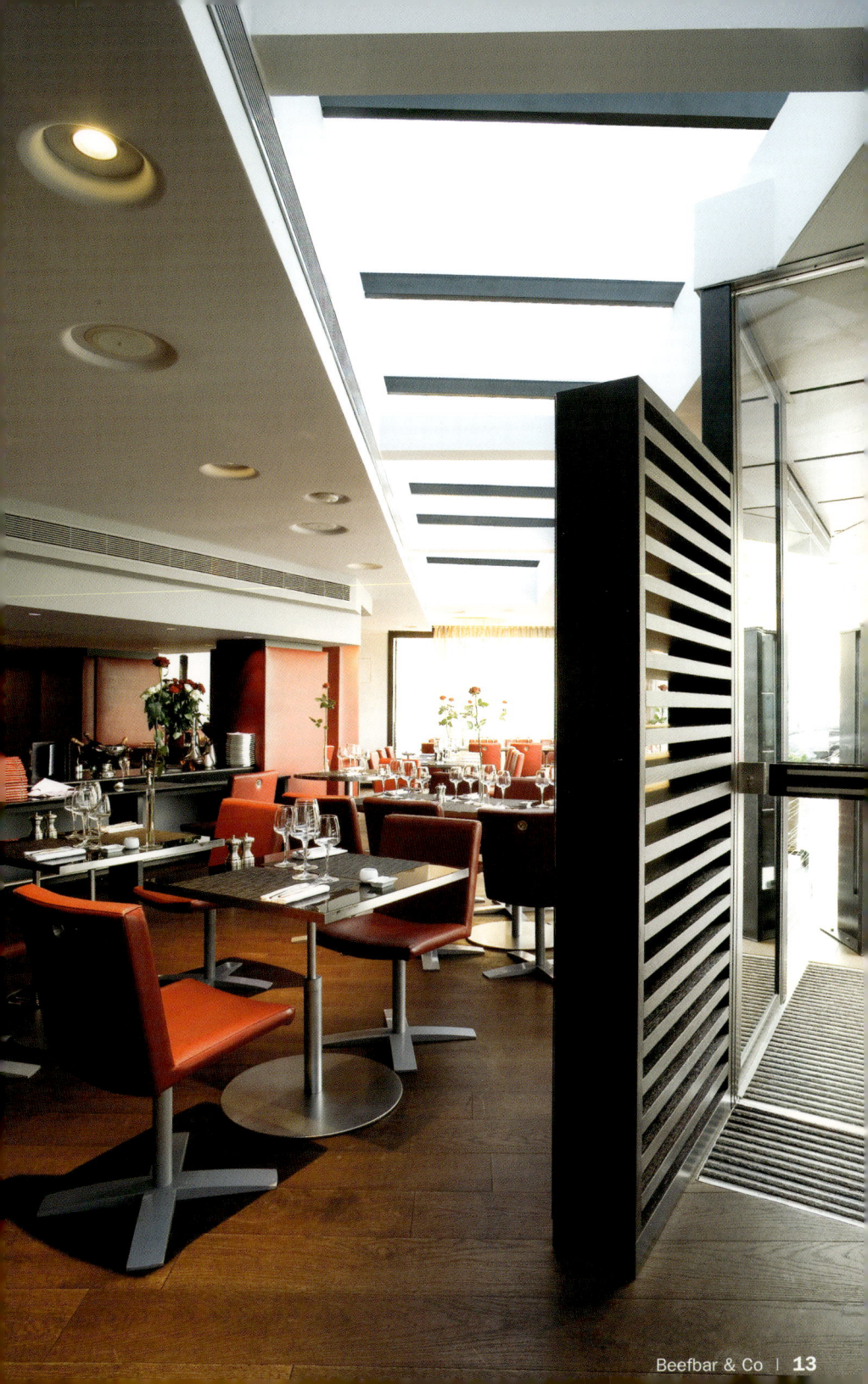

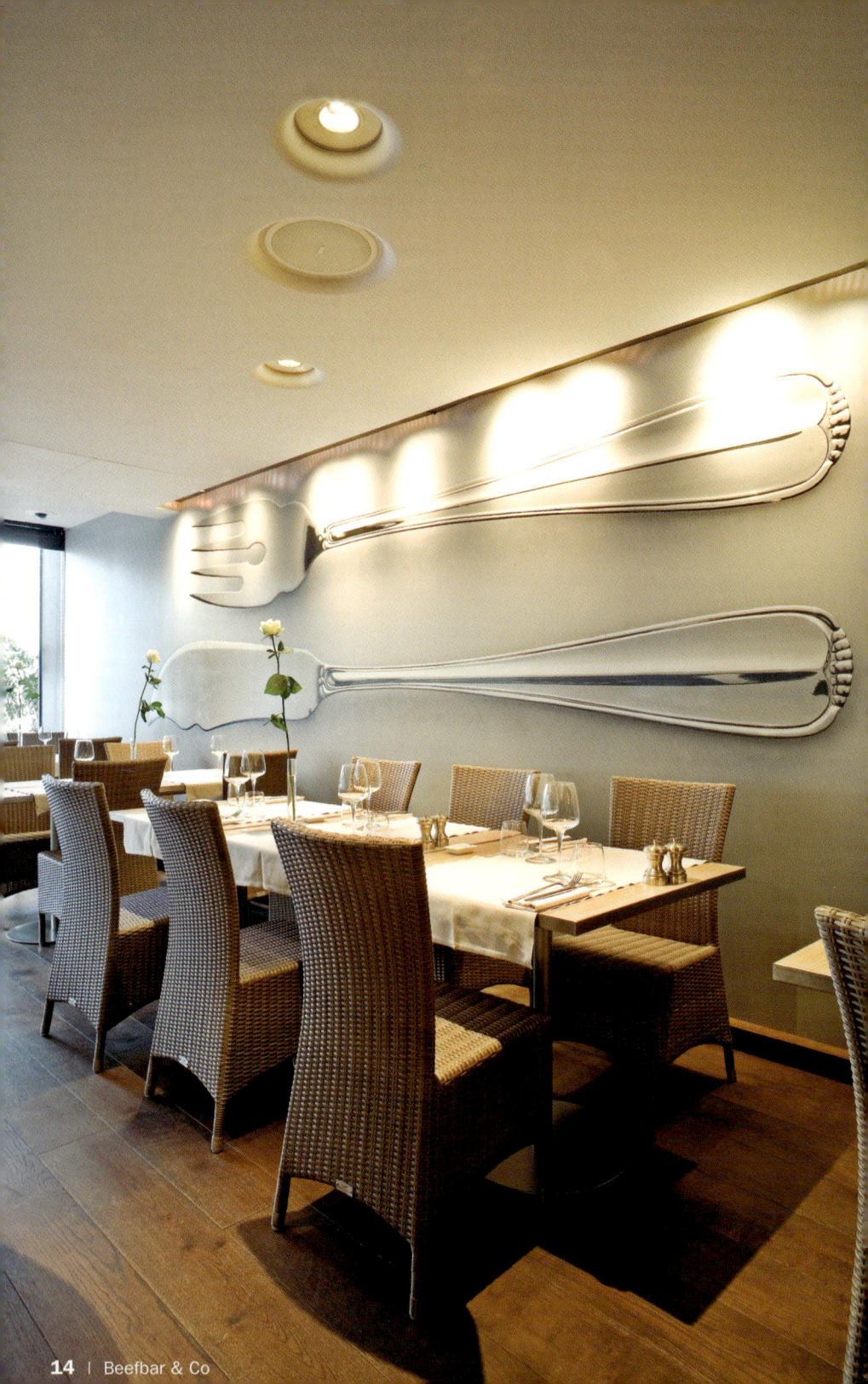

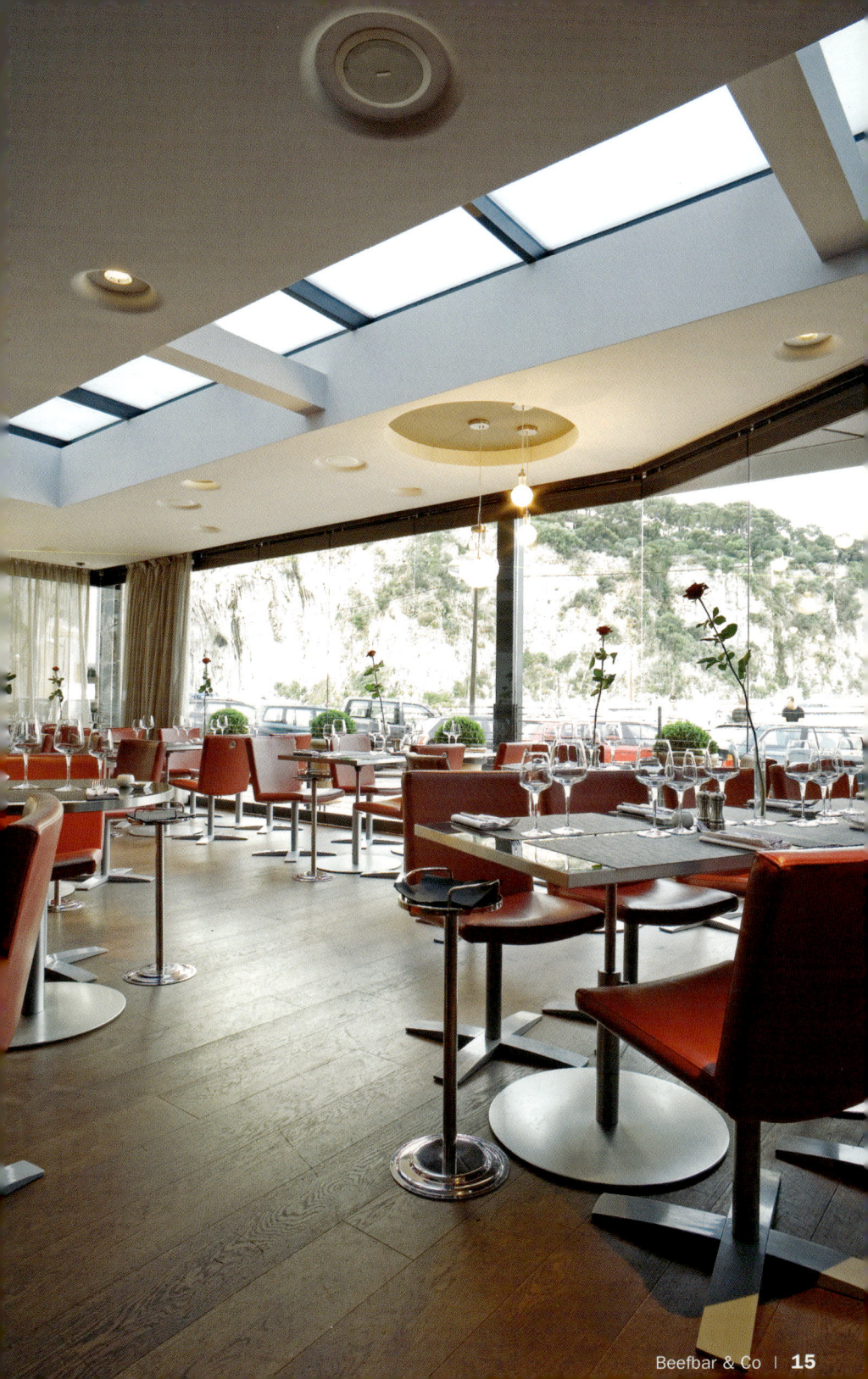

Before

Design: By the owners, Virginie Mouchneno, Fréderique Bouazes and Sebastian Arnaud

18 Rue du Congrès | 06000 Nice
Phone: +33 4 93 87 85 59
www.before-nice.com
Opening hours: Every day from 6 pm to 12:30 am
Special features: The best bar for pre-dinner drinks or lounge to start the night, with stunning djs and a variety of elaborate cocktails

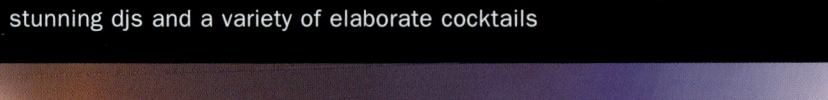

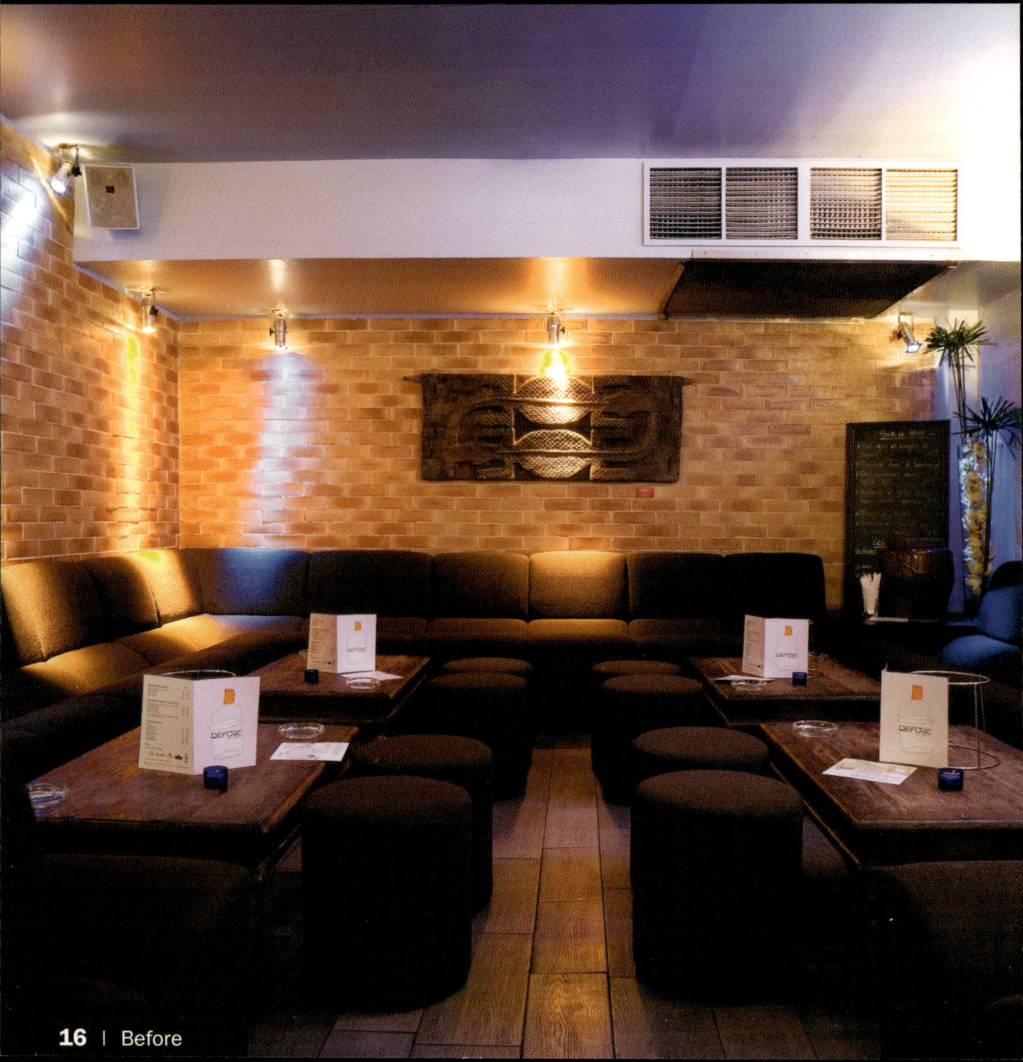

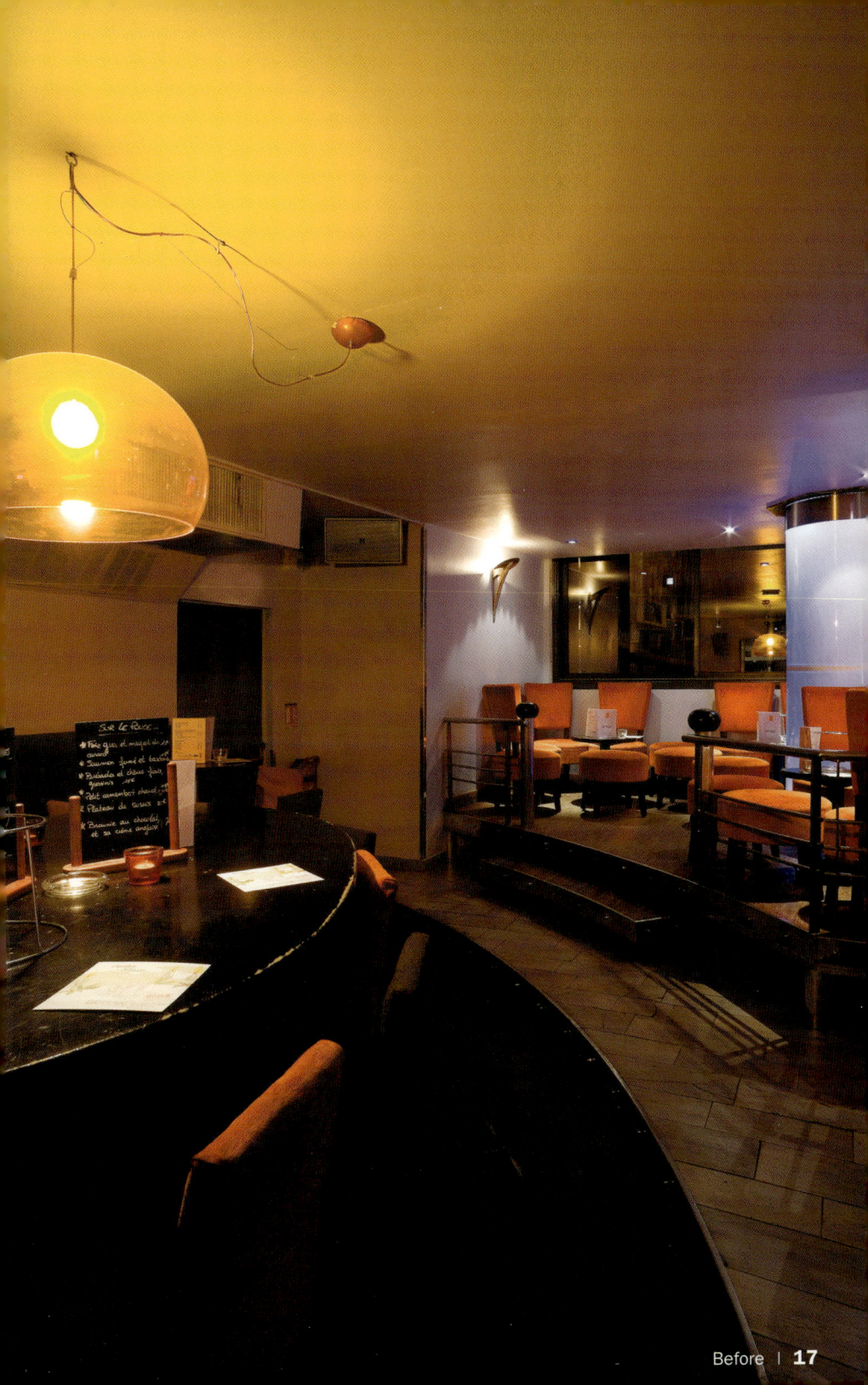

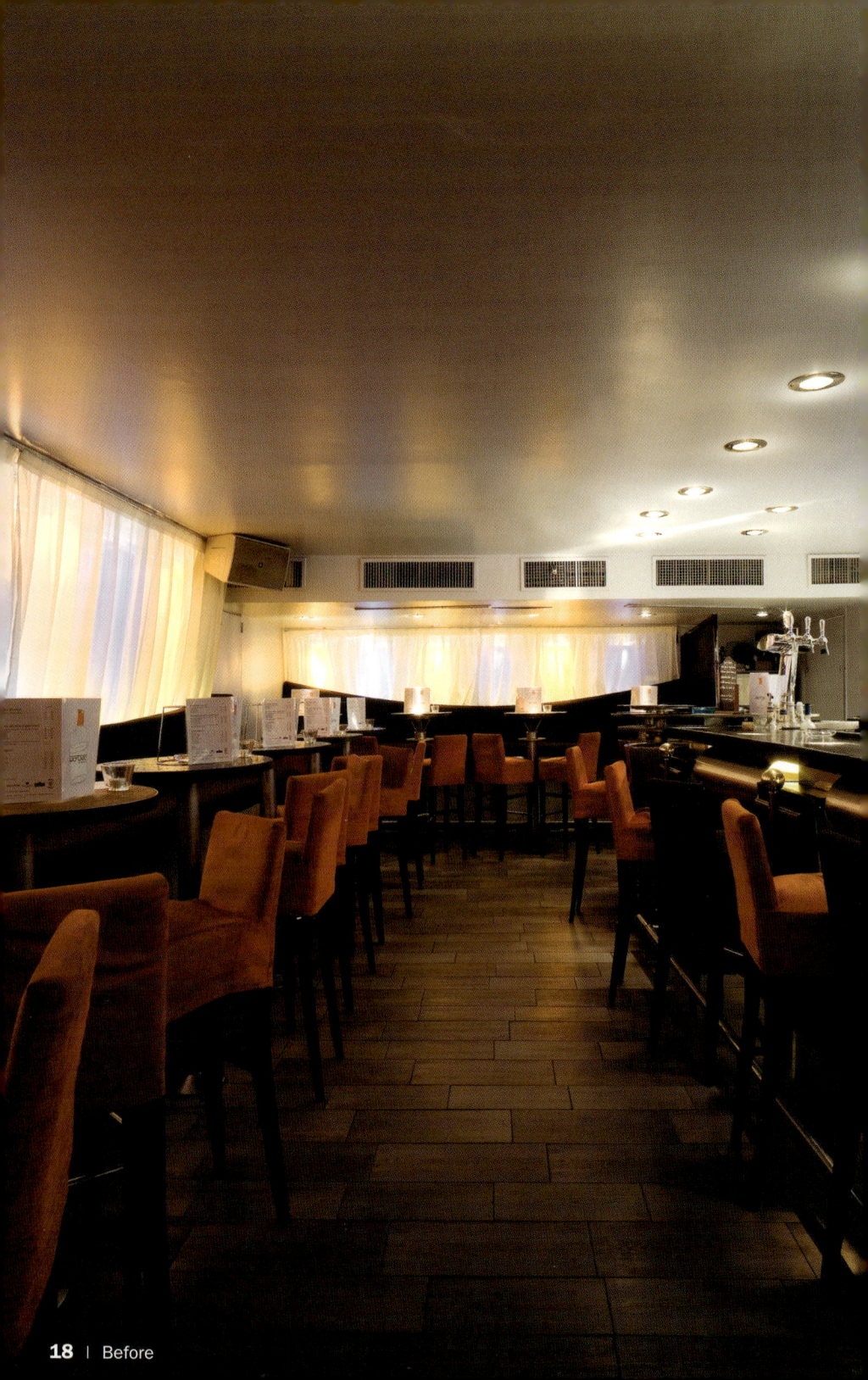

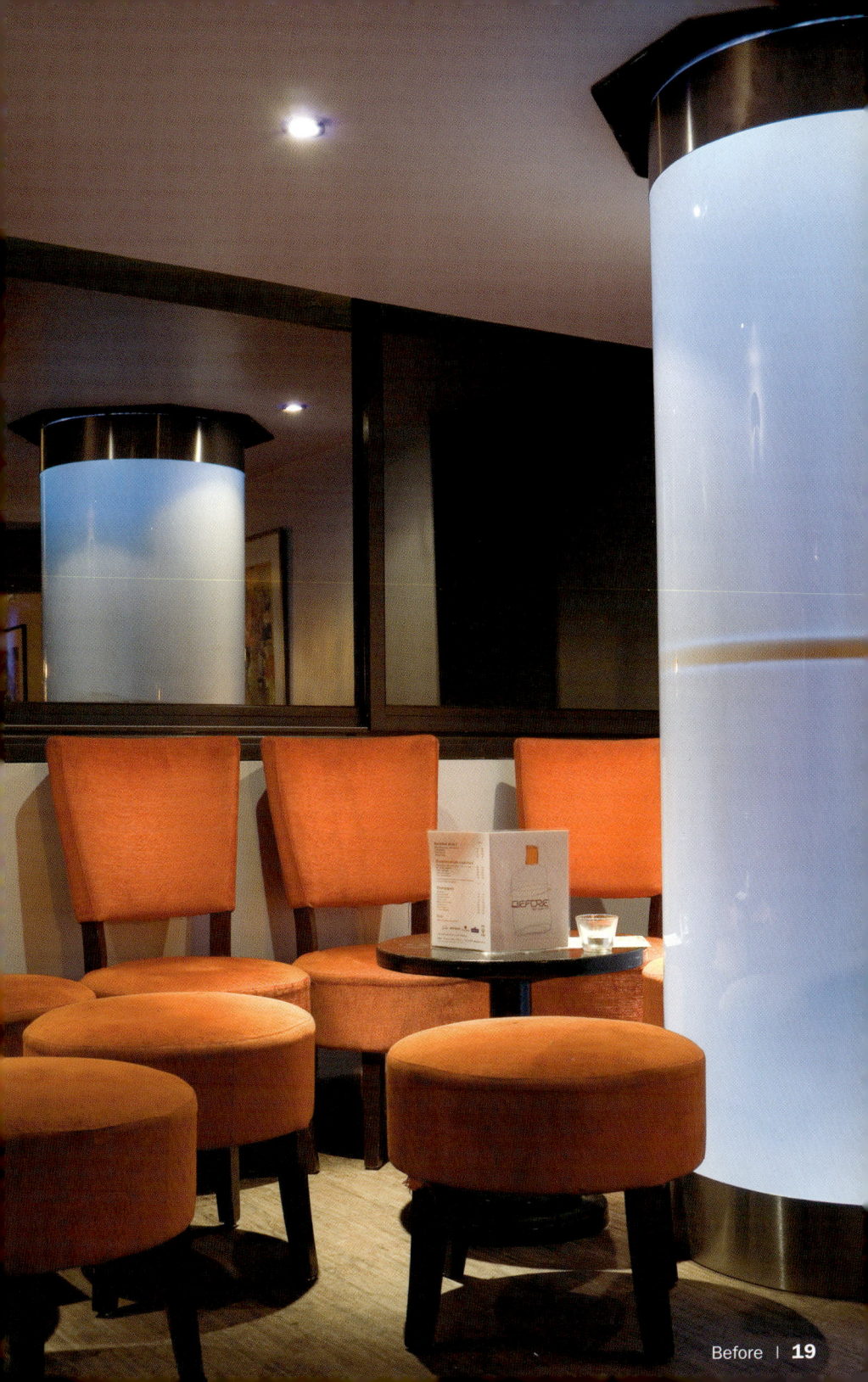

15 Rue des Frères Pradignac | 06400 Cannes
Phone: +33 6 18 09 70 28
www.dalton-group.com
Opening hours: From 8 pm to 2:30 am
Special features: Having a drink at the elegant bar or a Lebanese gourmet dinner in
the 1001 Nights-styled "Harem Restaurant", both is possible in this cosmopolitan
location with two very contrasting sides

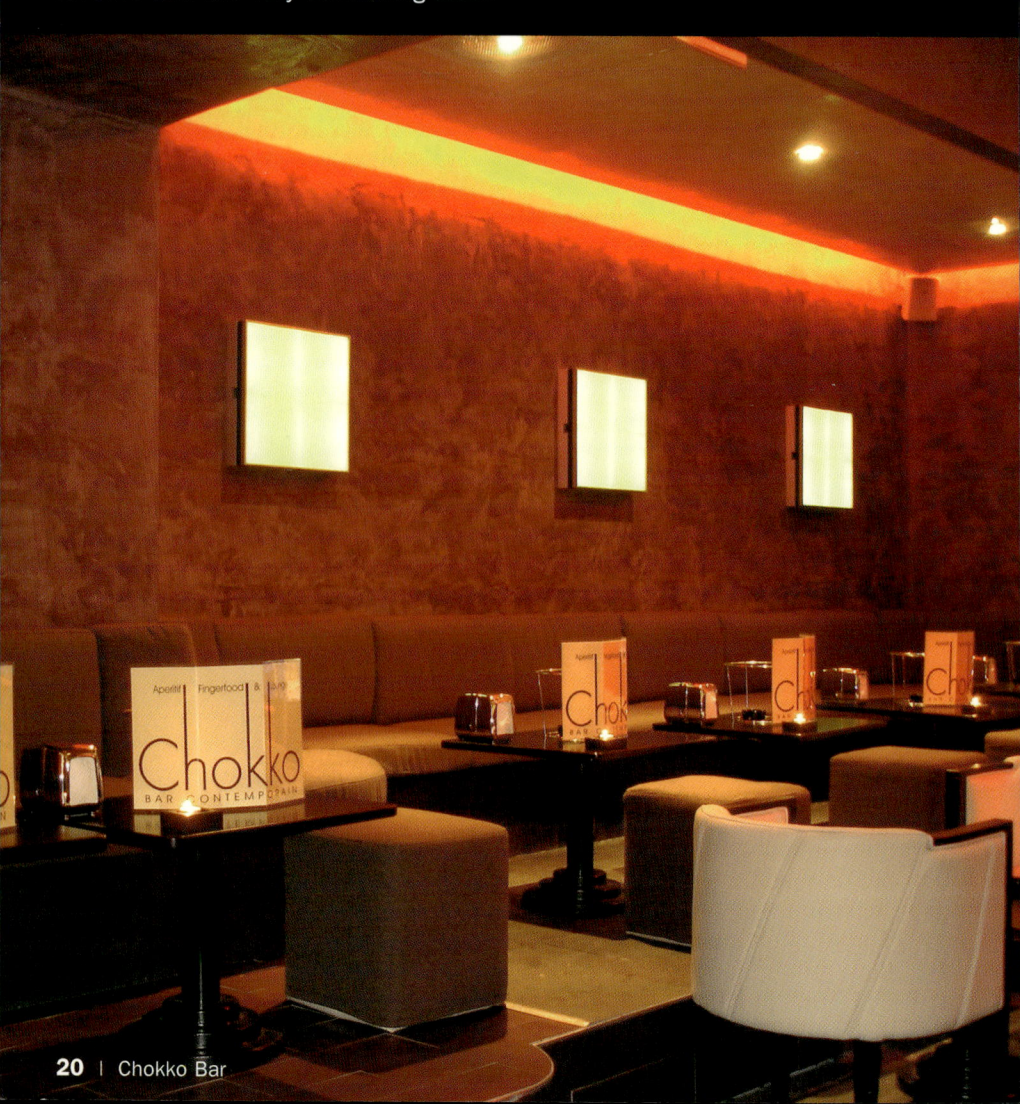

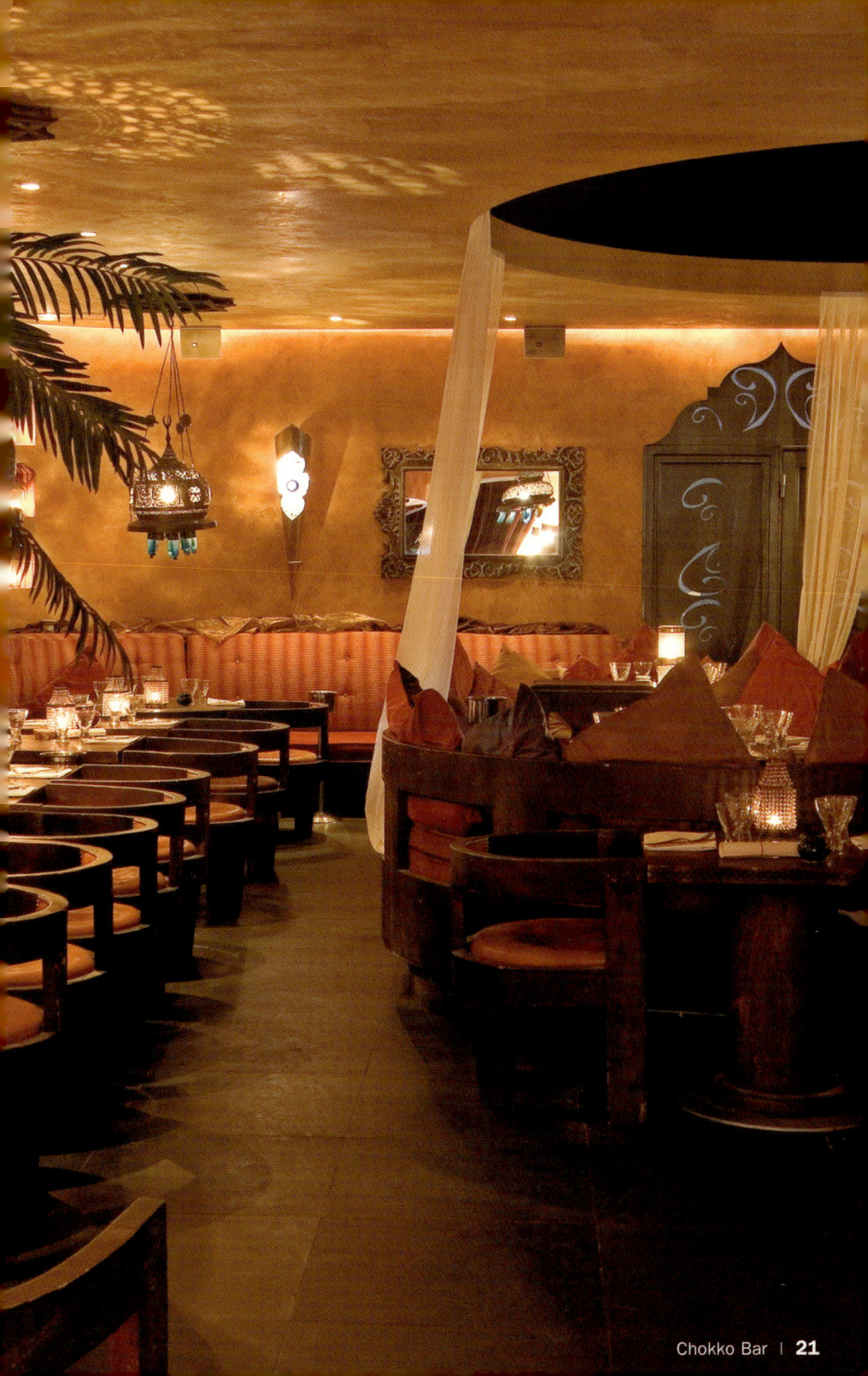

Fondation Maeght

Design: Josep-Lluis Sert

06570 Saint-Paul de Vence
Phone: +33 4 93 32 81 63
www.fondation.maeght.com
Opening hours: Every day, from October to June, from 10 am to 12:30 pm and from 2:30 pm to 6 pm; from July to September, from 10 am to 7 pm
Special features: Private art foundation built in 1964 by a disciple of Le Corbusier to represent one of the earliest examples of contemporary architecture in the area

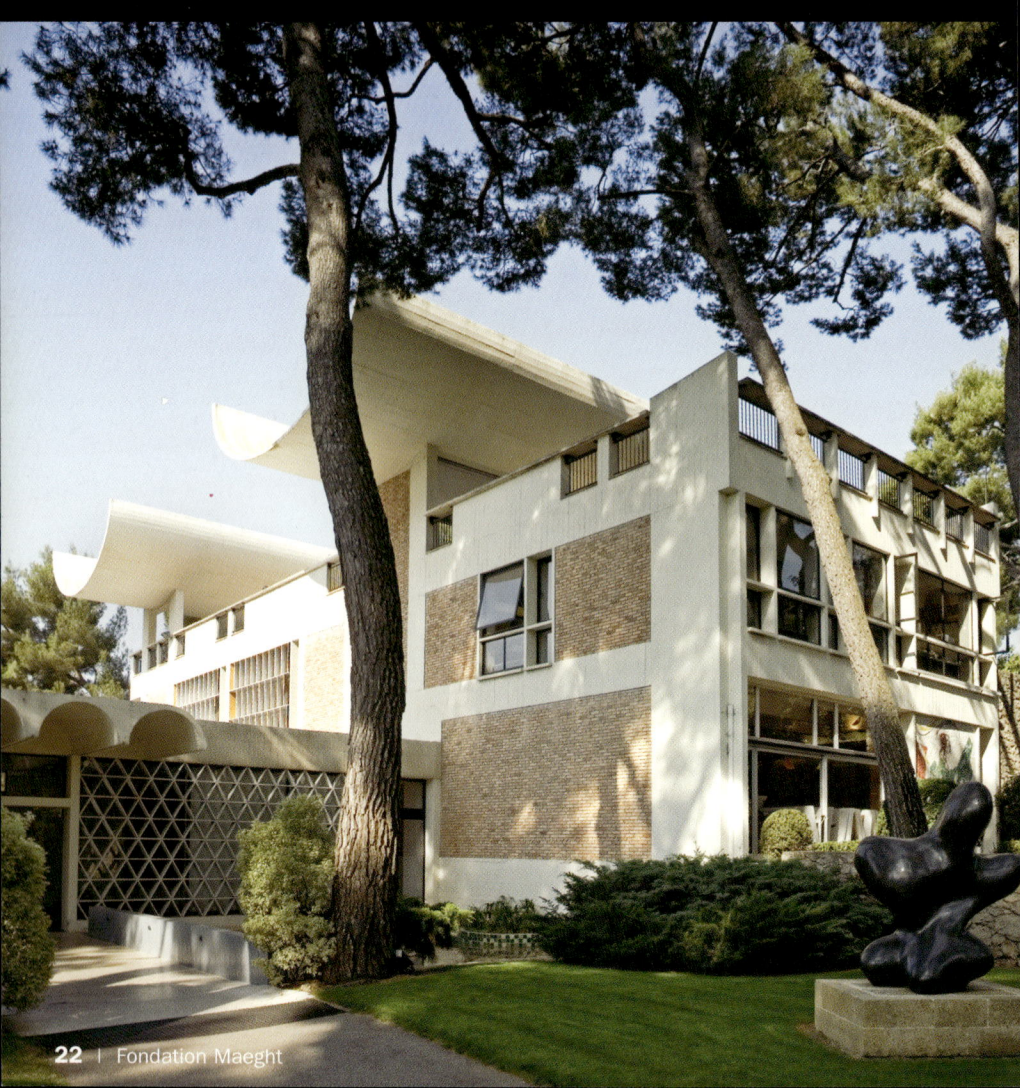

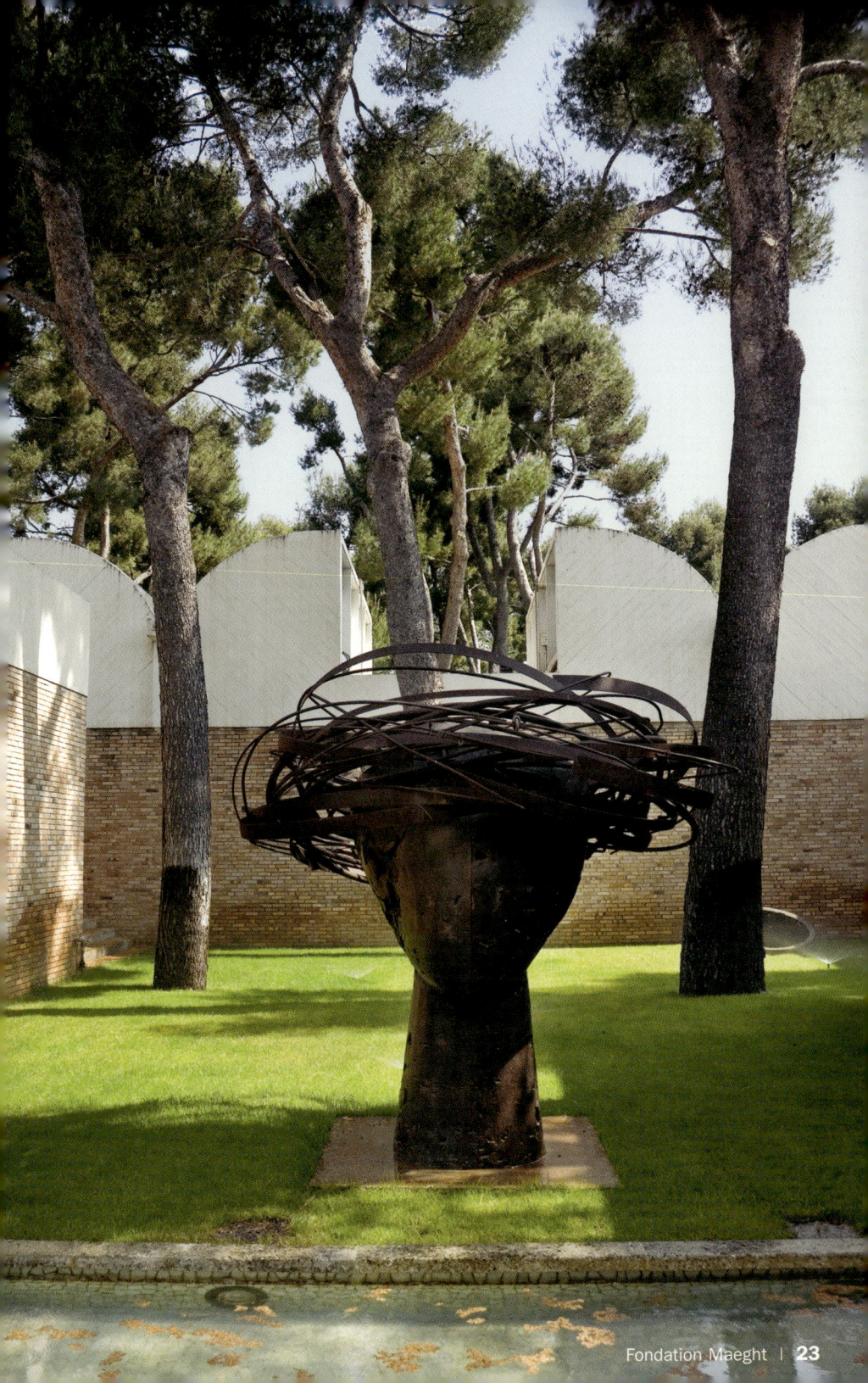

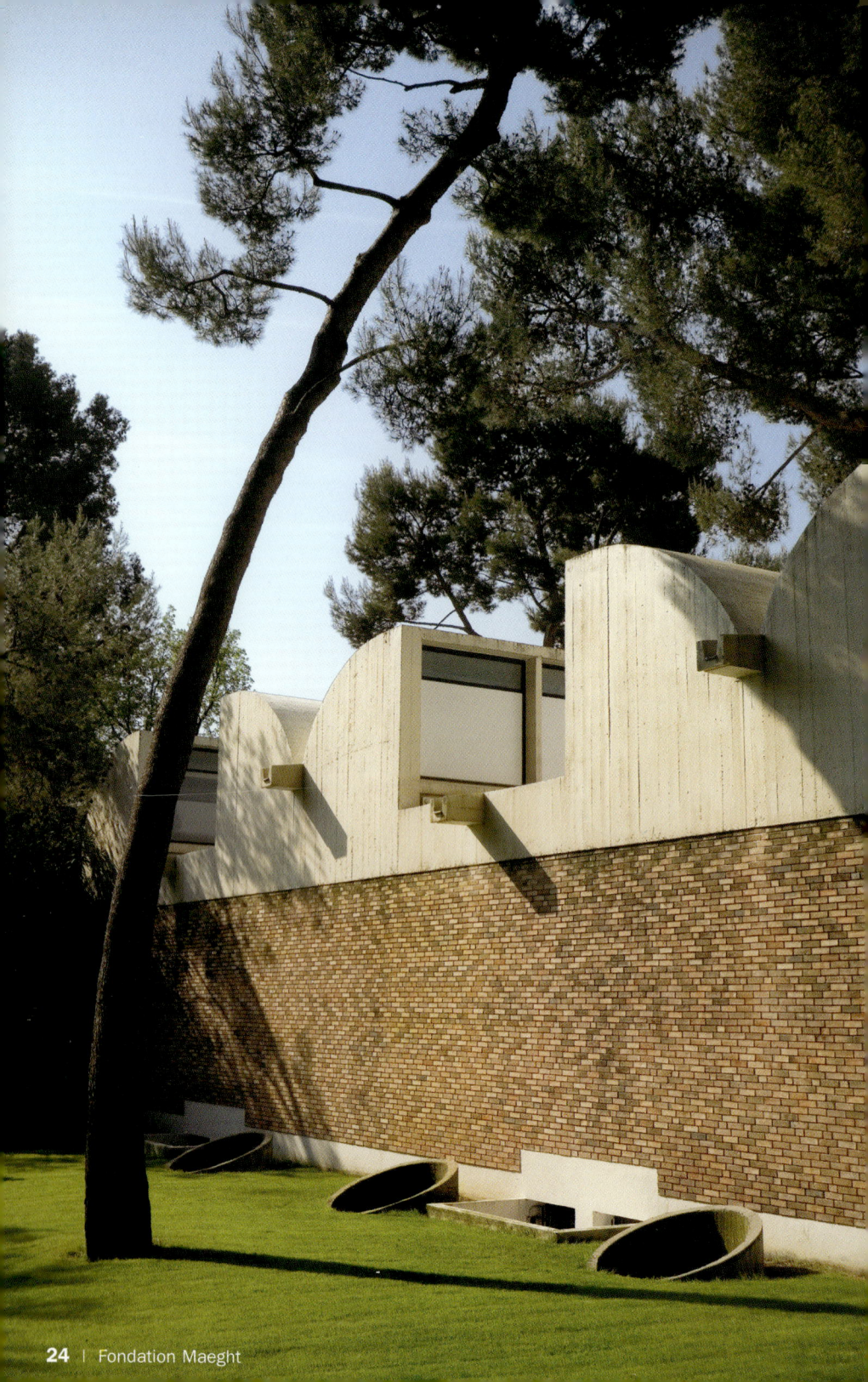

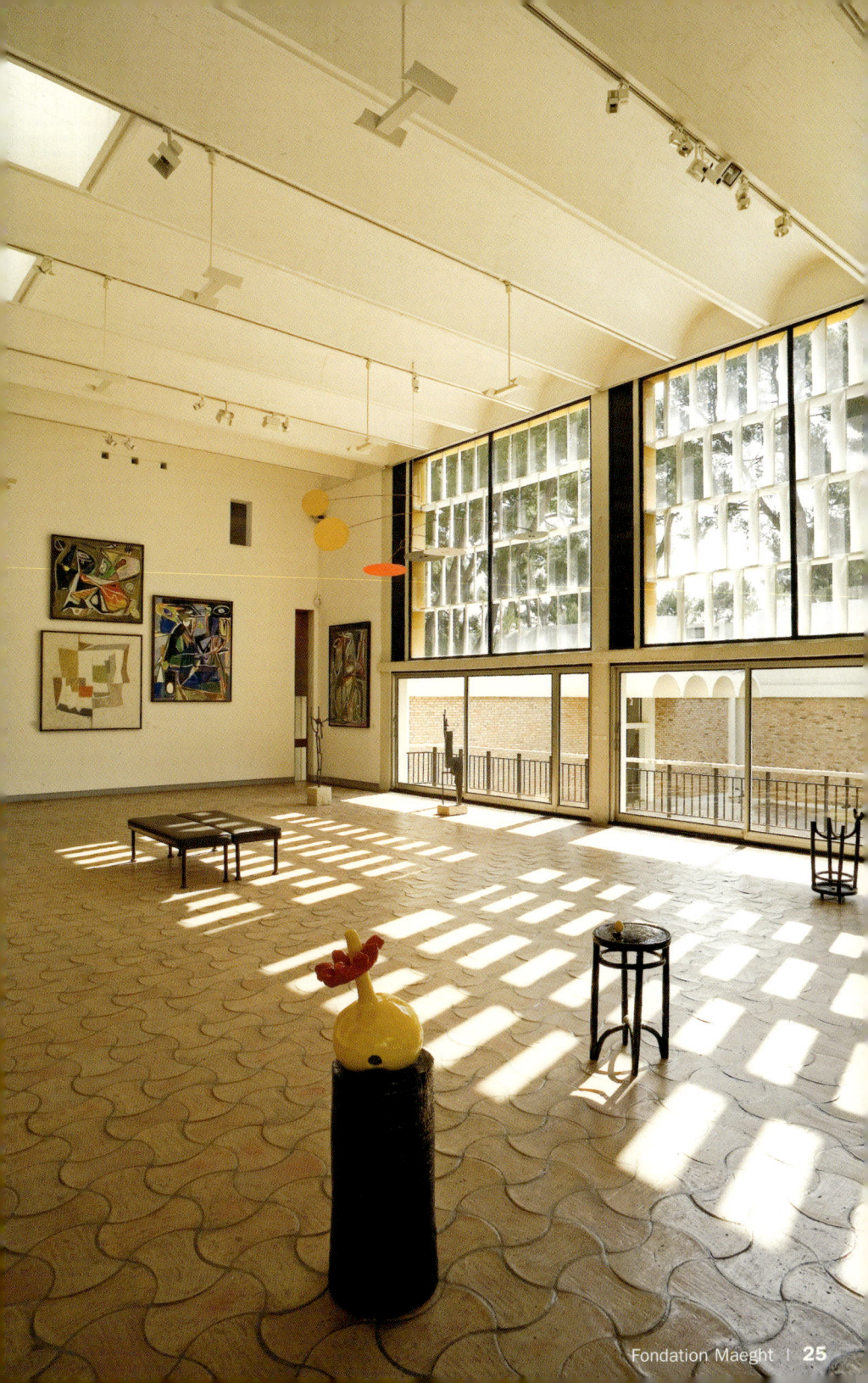

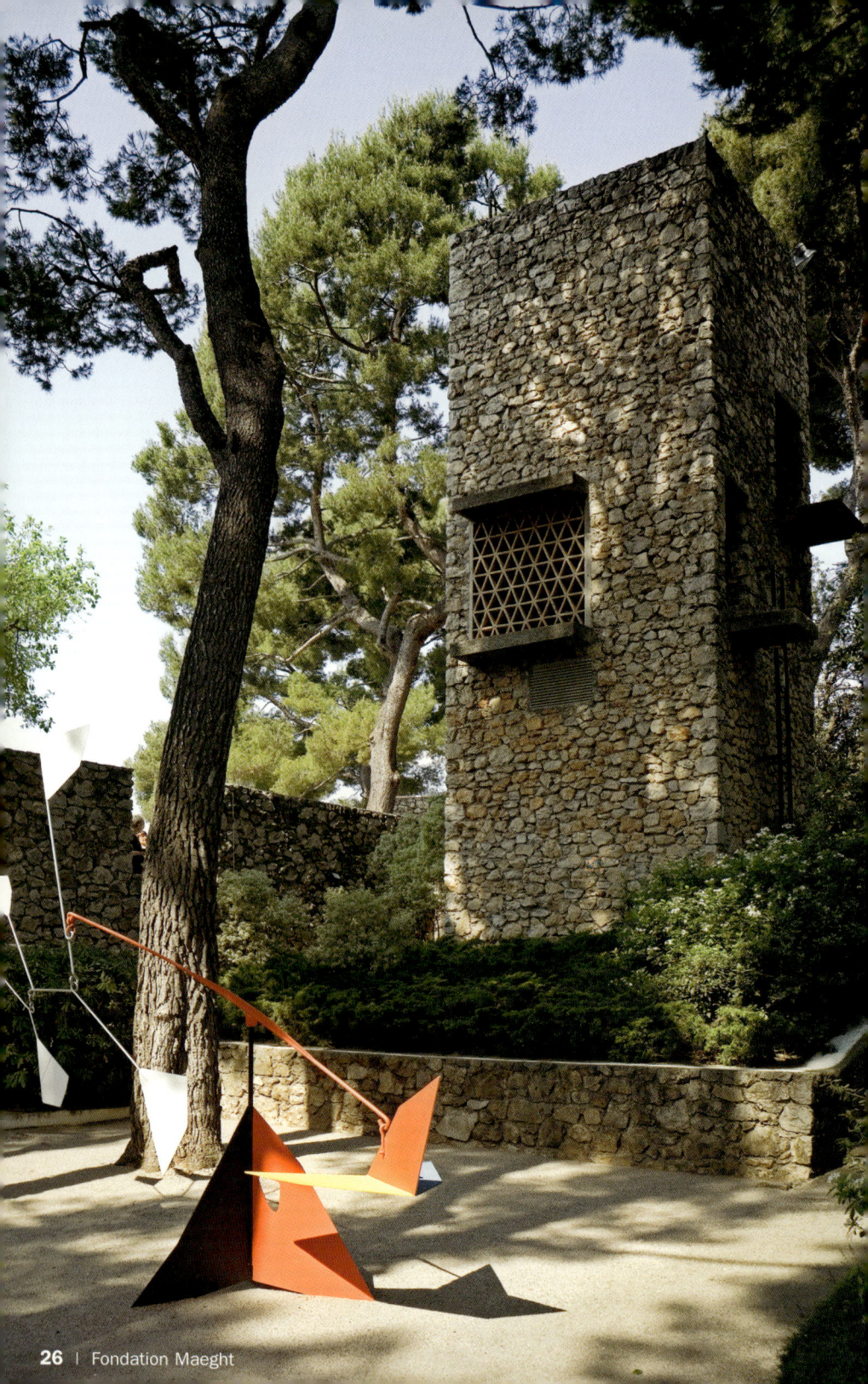

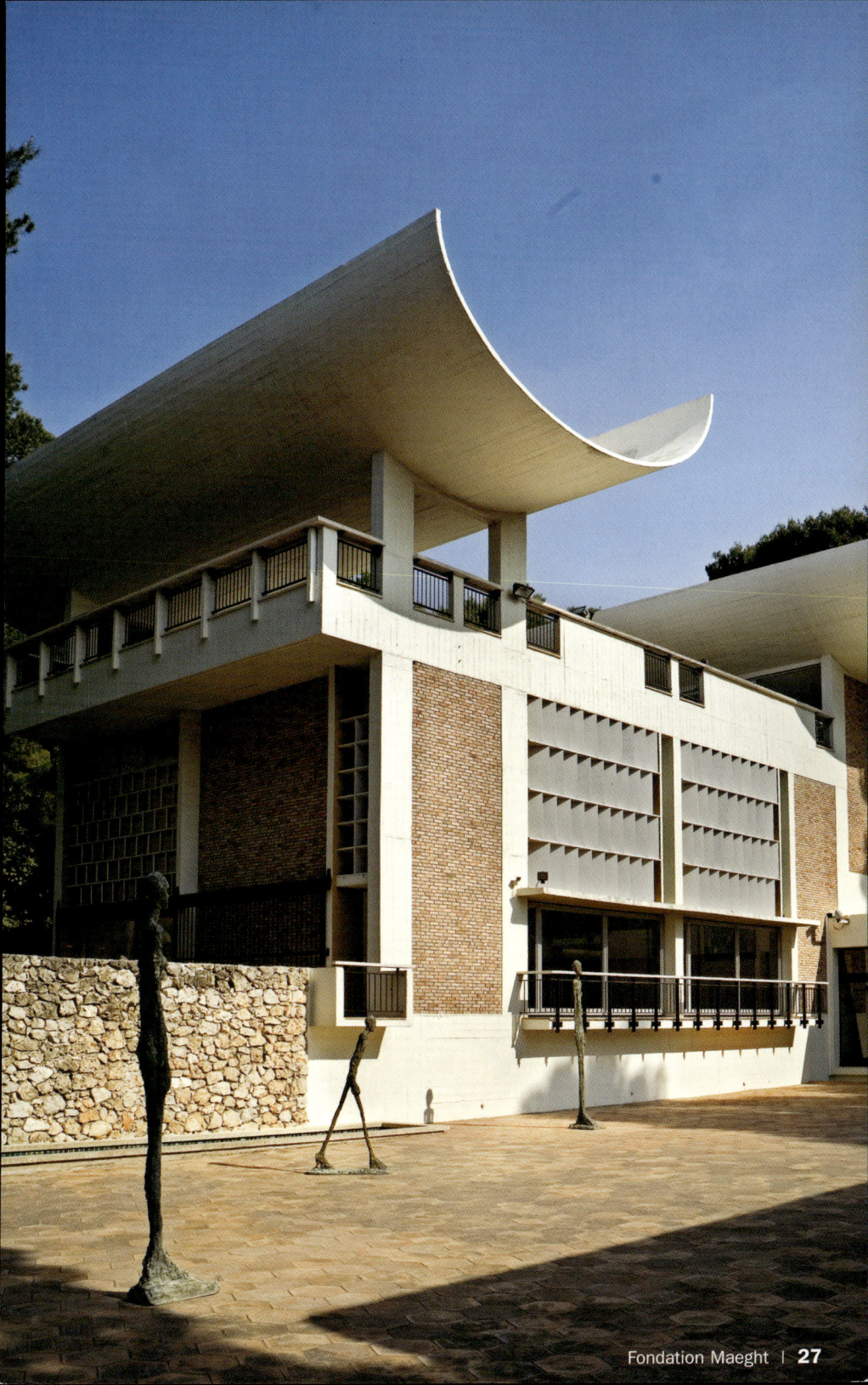

Hôtel 3,14

Design: Alexandra Ellena

5 Rue François Einesy | 06400 Cannes
Phone: +33 4 92 99 72 00
www.3-14hotel.com
Opening hours: Every day, open 24 hours
Special features: Each of the 5 floors in the hotel is decorated to represent a
different continent. Only 50 meters from La Croisette boulevard where the hotel
propose his private beach

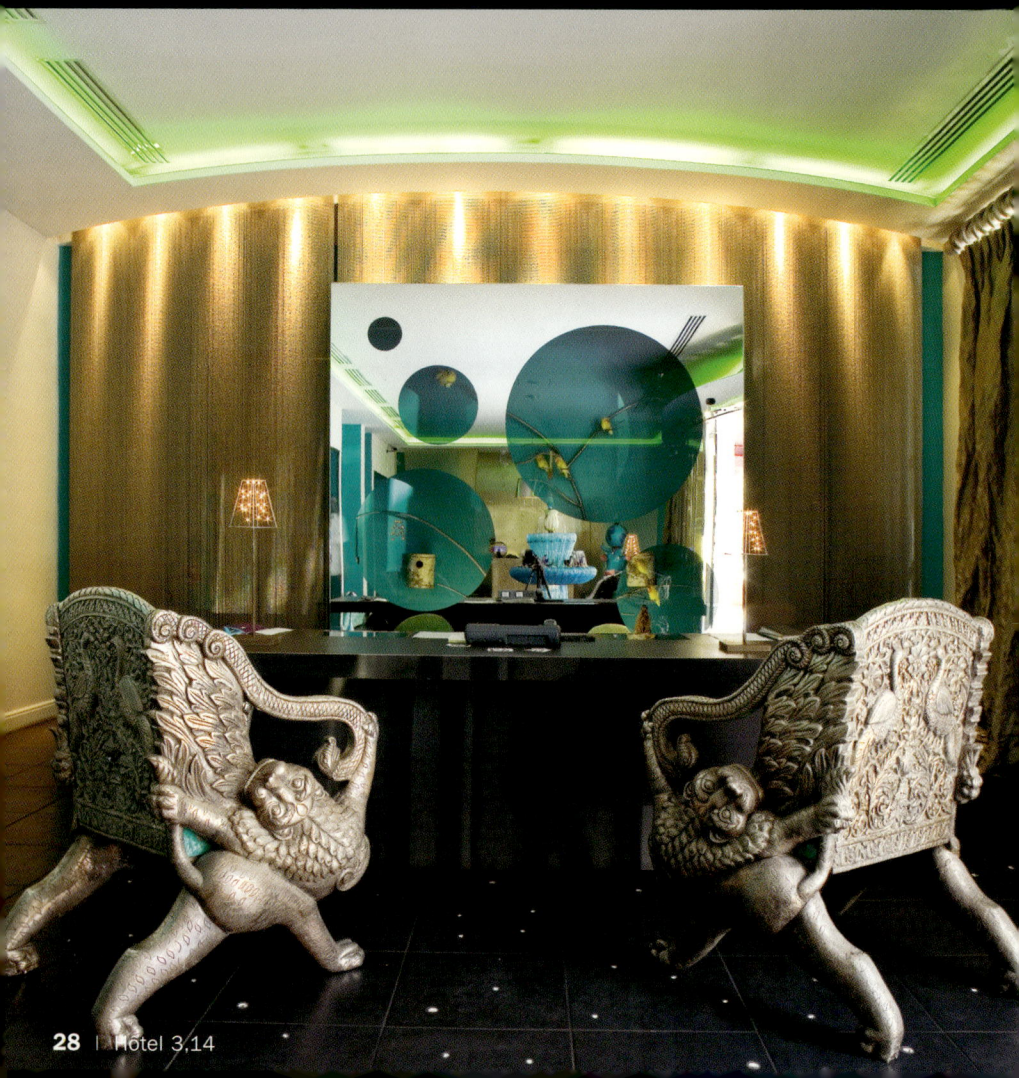

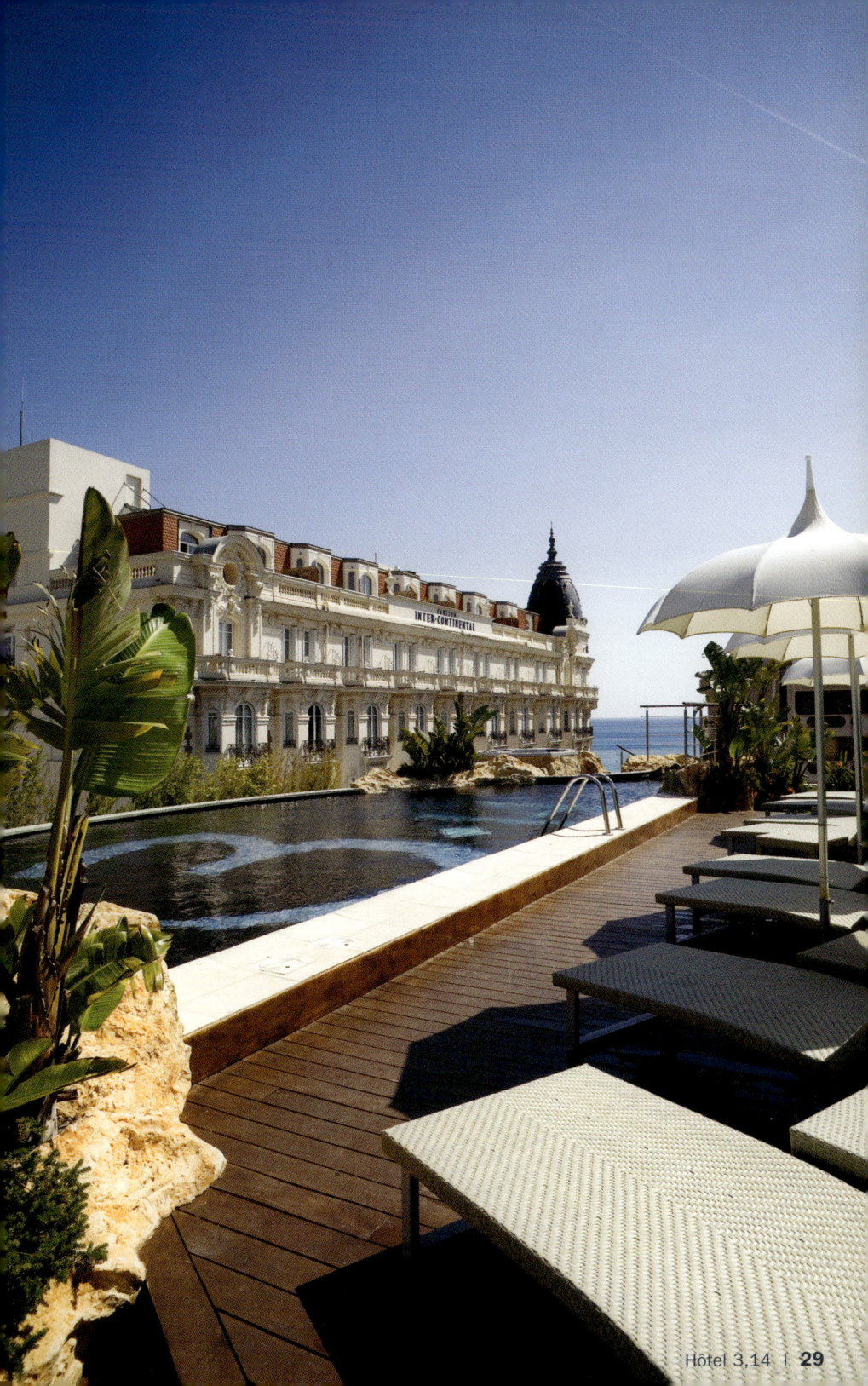

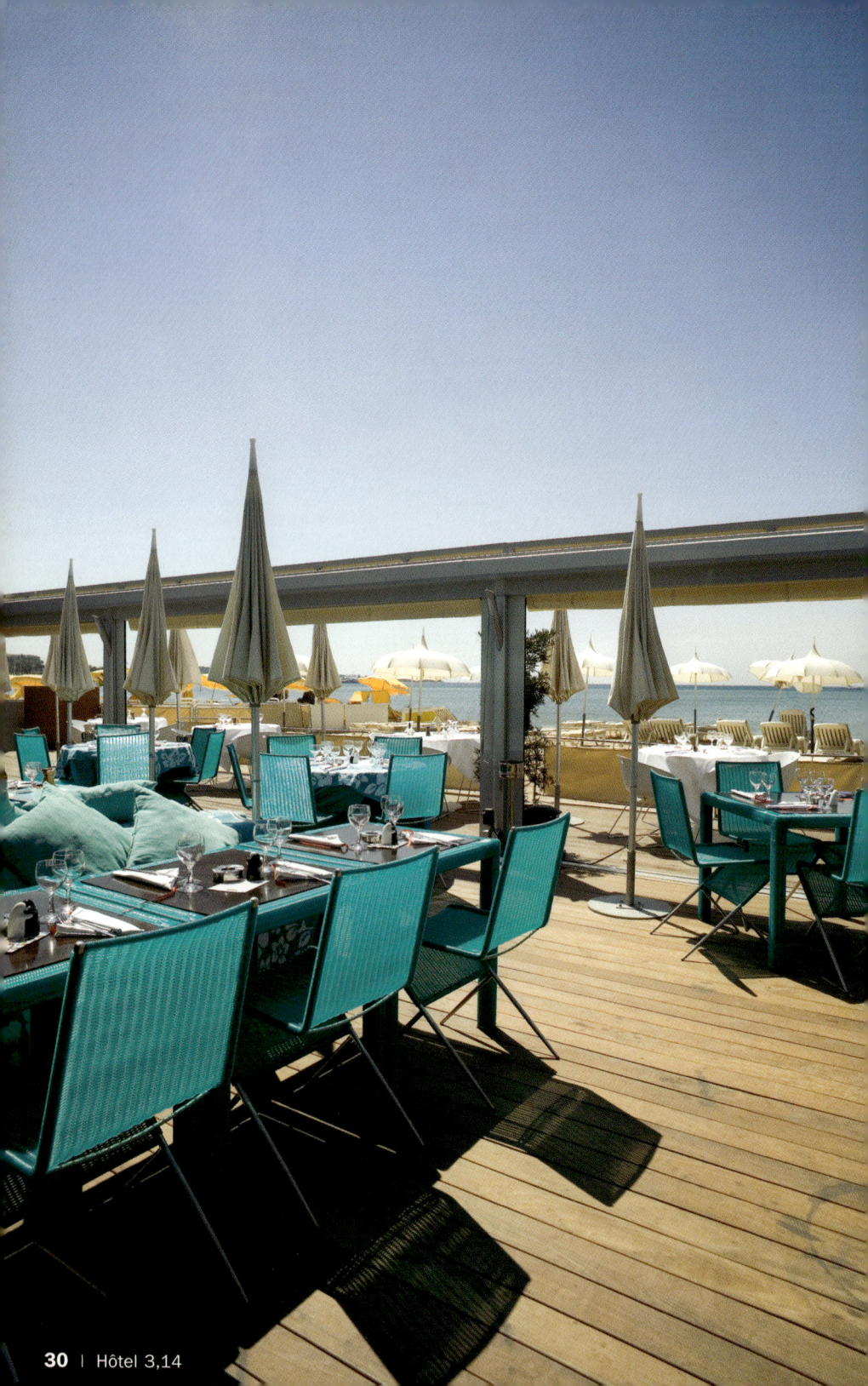

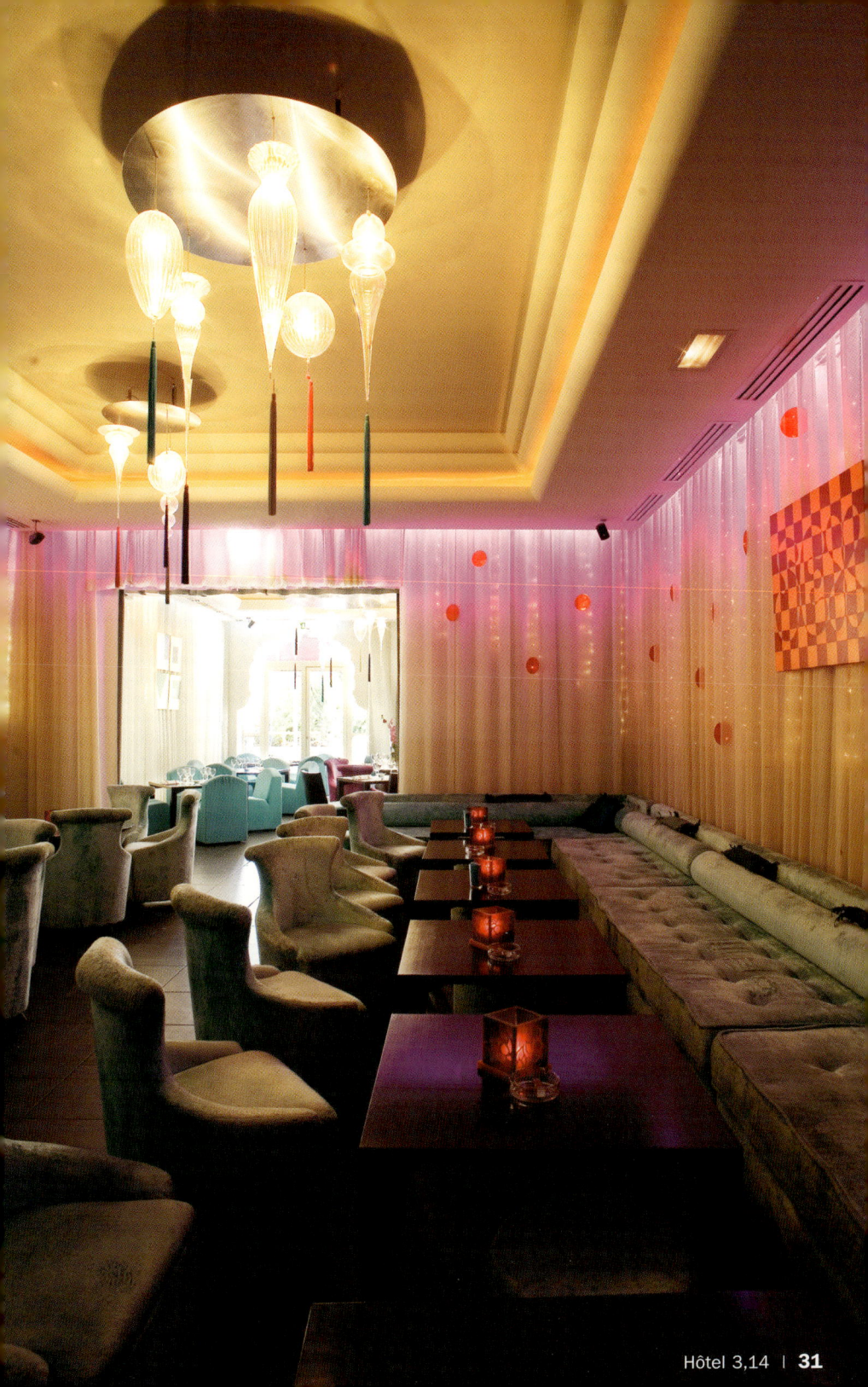

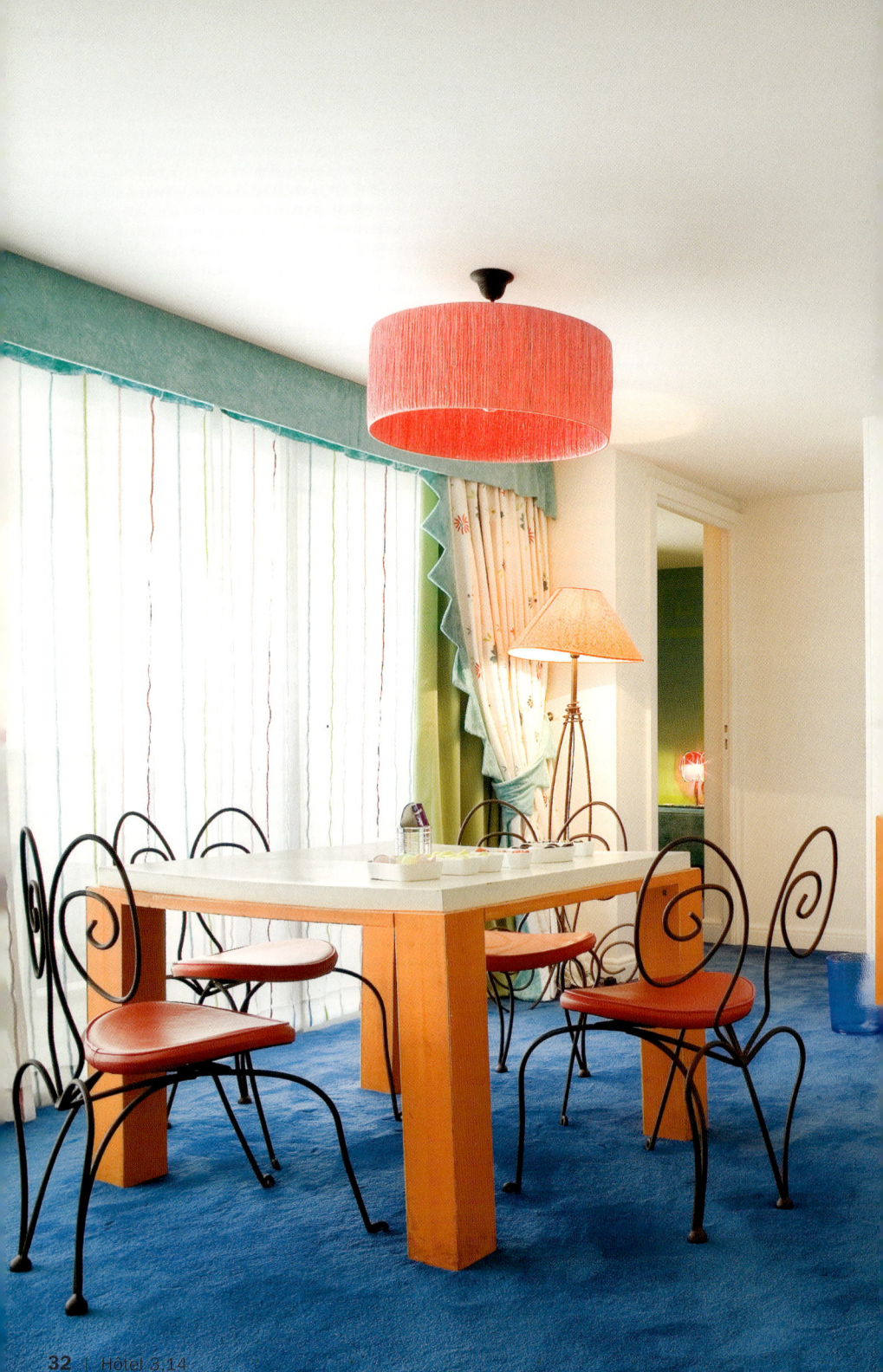

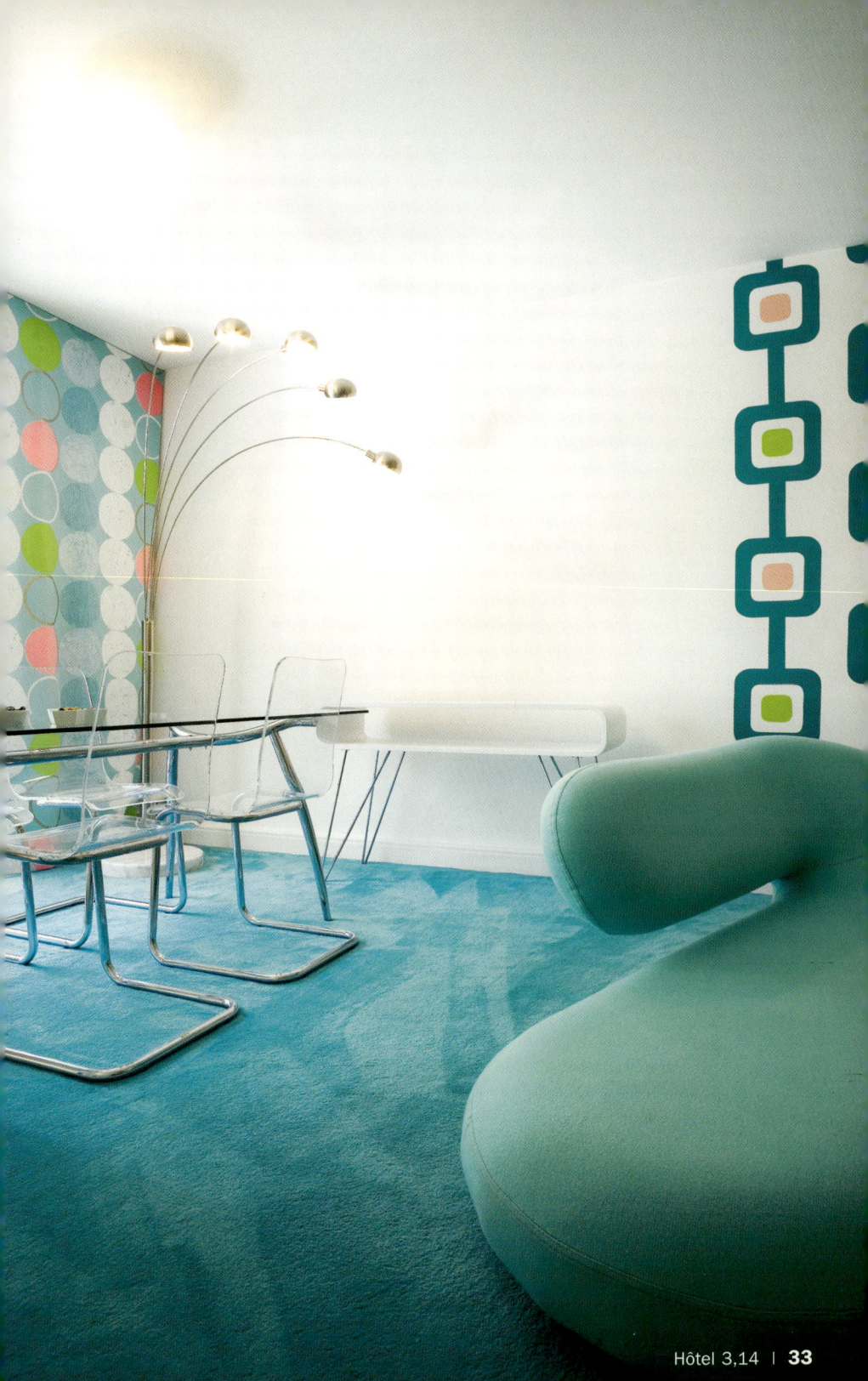

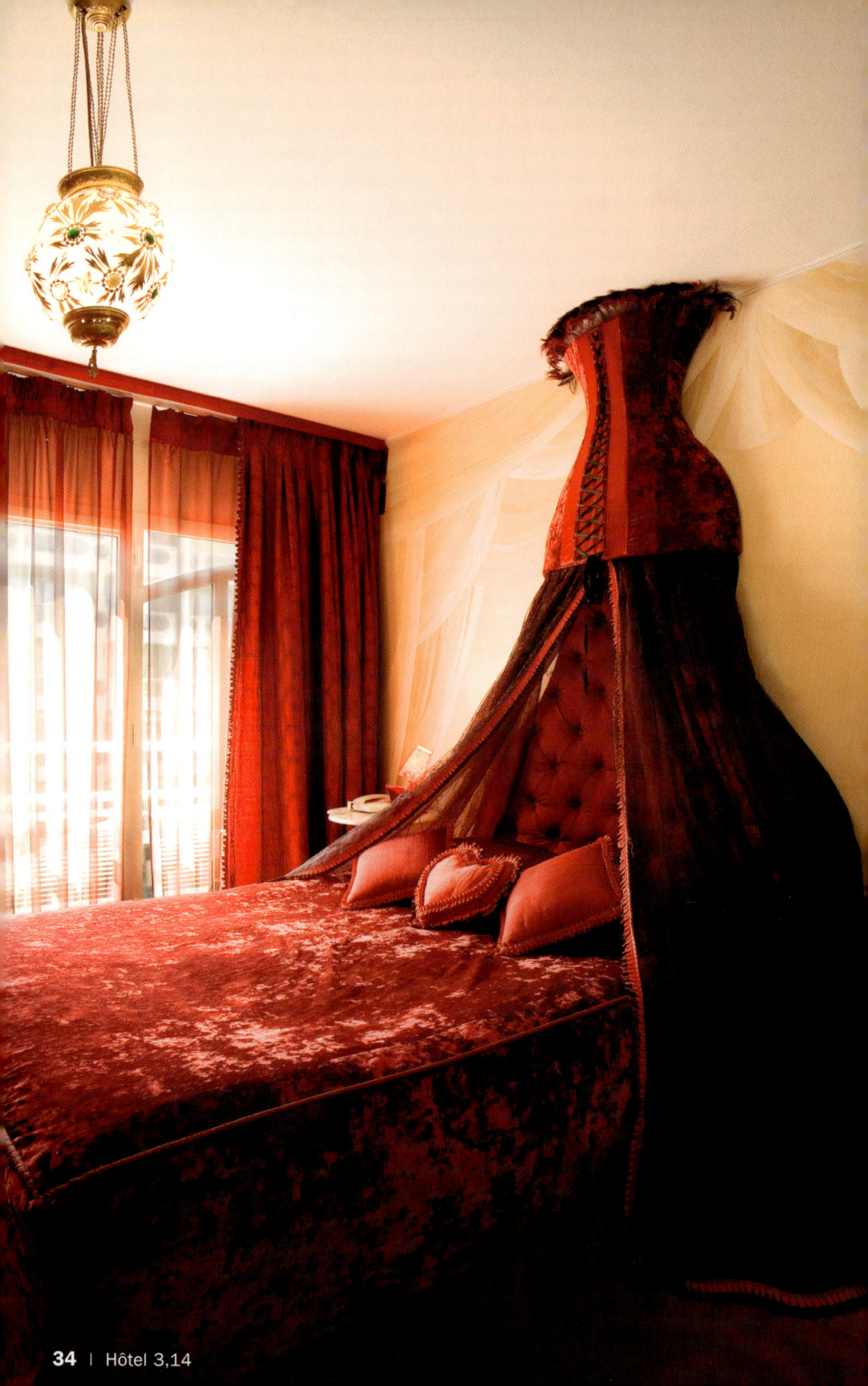

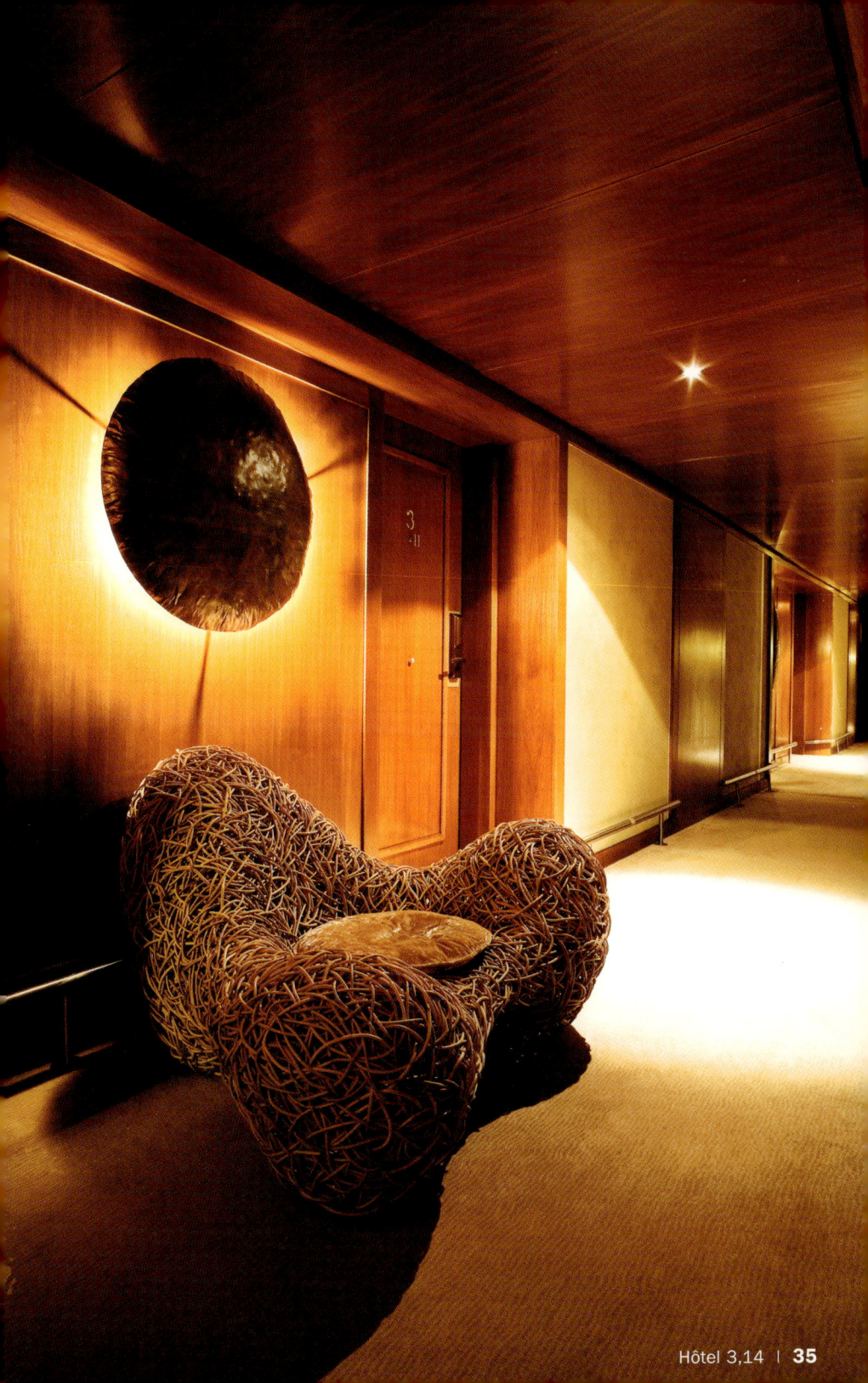

Hôtel Beau Rivage

Design: Jean-Michel Wilmotte

24 Rue Saint François de Paule | 06300 Nice
Phone: +33 4 92 47 82 82
www.nicebeaurivage.com
Opening hours: Open 24 hours
Special features: Restaurant, bar and sunbeds at the large private beach open from
April to October. The hotel combines modern styles with the traditional *niçois*

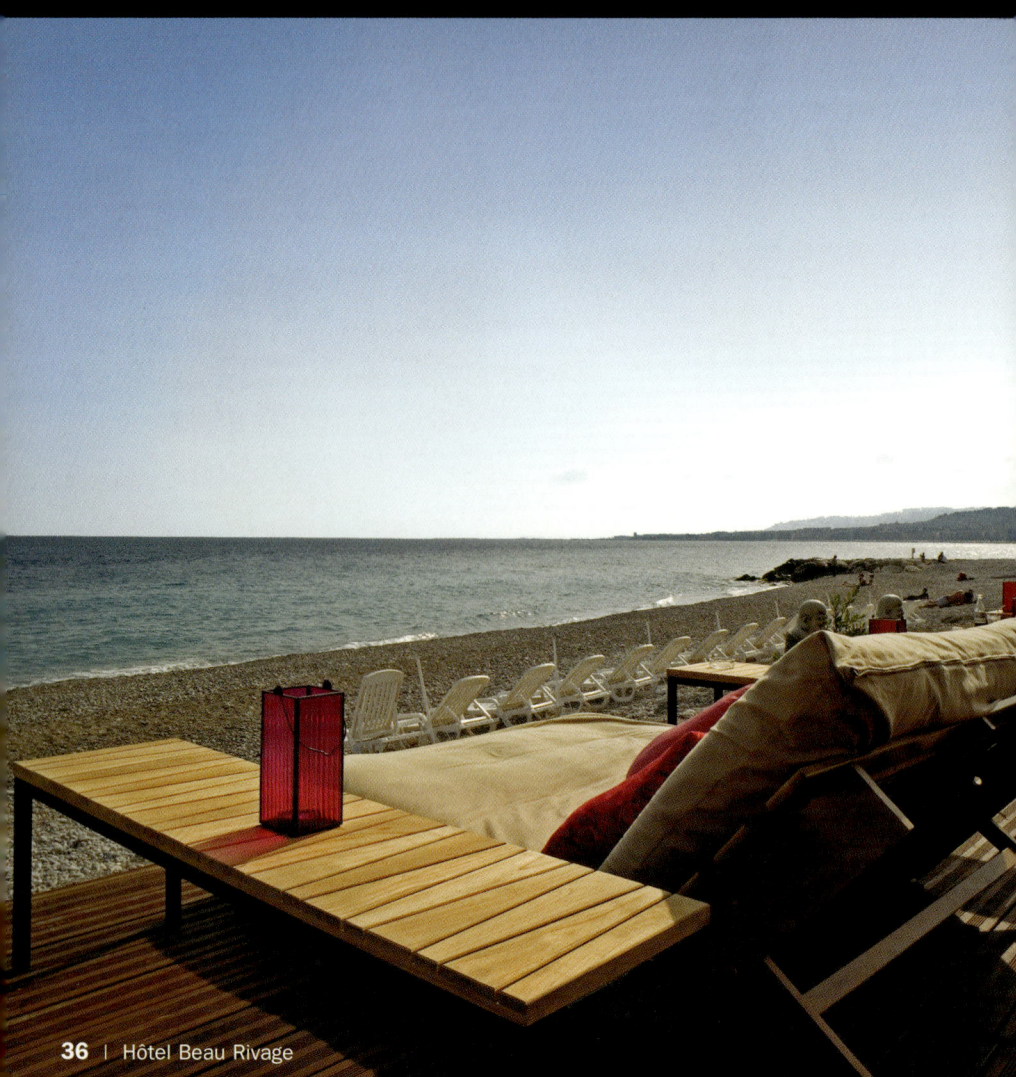

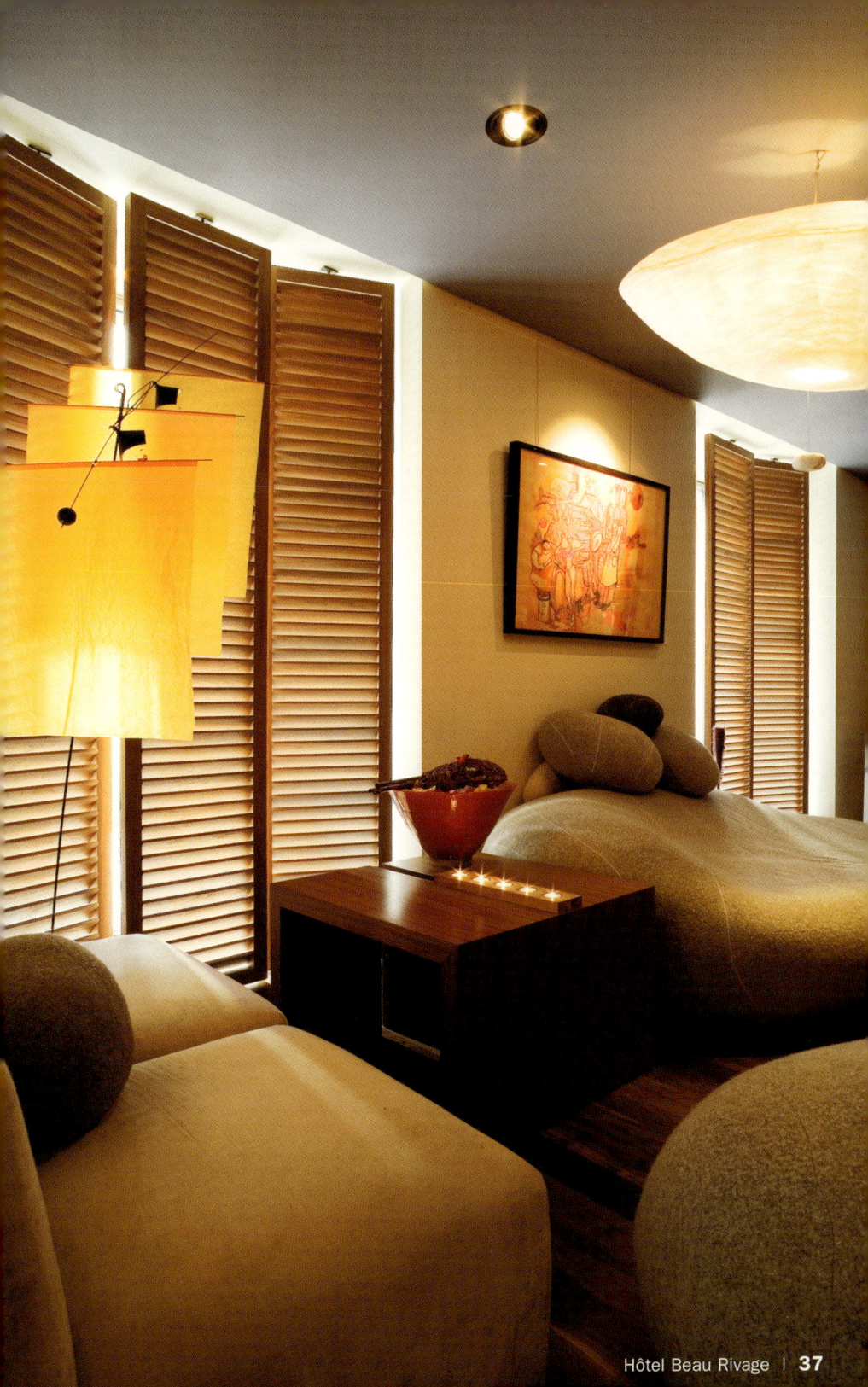

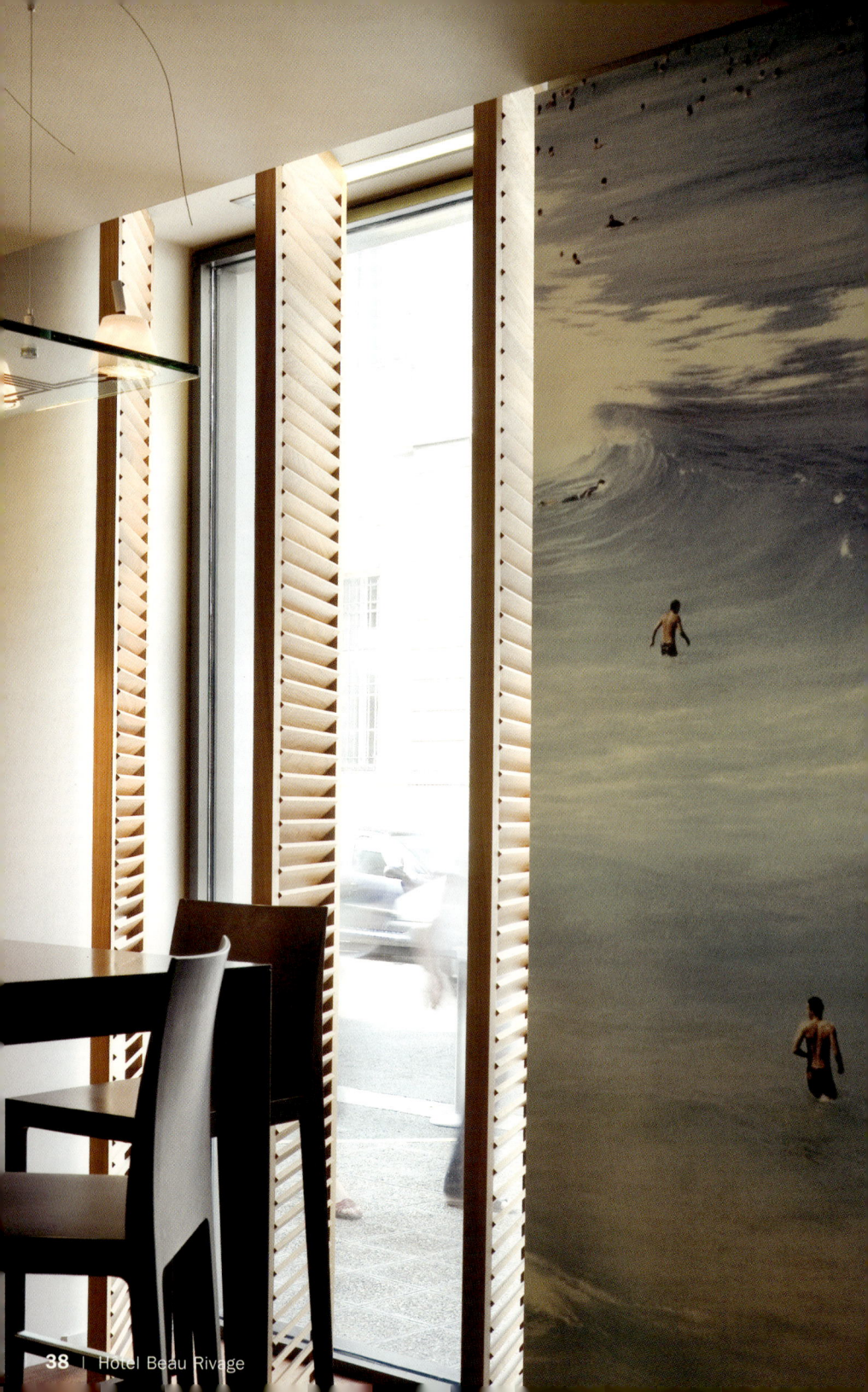

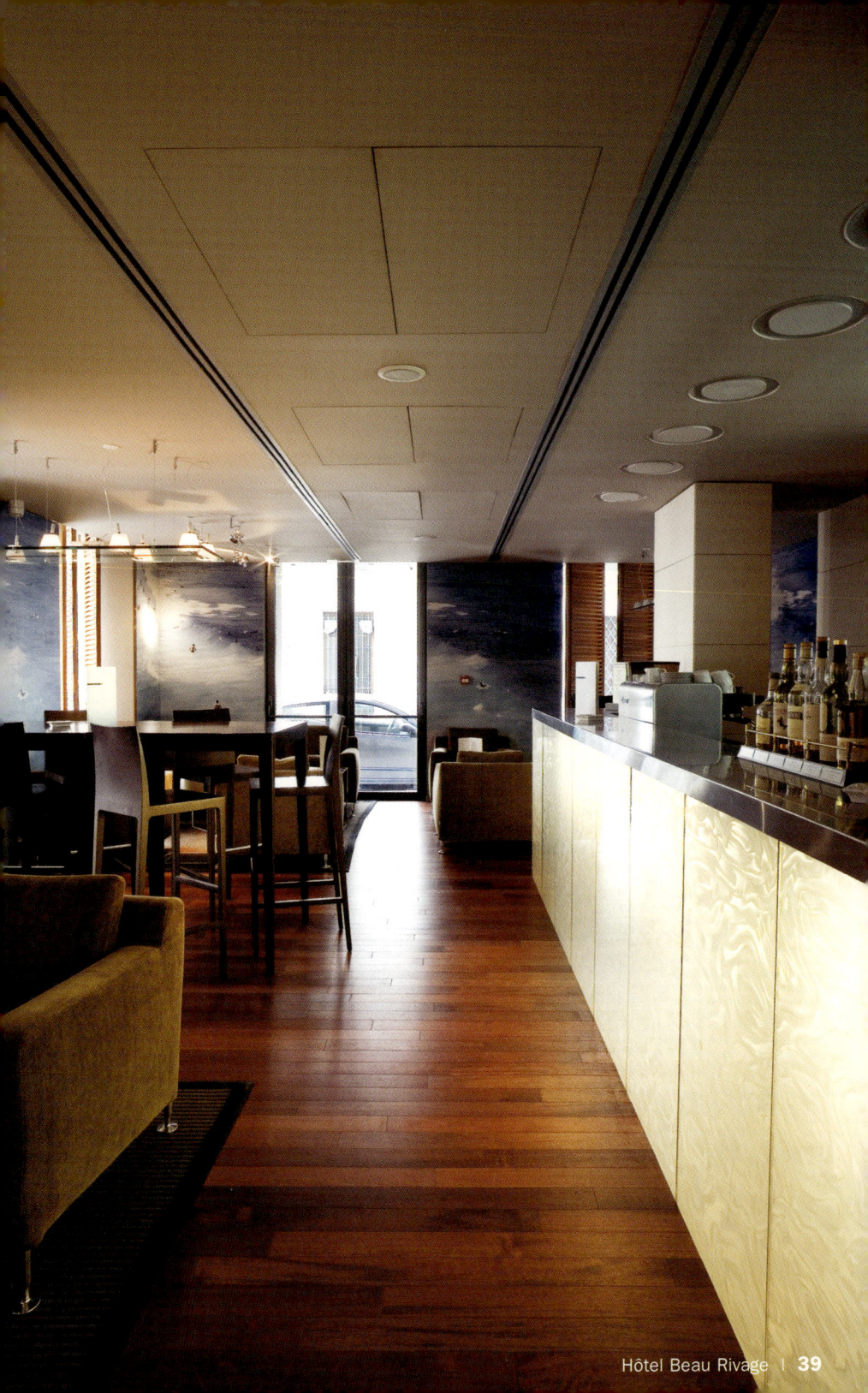

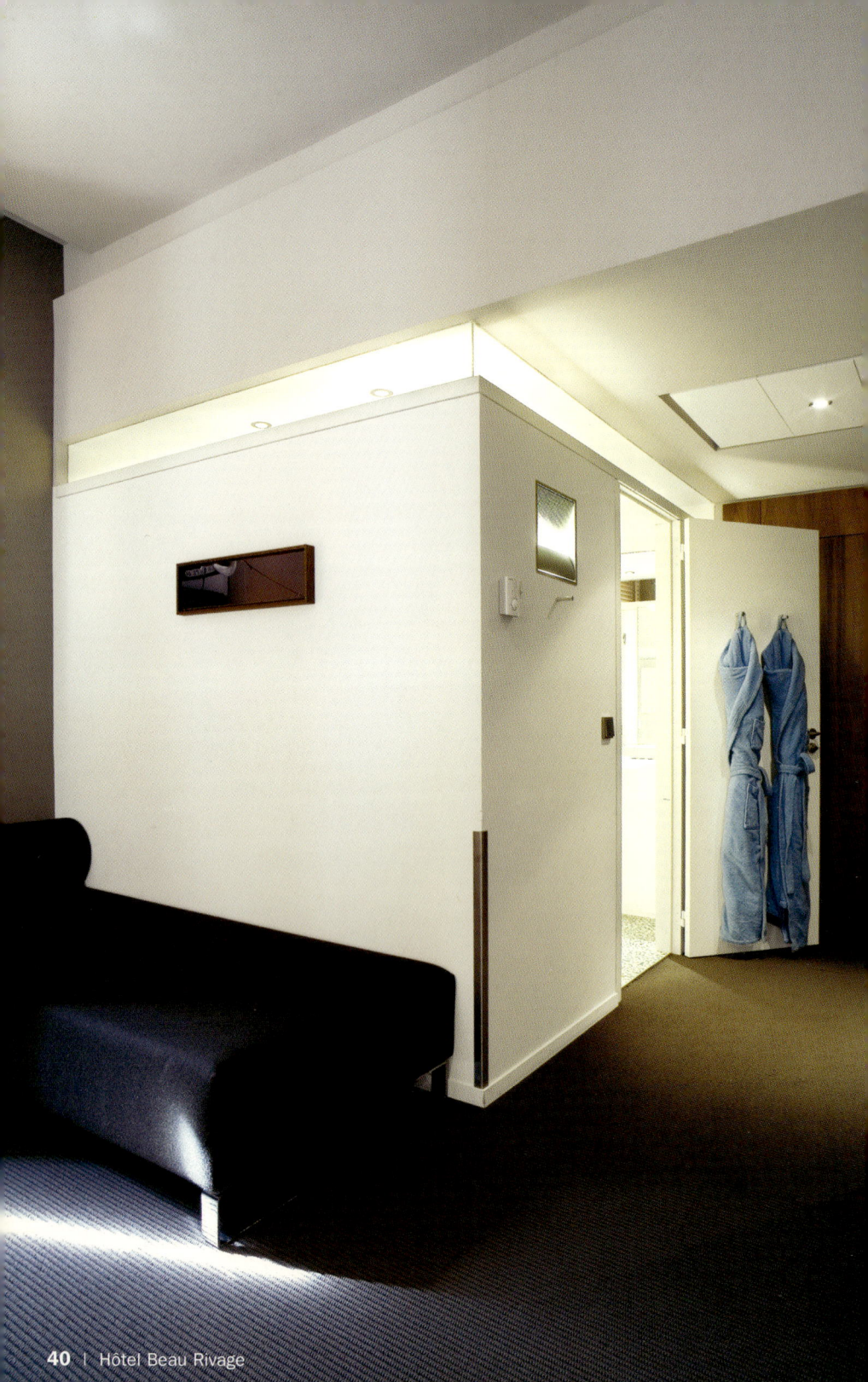

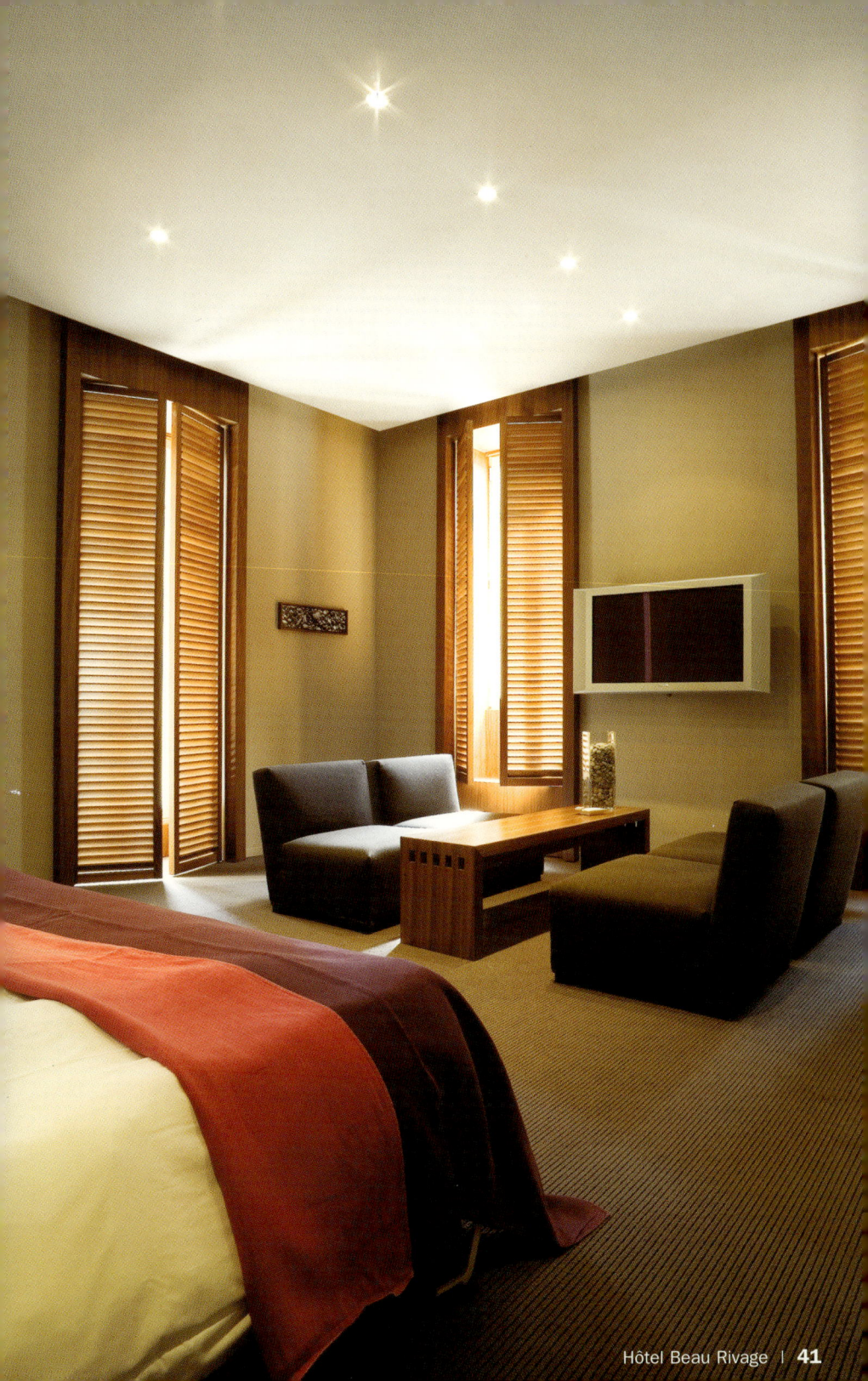

Hôtel Byblos
Saint-Tropez

Design: Mireille Chevanne

Avenue Paul Signac | 83990 Saint-Tropez
Phone: +33 4 94 56 68 00
www.byblos.com
Opening hours: Every day, open 24 hours
Special features: Les Caves du Roy, the hypest disco in Saint-Tropez, and the Spoon
Byblos, the Mediterranean variation of Alain Ducasse's Parisian Food & Wine

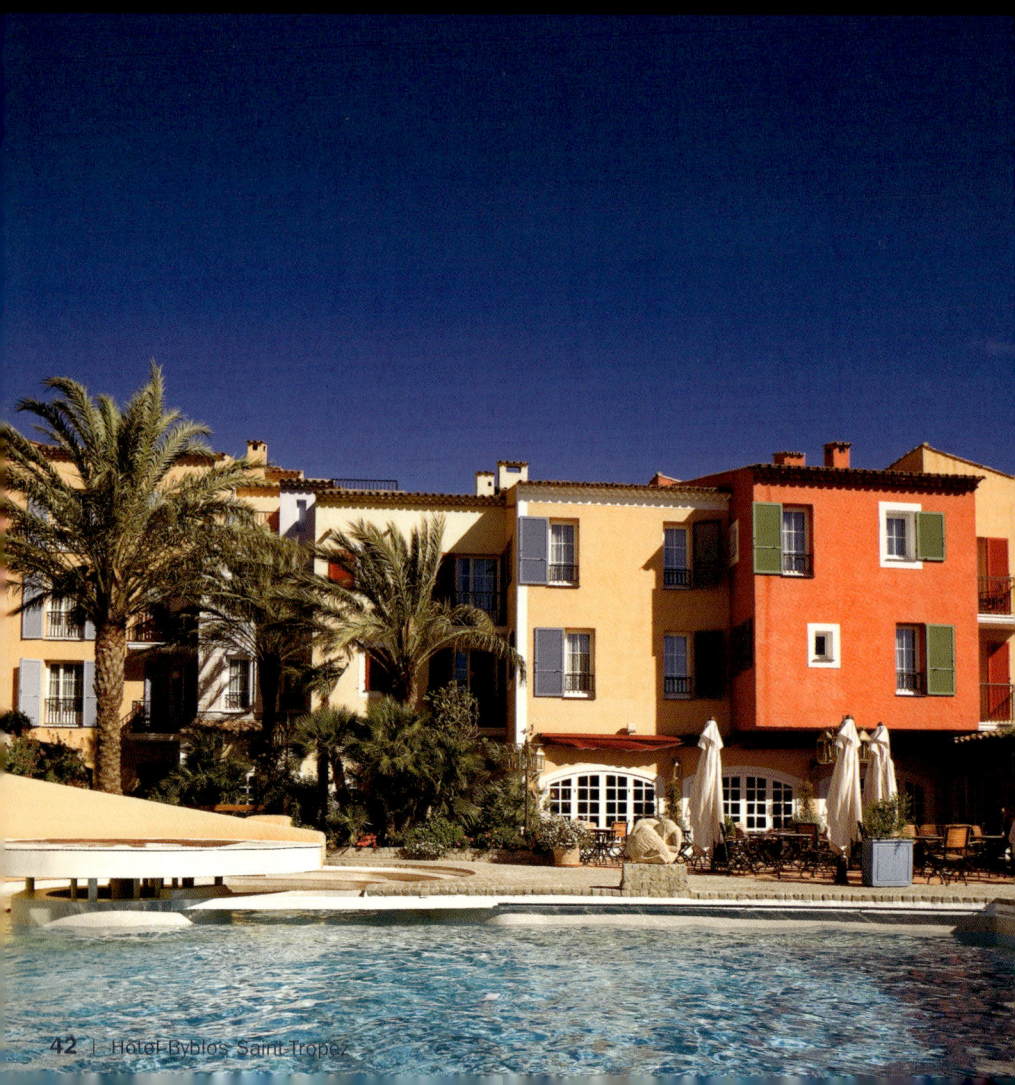

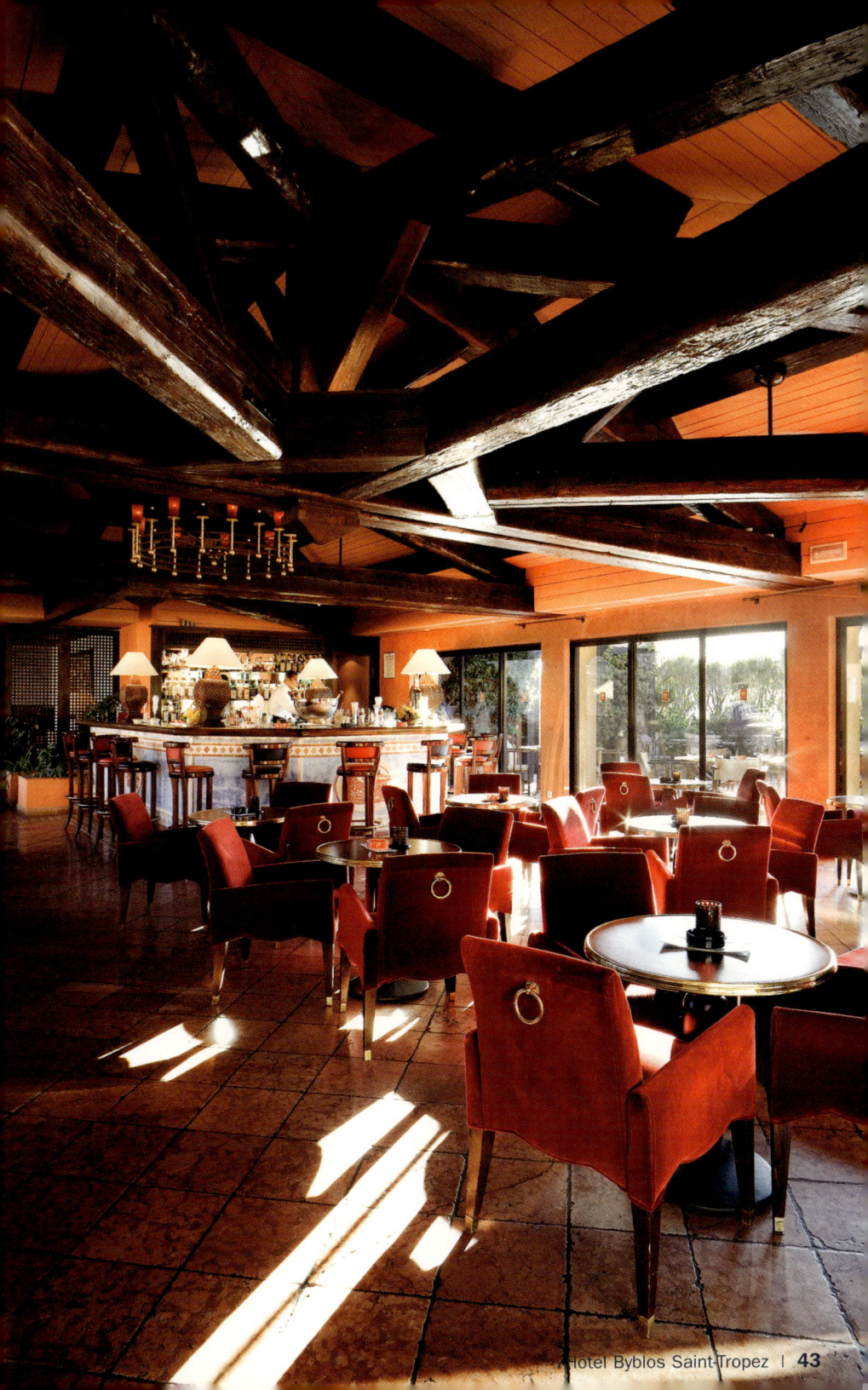

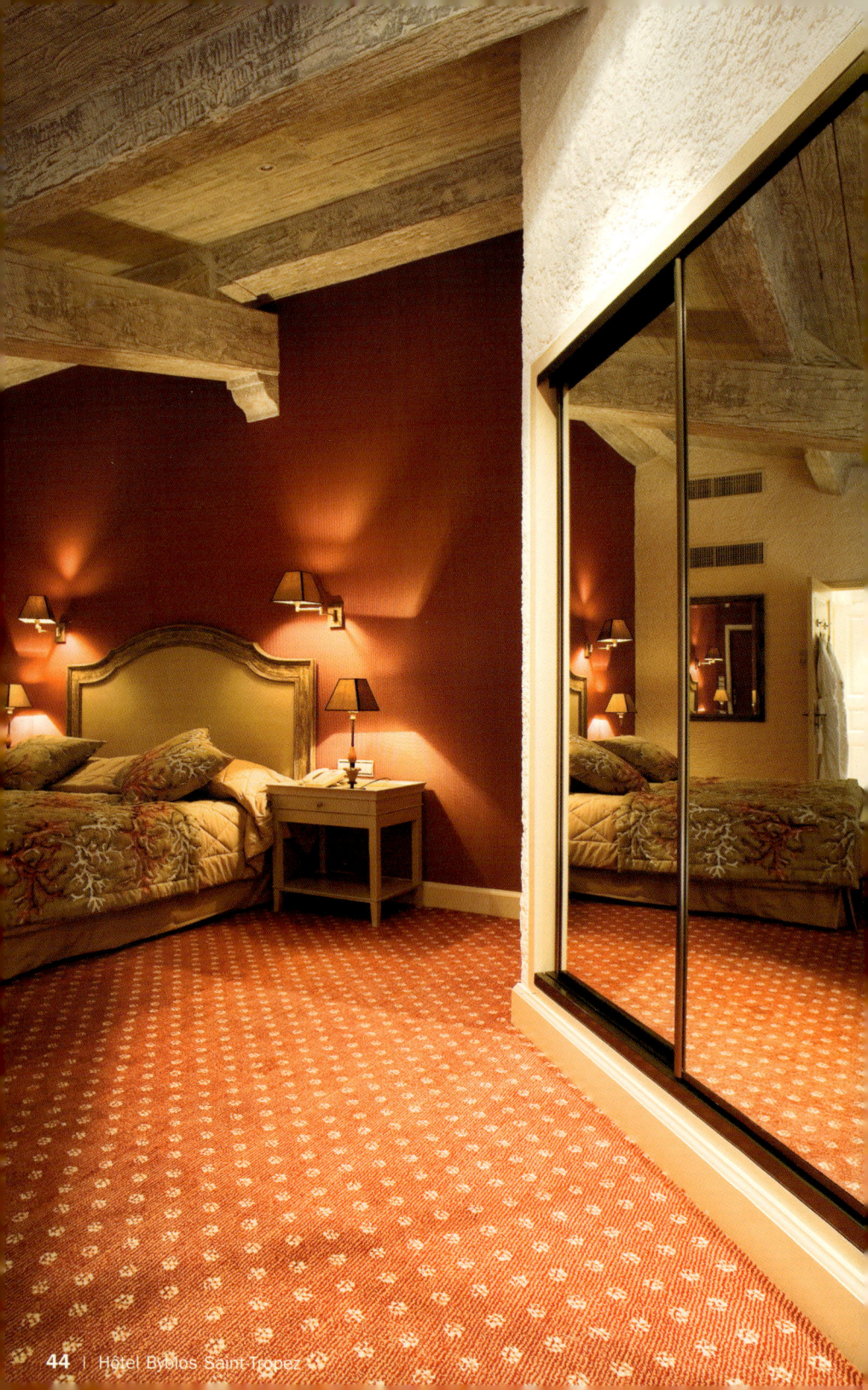

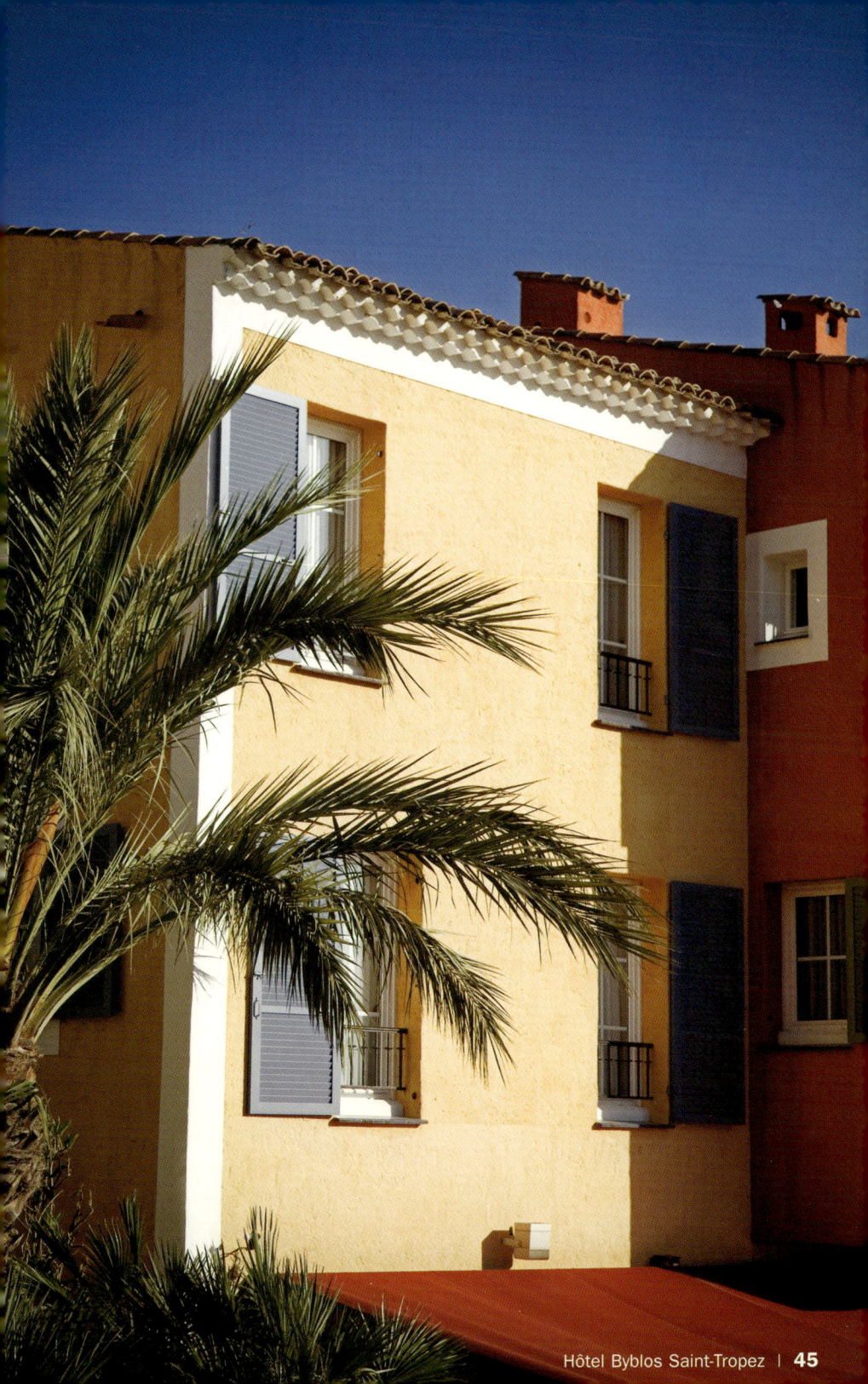

Hôtel Columbus
Monaco

Design: Amanda Rosa

23 Avenue des Papalins I 98000 Monte-Carlo
Phone: +377 92 05 90 00
www.columbushotels.com
Opening hours: Every day, open 24 hours, restaurant every day from 7 pm to 10:30 pm
Special features: Located in Fontvieille, the Chelsea of Monaco, the hotel offers
private salons for up to 90 people and a beautiful outdoor terrace for receptions
and parties

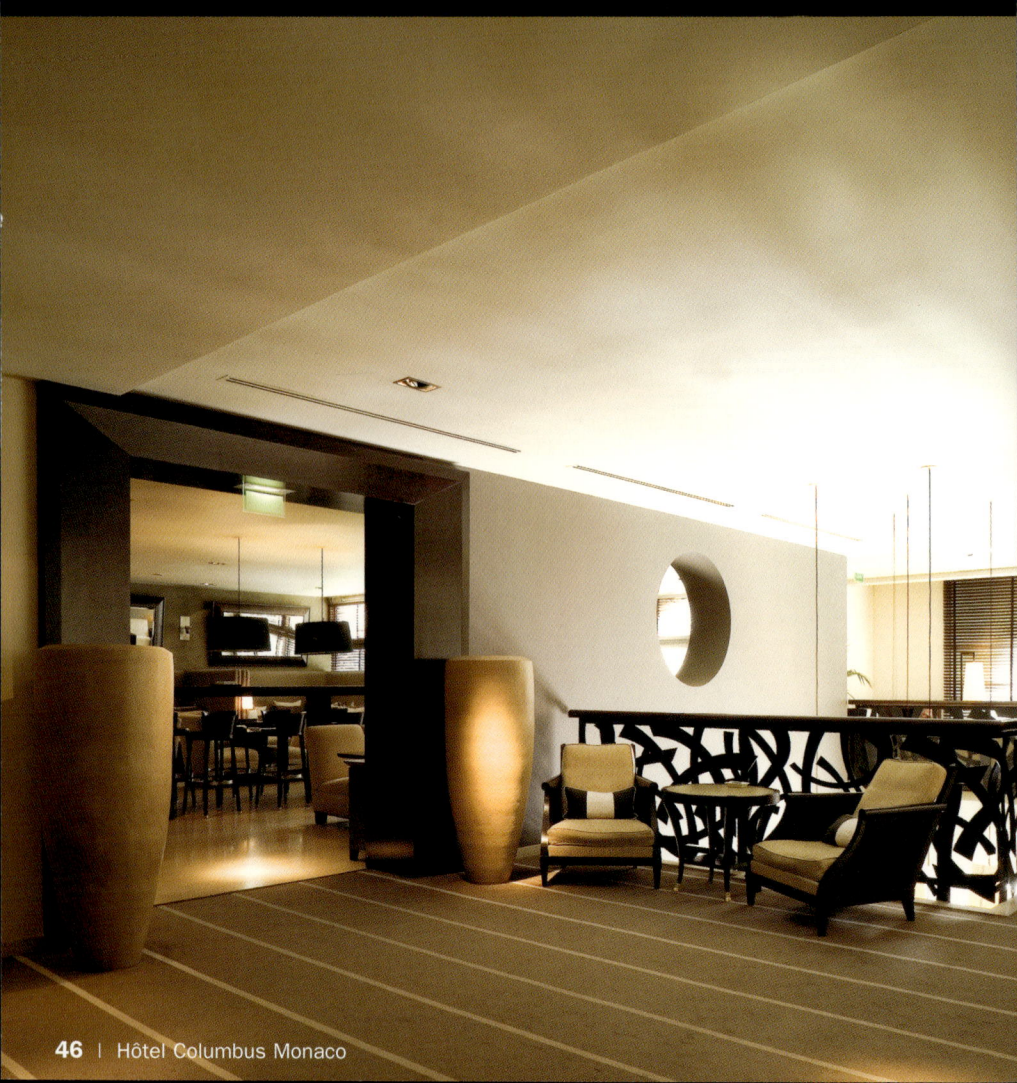

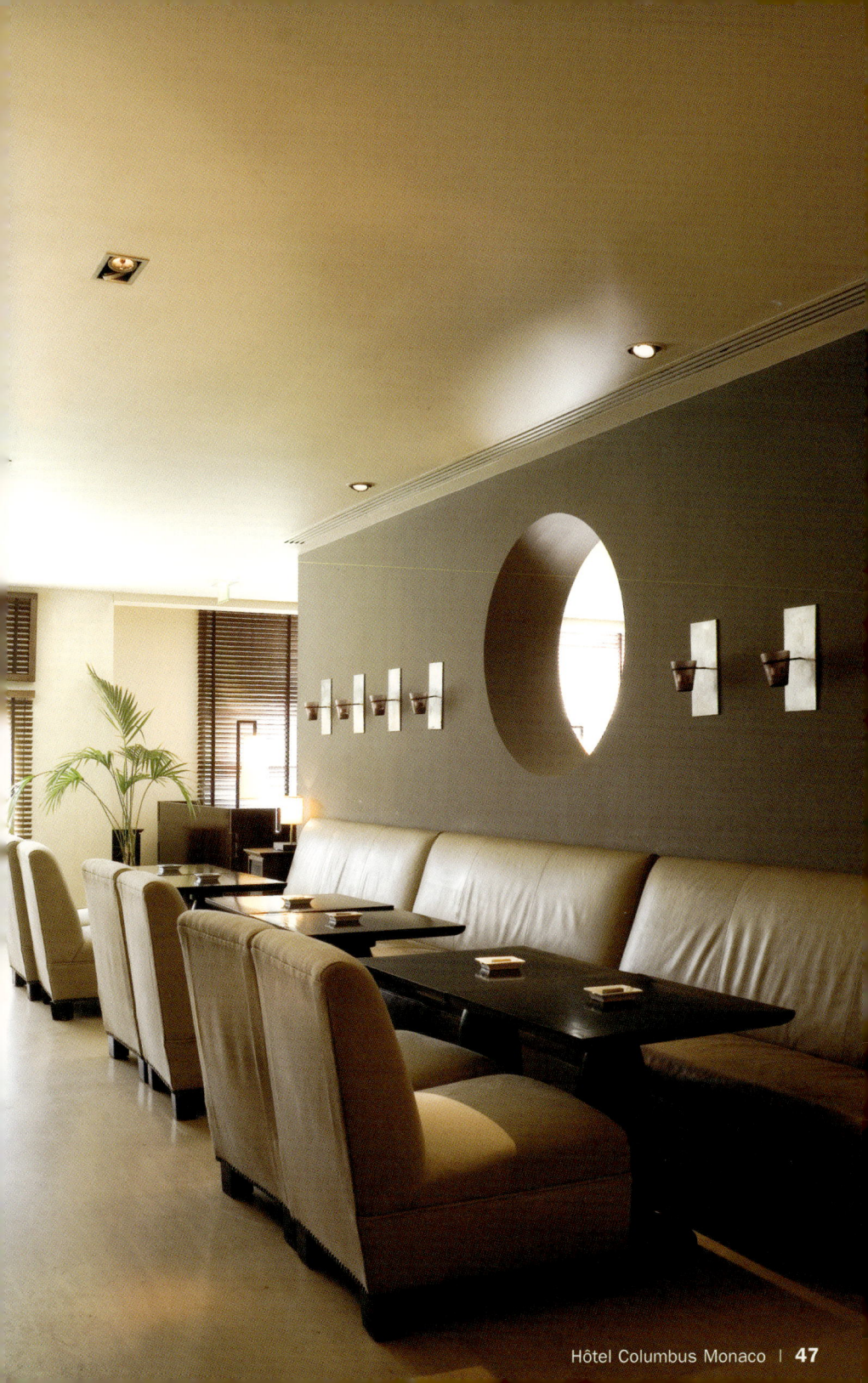

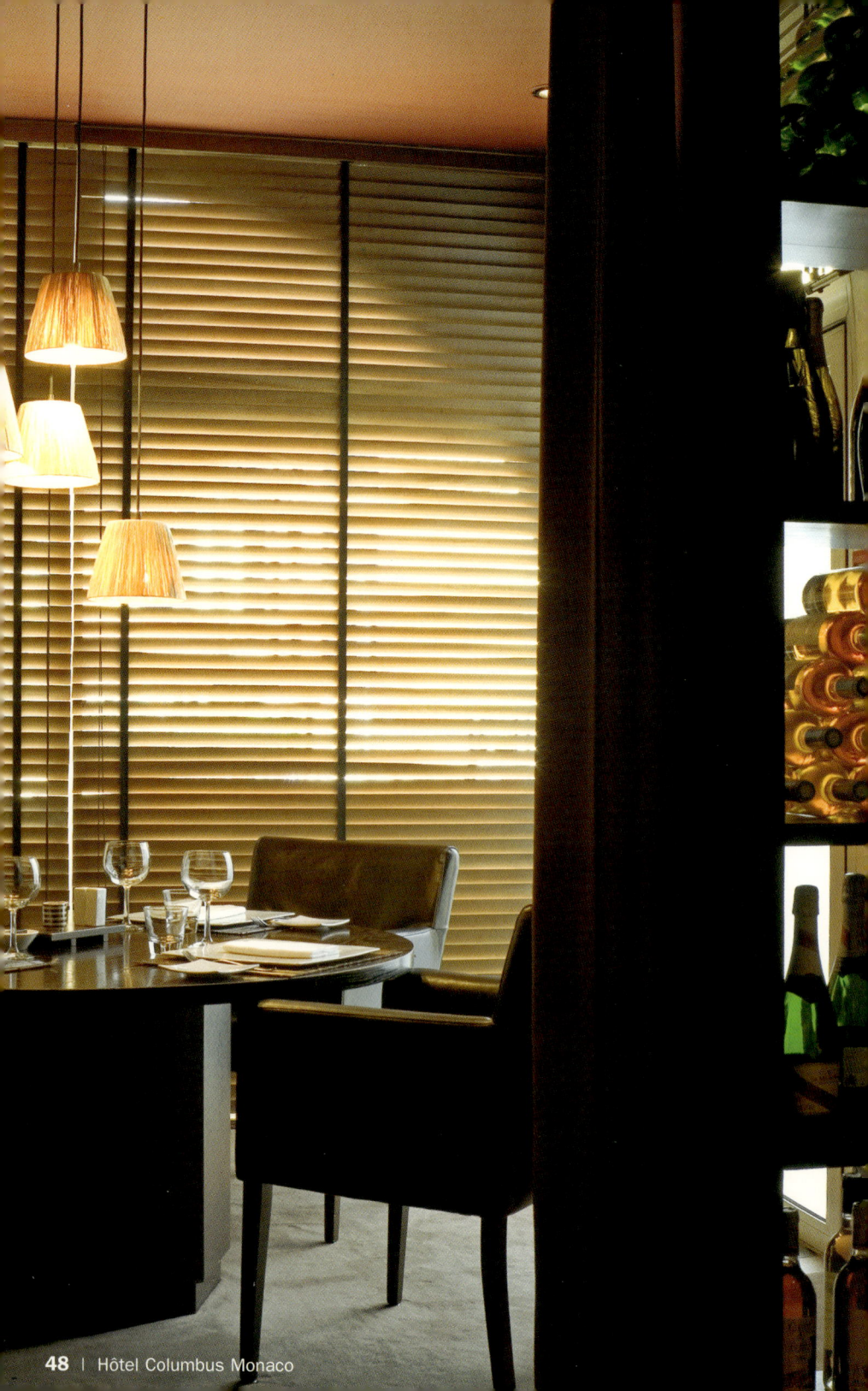

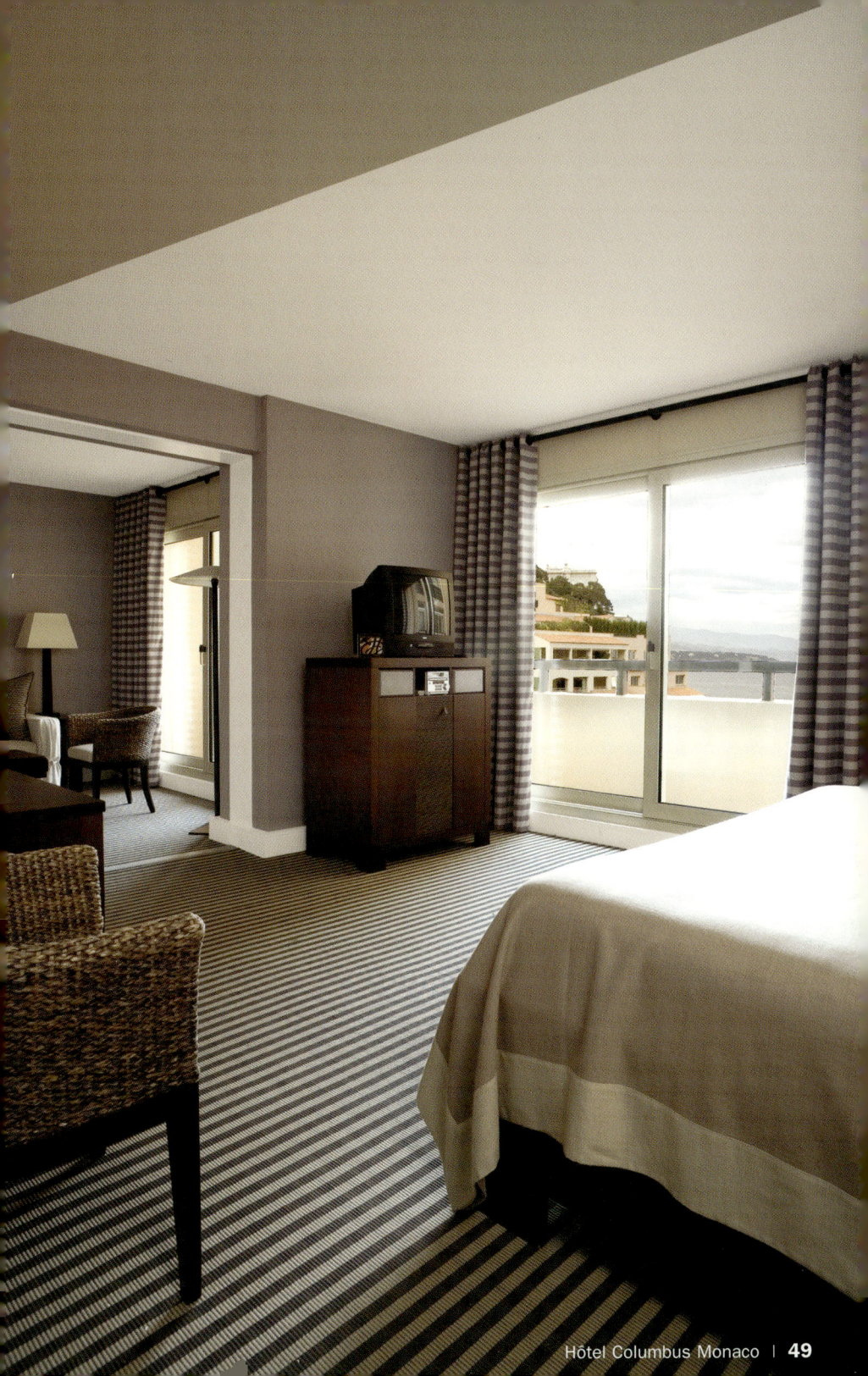

Hôtel HI

Design: Matali Crasset

3 Avenue des Fleurs | 06000 Nice
Phone: +33 4 97 07 26 26
www.hi-hotel.net
Opening hours: Every day, open 24 hours, hammam from 10 am to 11 pm
Special features: There is a hammam in the hotel, including massage and bath
zones and a relaxation room, as well as a "Happy Bar", open 24 hours. Rooms are
furnished under 9 concepts or decorative themes

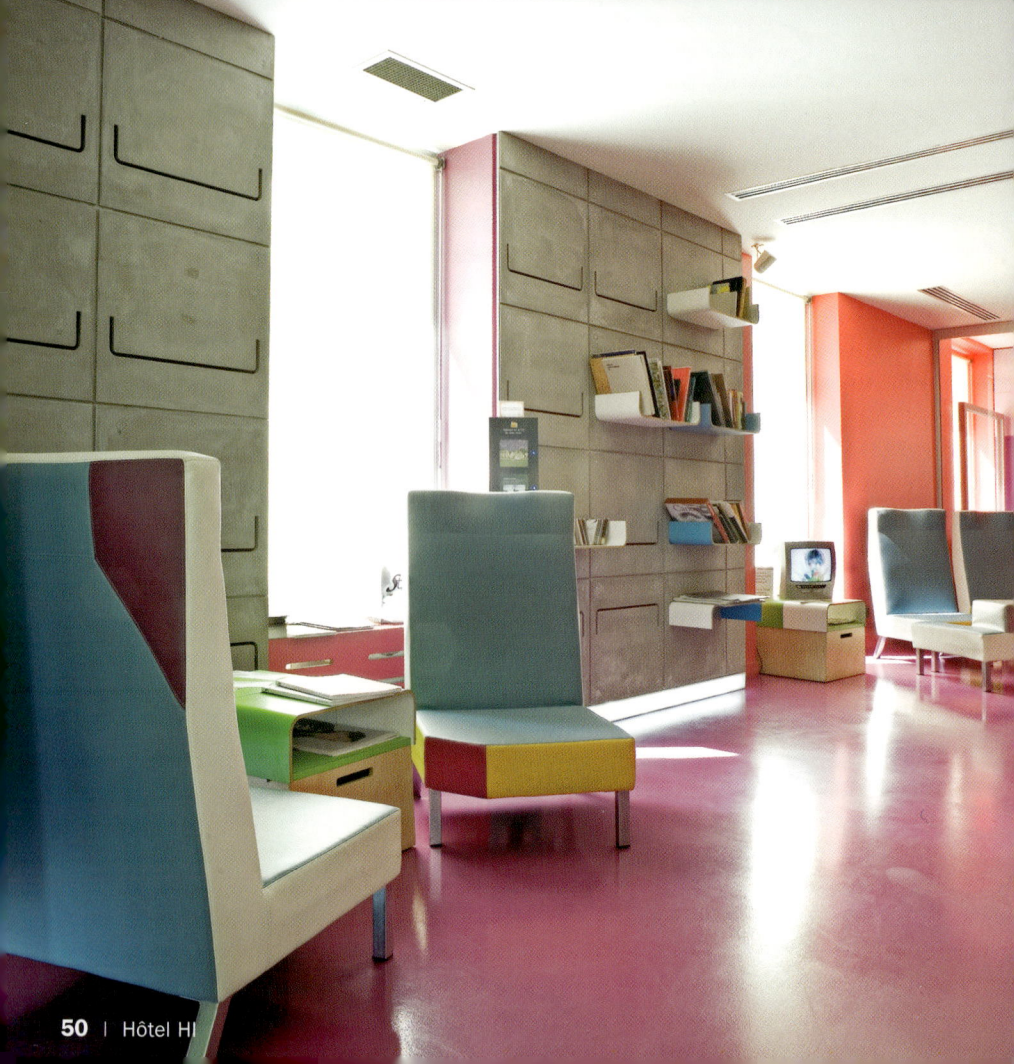

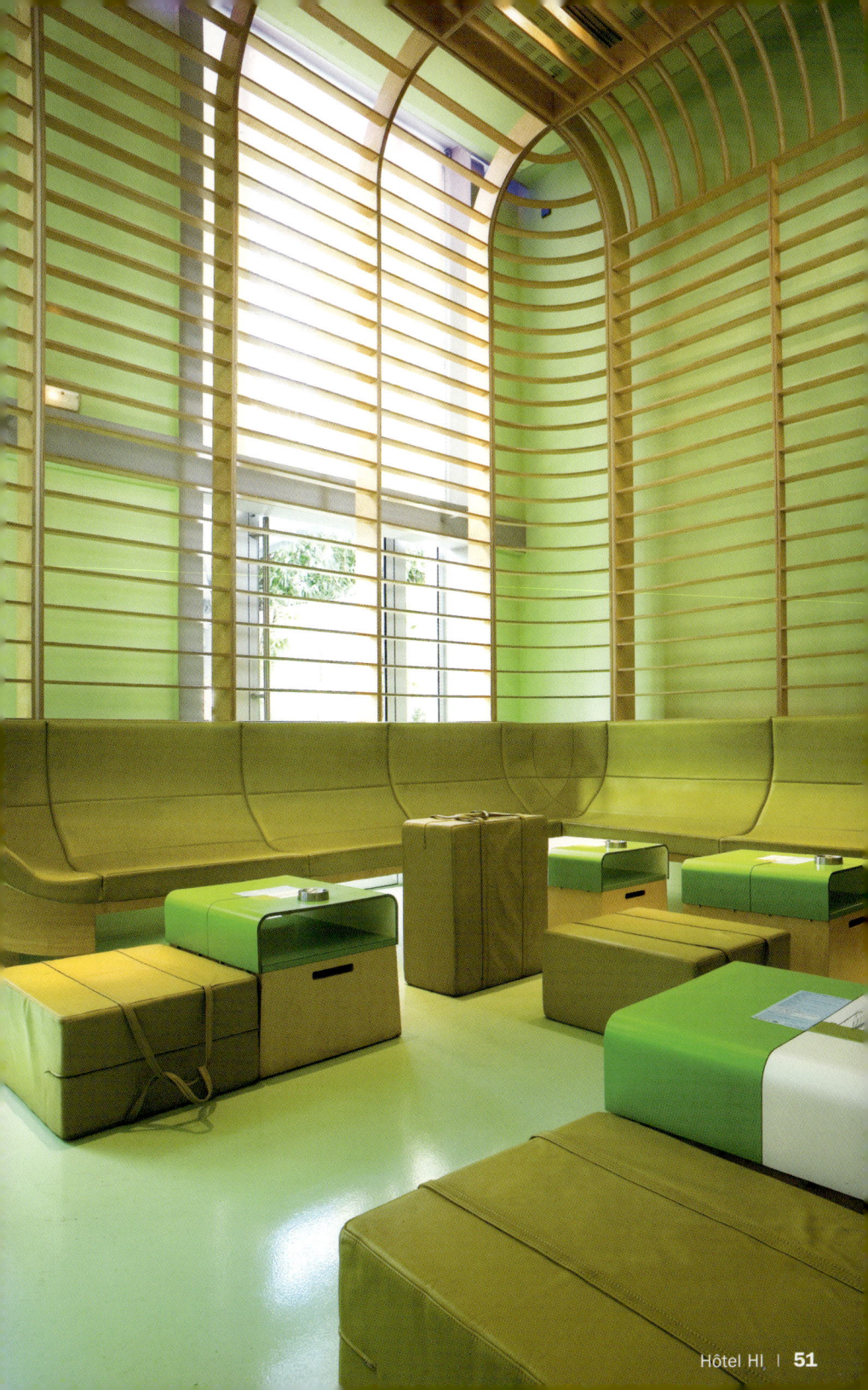

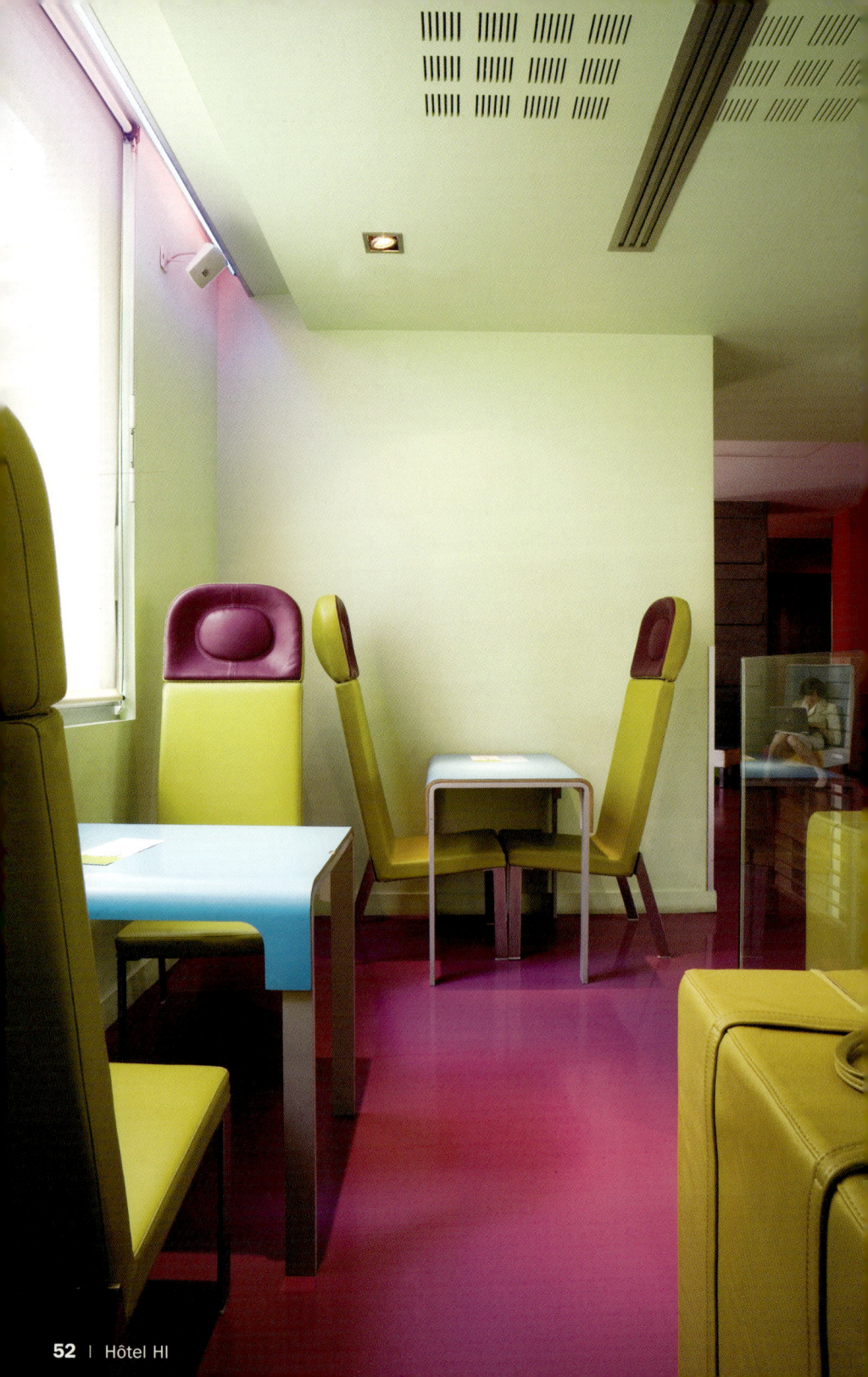

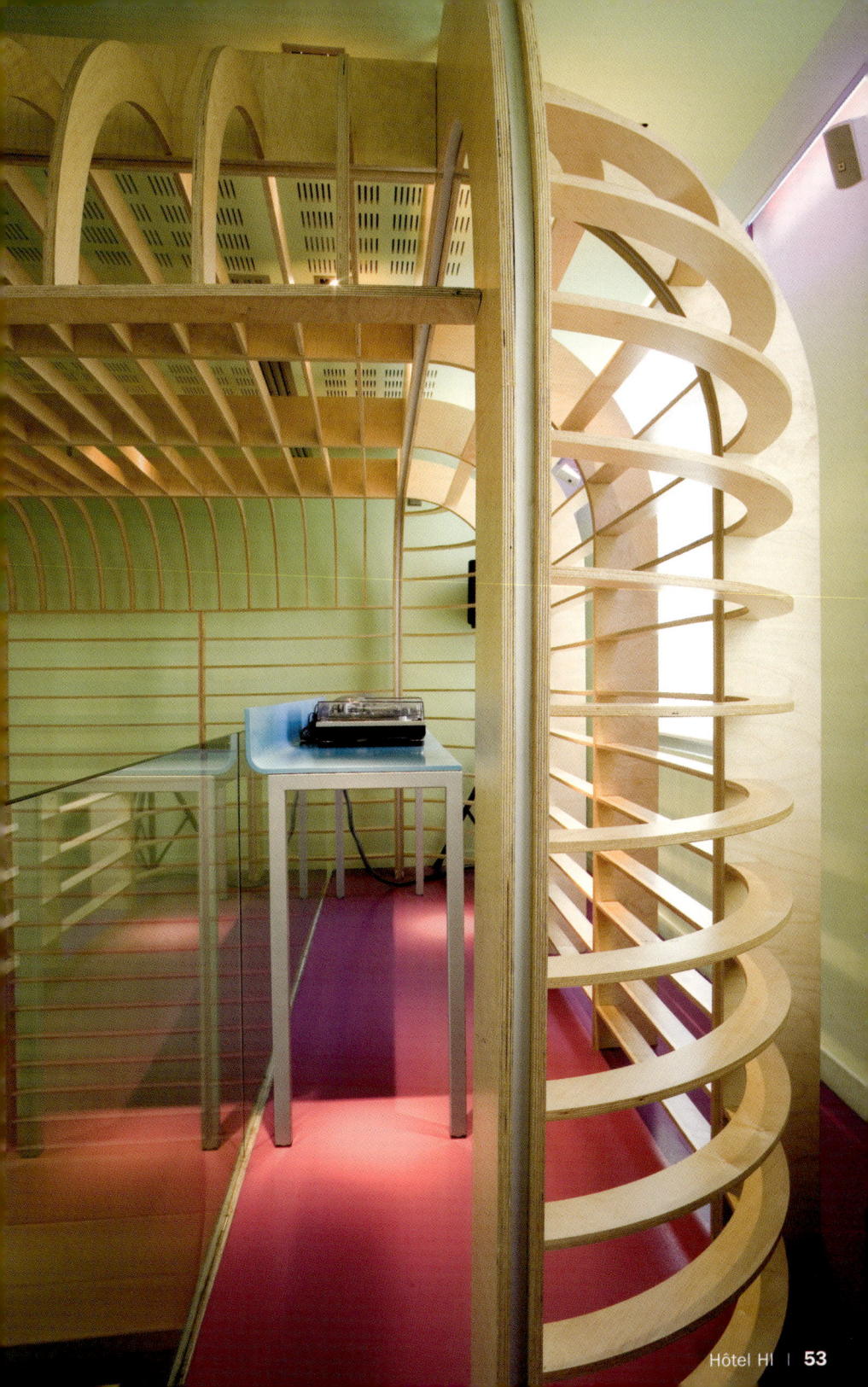

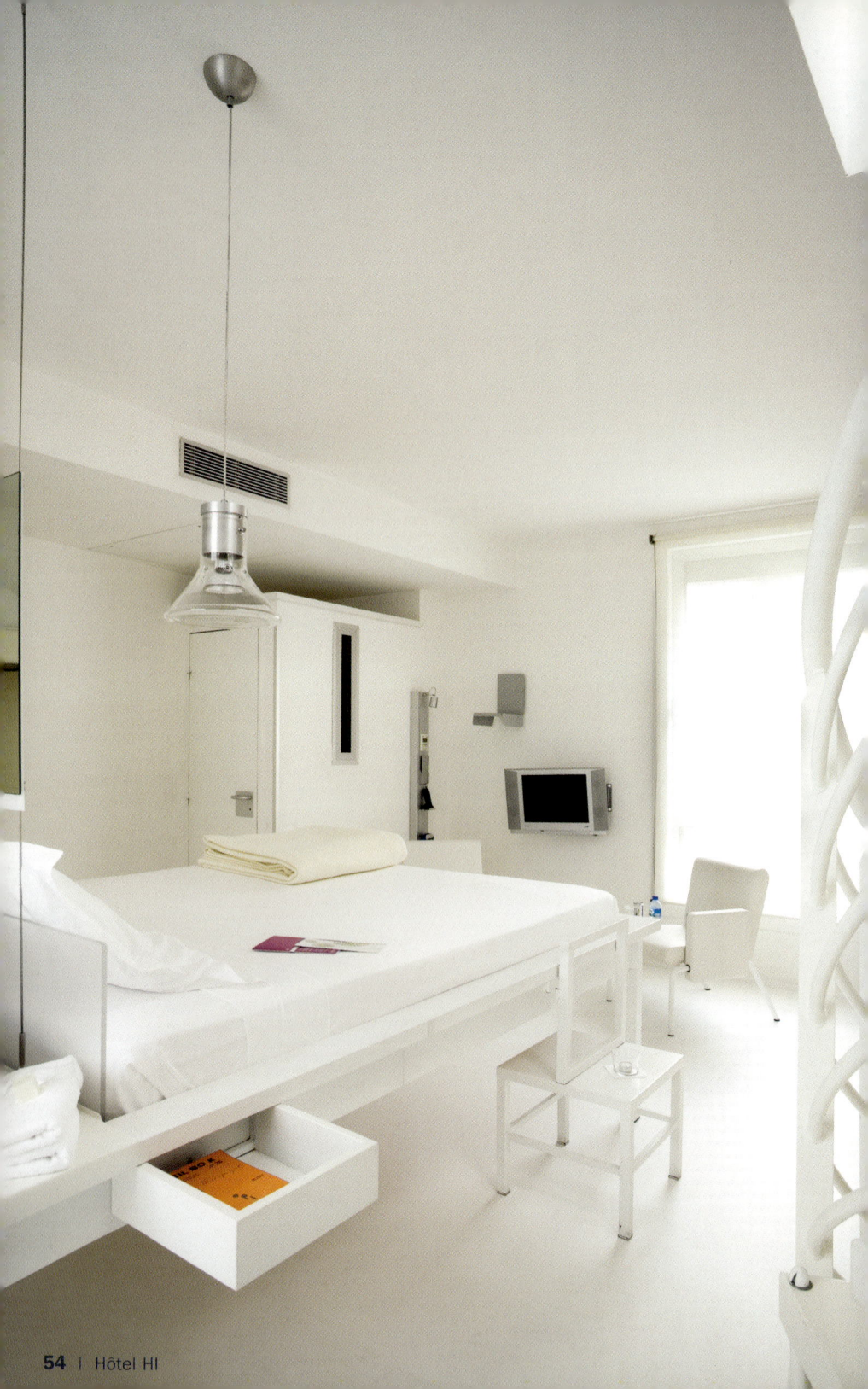

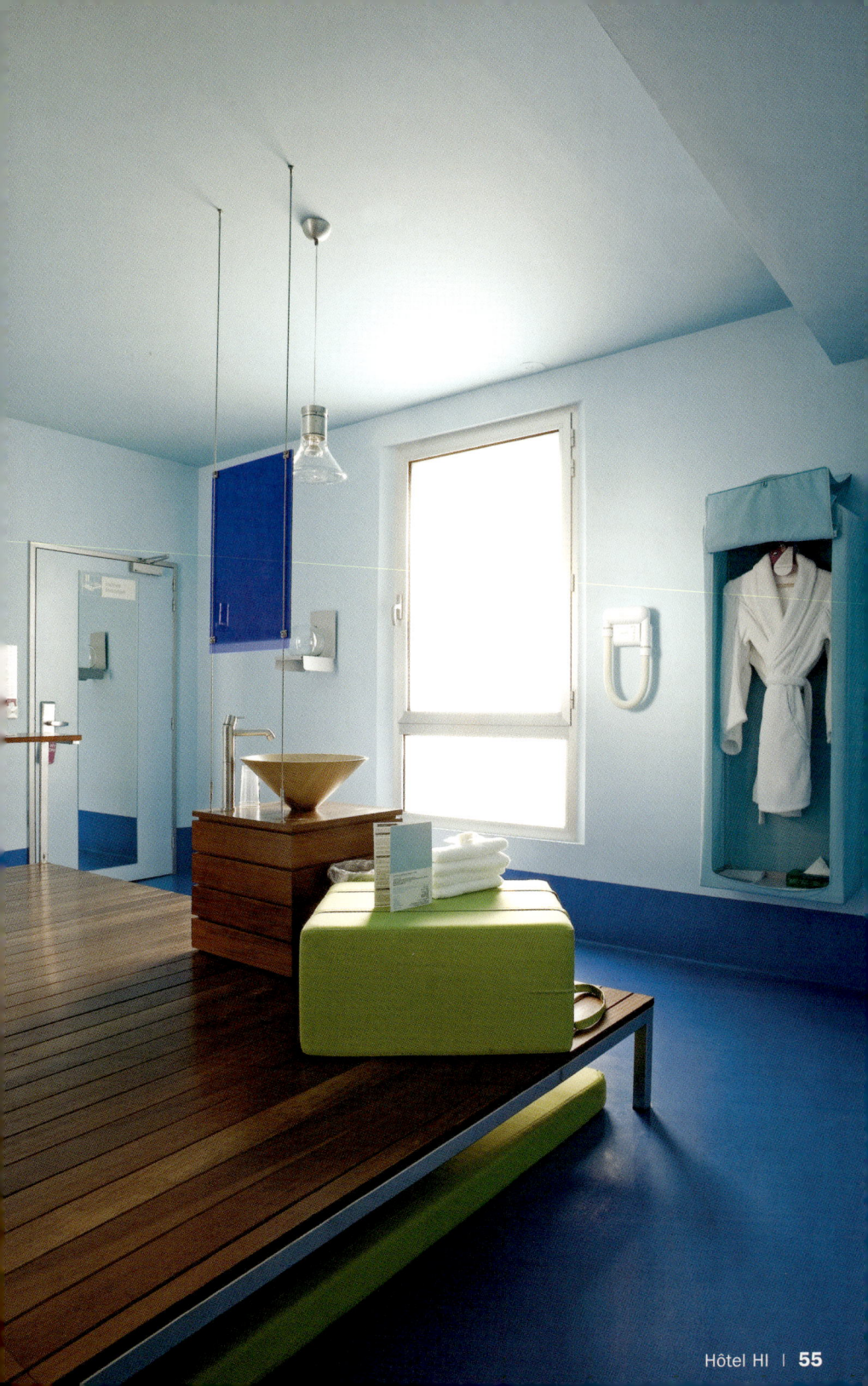

Hôtel Martinez

Design: ECART Paris

73 La Croisette | 06406 Cannes Cedex
Phone: +33 4 92 98 73 00
www.hotel-martinez.com
Opening hours: Every day, open 24 hours
Special features: The Hôtel Martinez is considered one of Europe's finest luxury resorts. The panoramic apartments on the 7th floor are among the most beautiful suites with sea view you can find

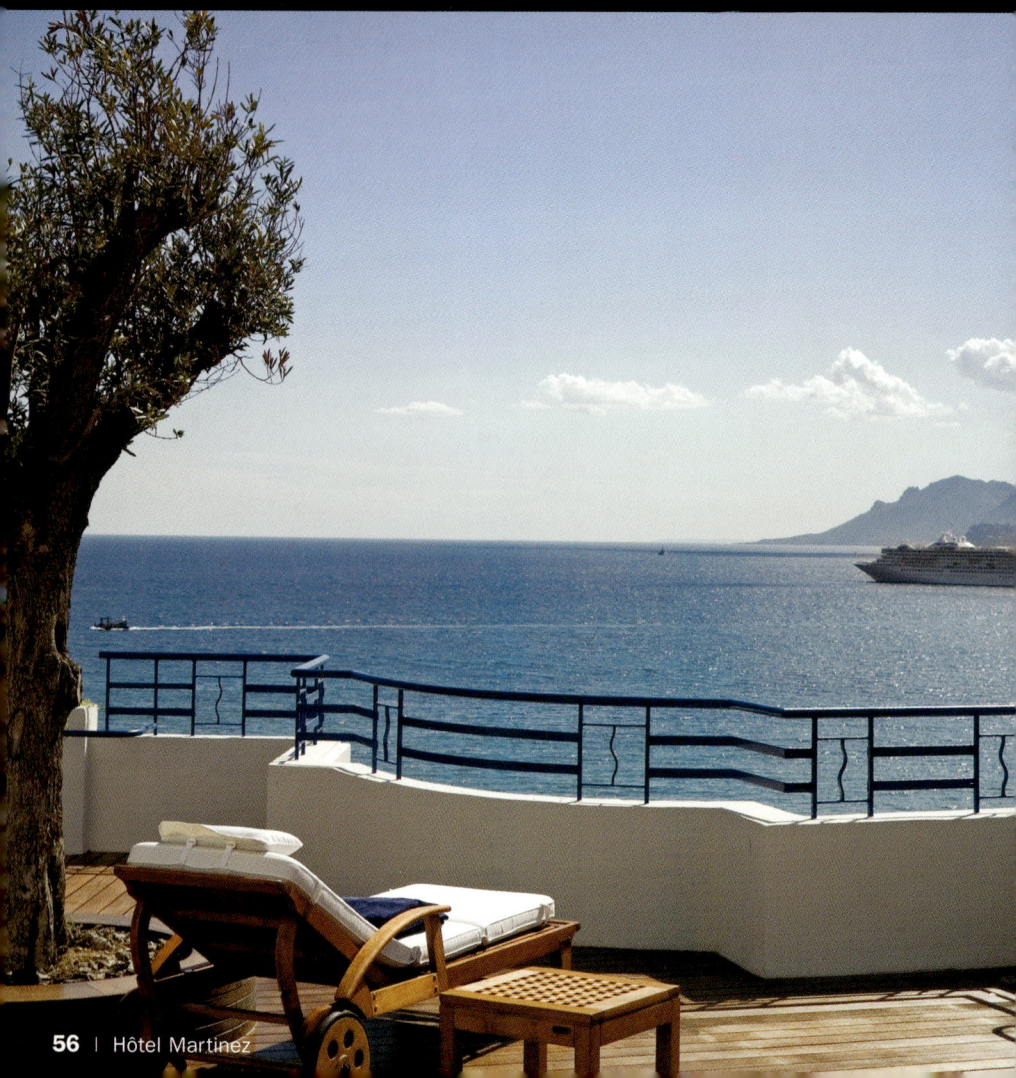

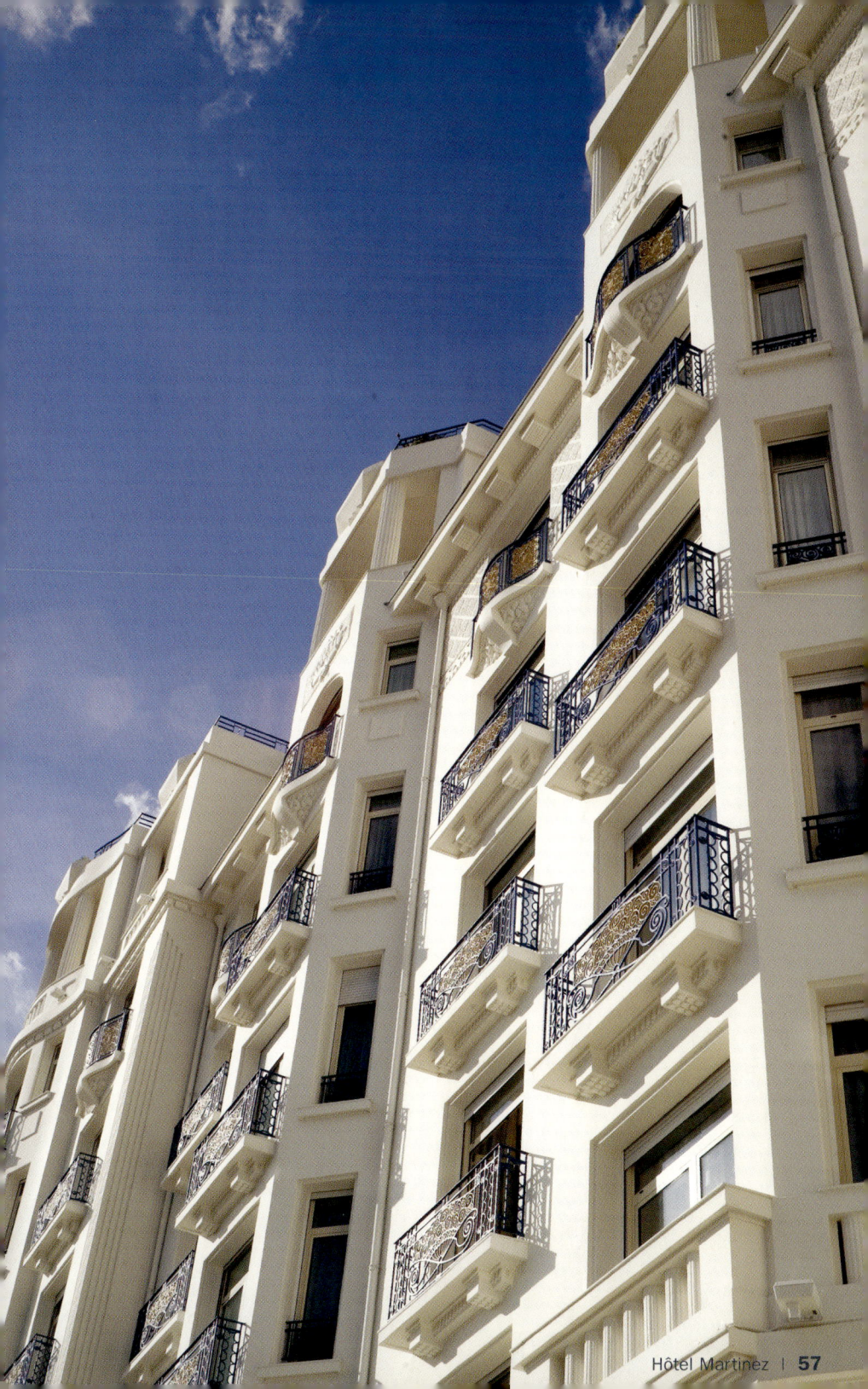

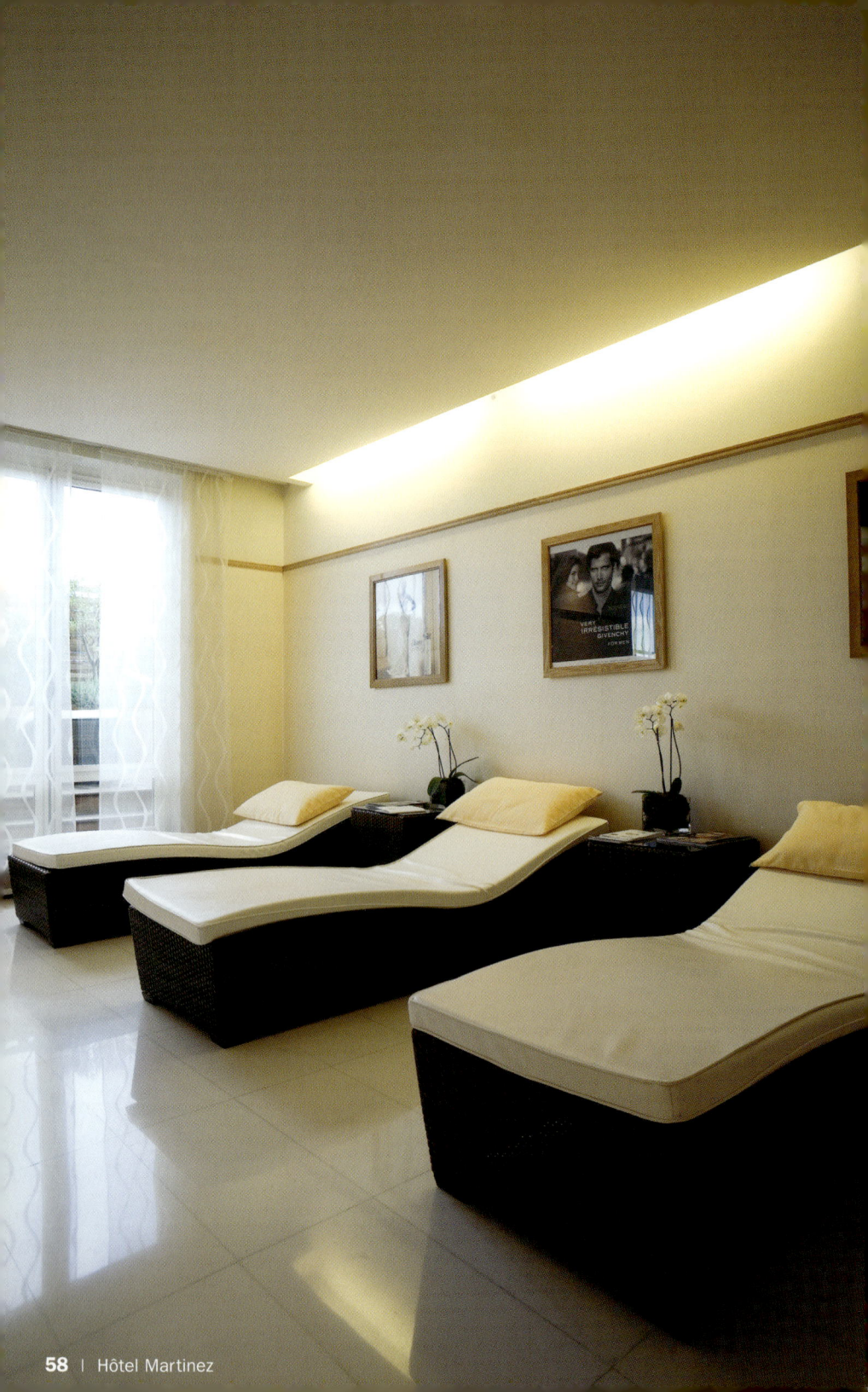

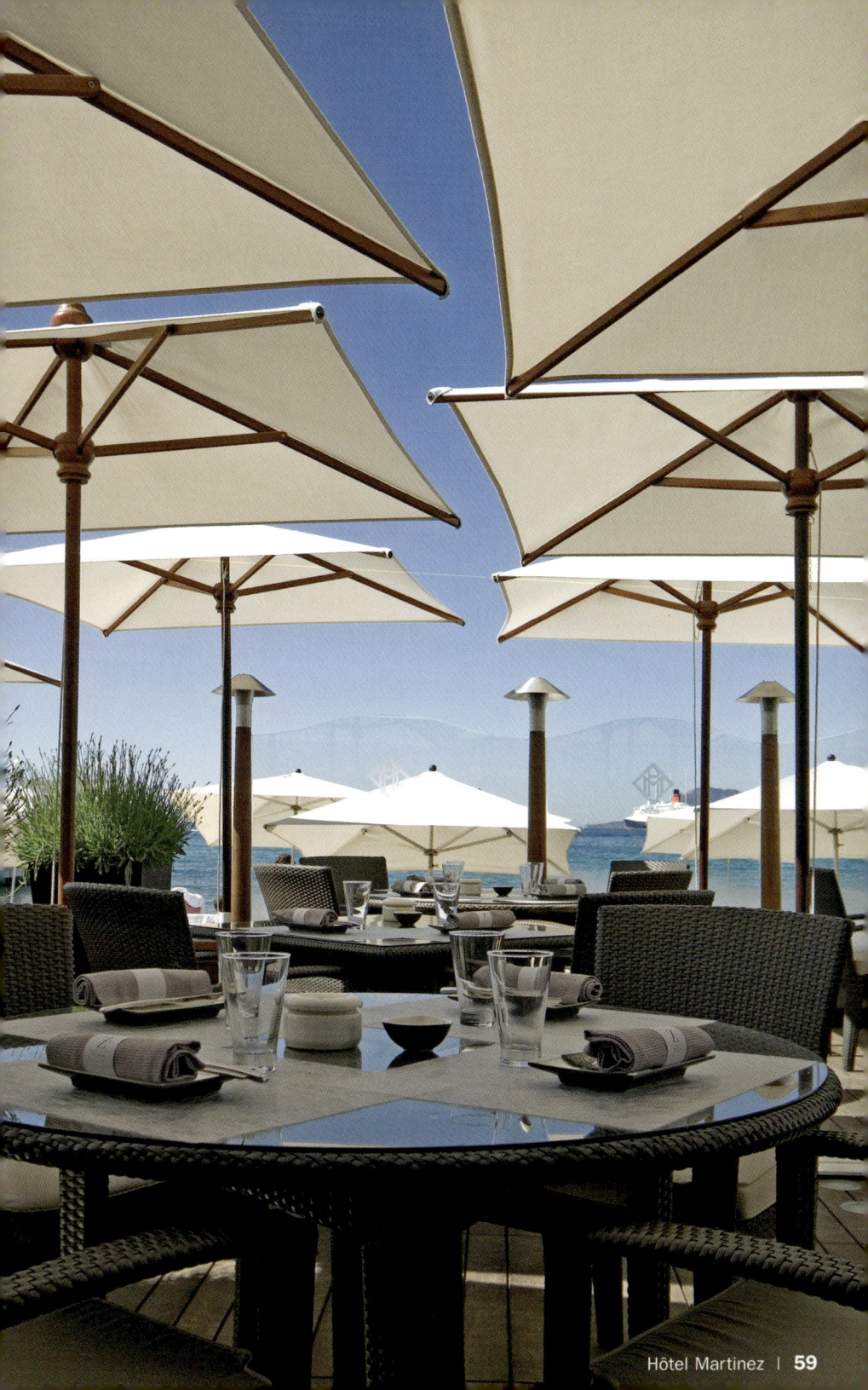

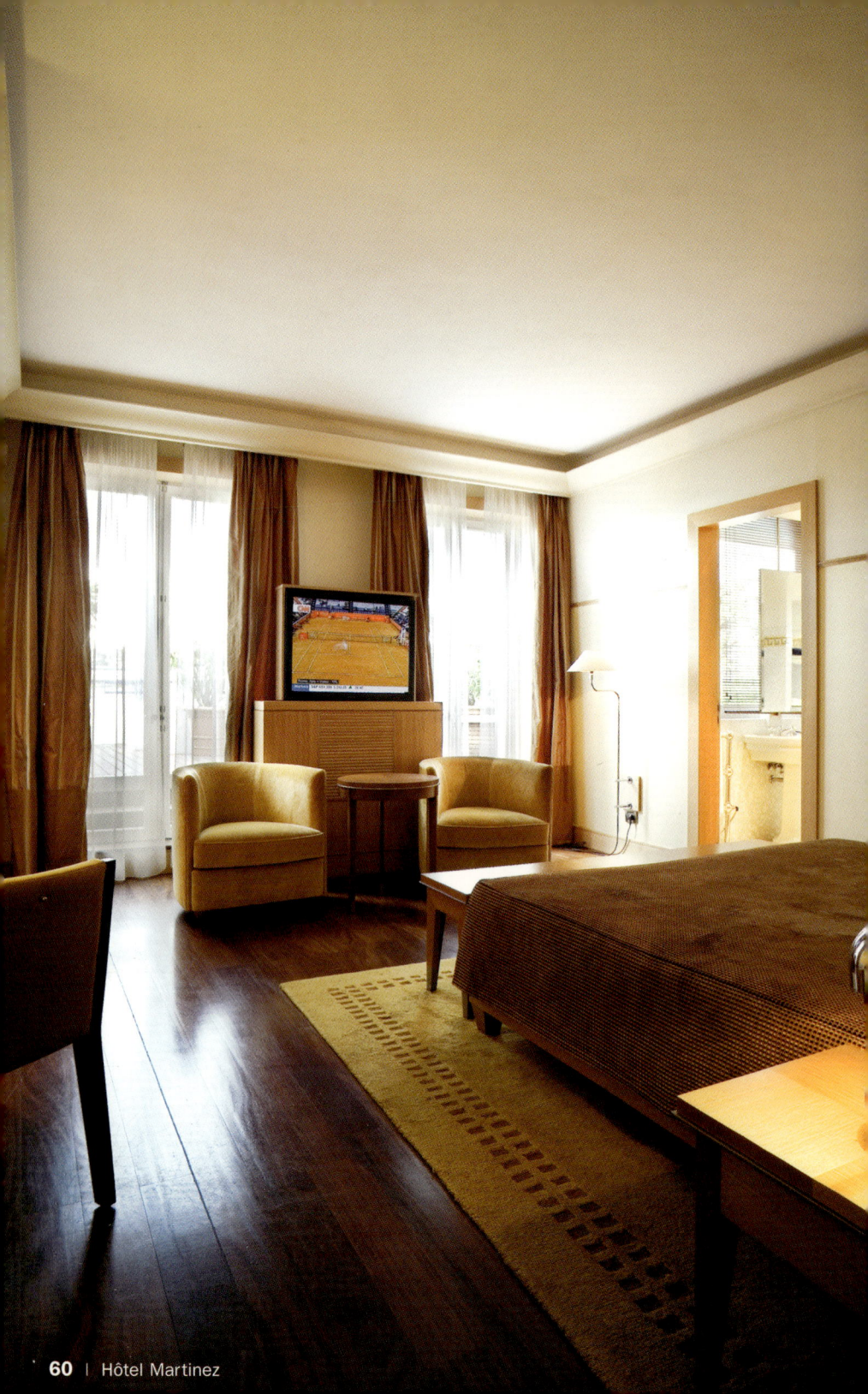

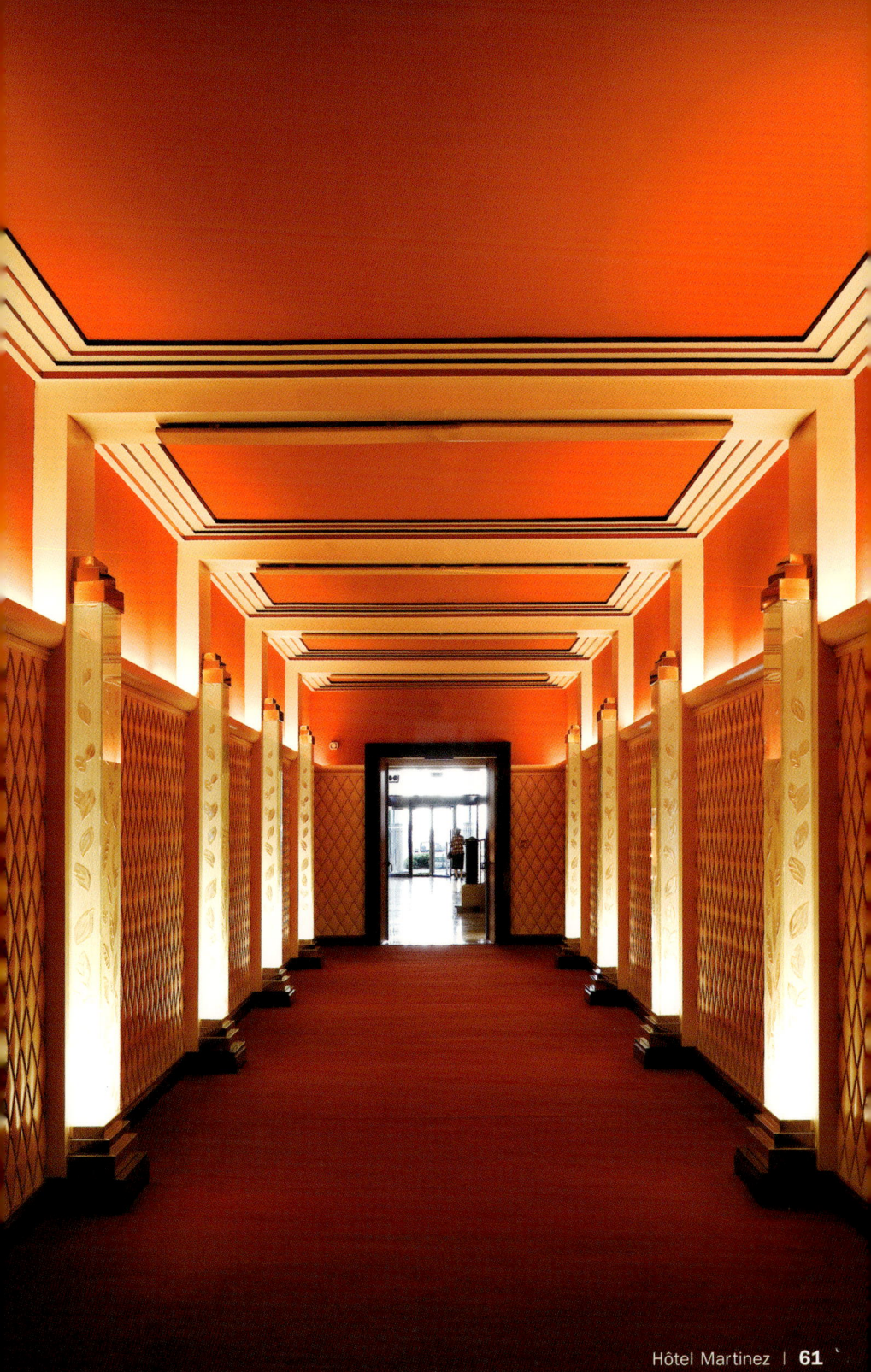

Hôtel Villa Marie

Design: Jean Louis Sibuet

Route des Plages/Chemin Val Rian | 83350 Ramatuelle
Phone: +33 4 94 97 40 22
www.villamarie.fr
Opening hours: From the end of April to the beginning of October, open 24 hours
Special features: A beautiful villa on the hill of Ramatuelle, surrounded by a pine
forest. There is an excellent restaurant and a spa in the hotel

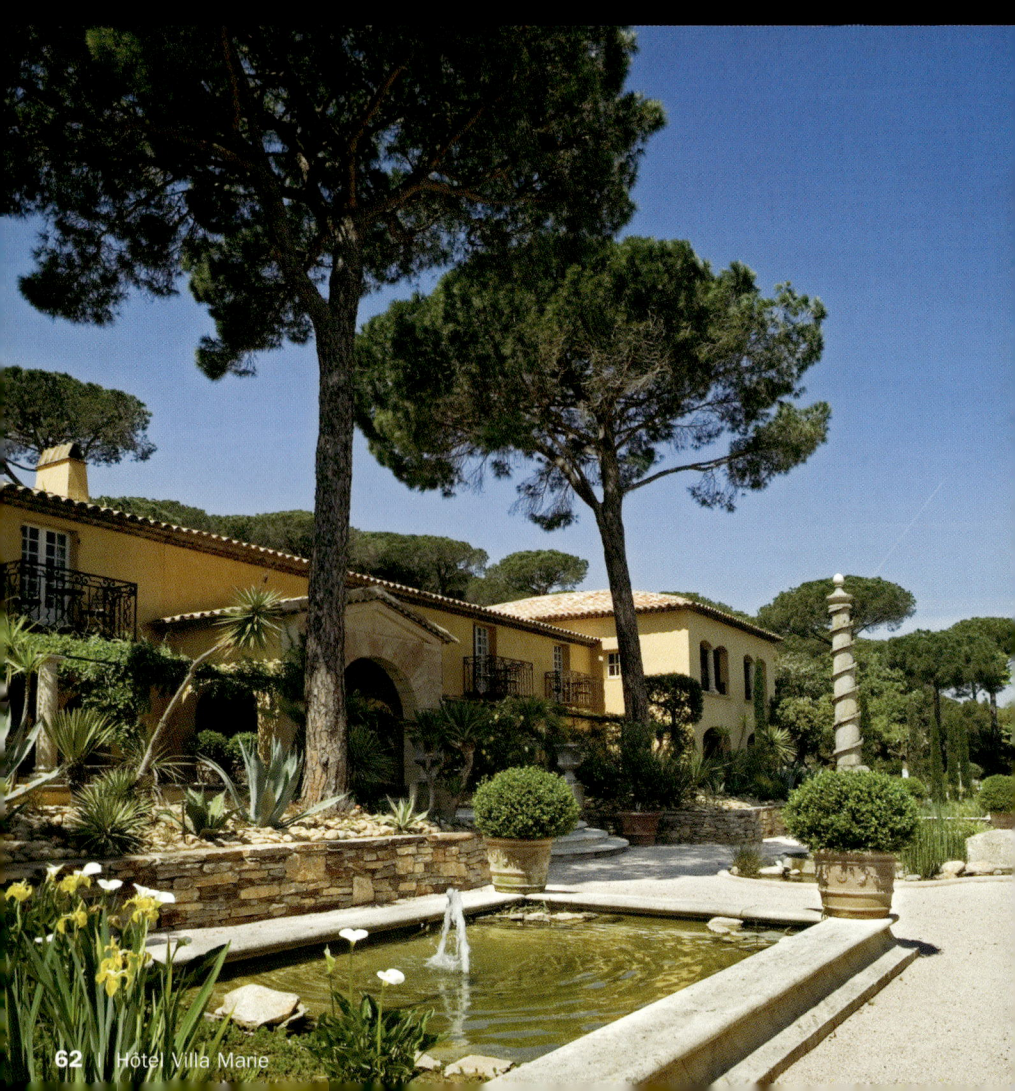

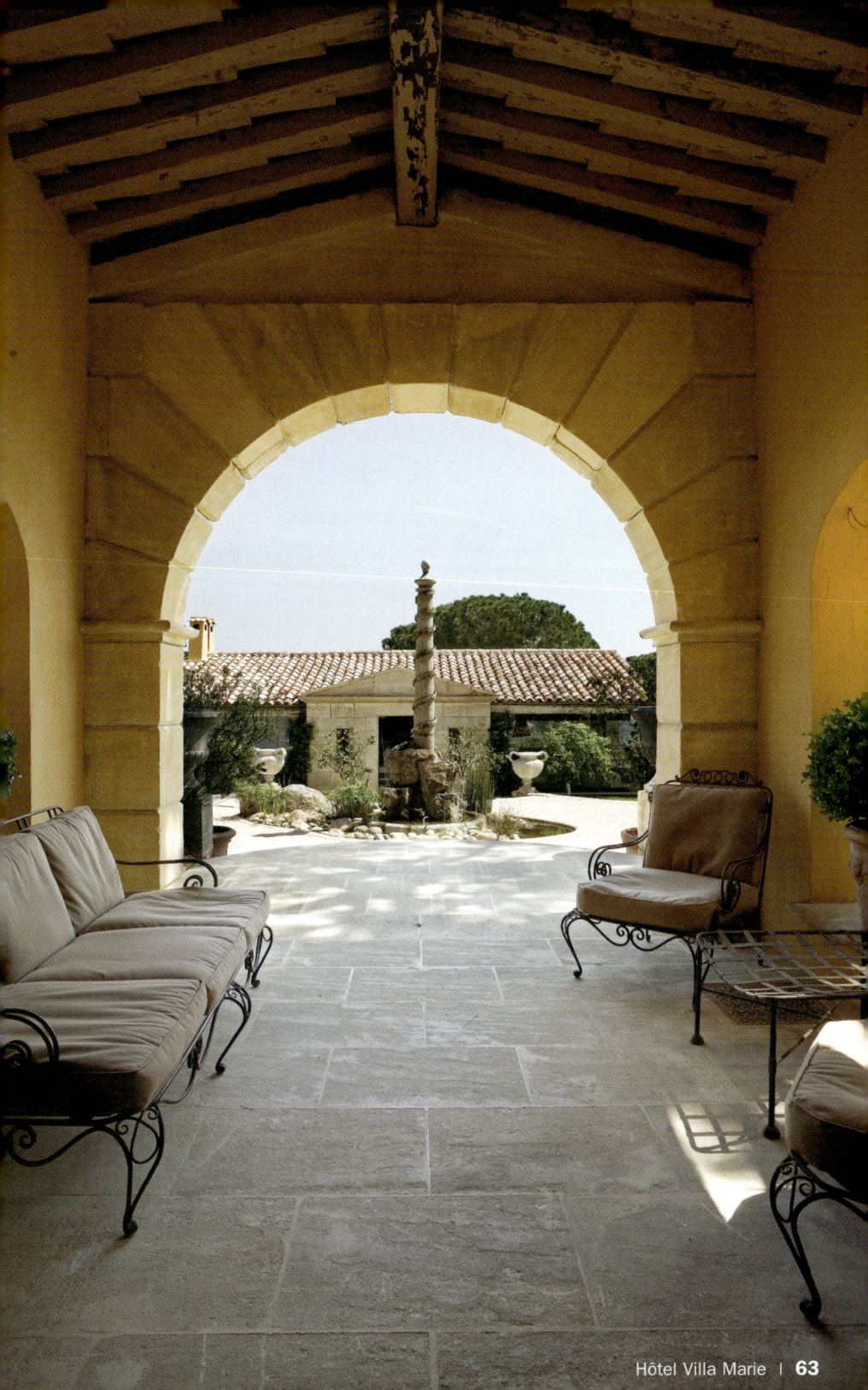

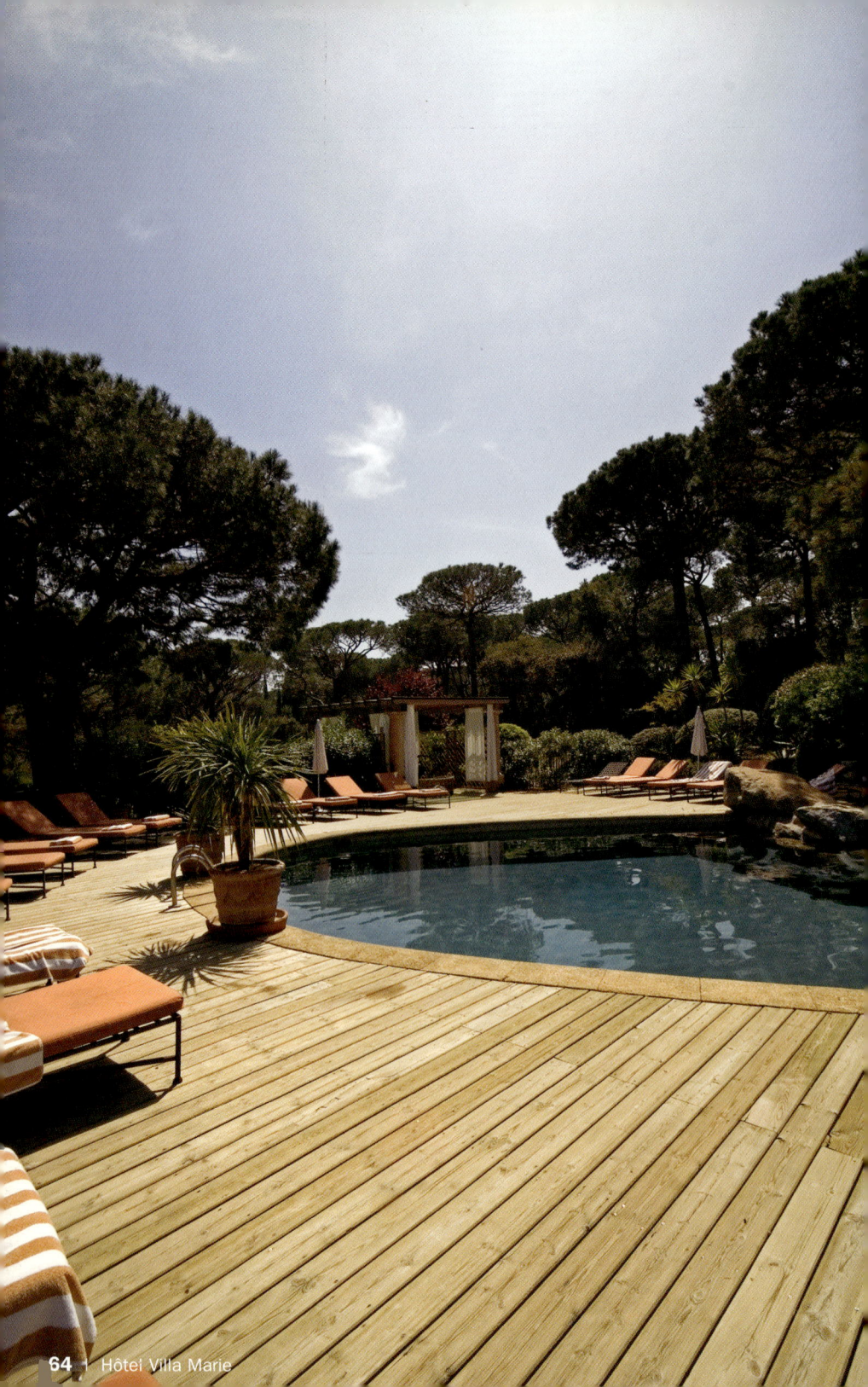

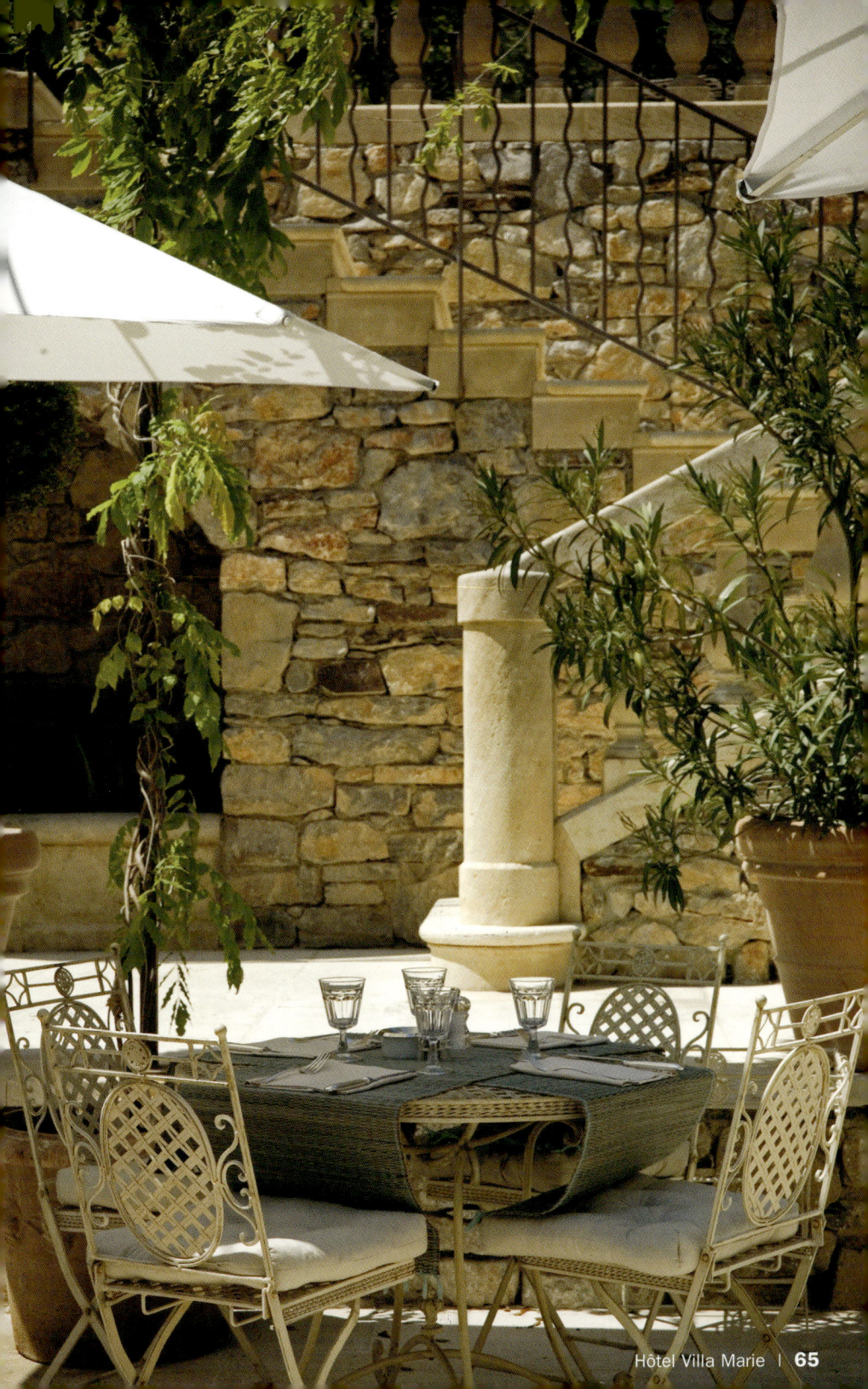

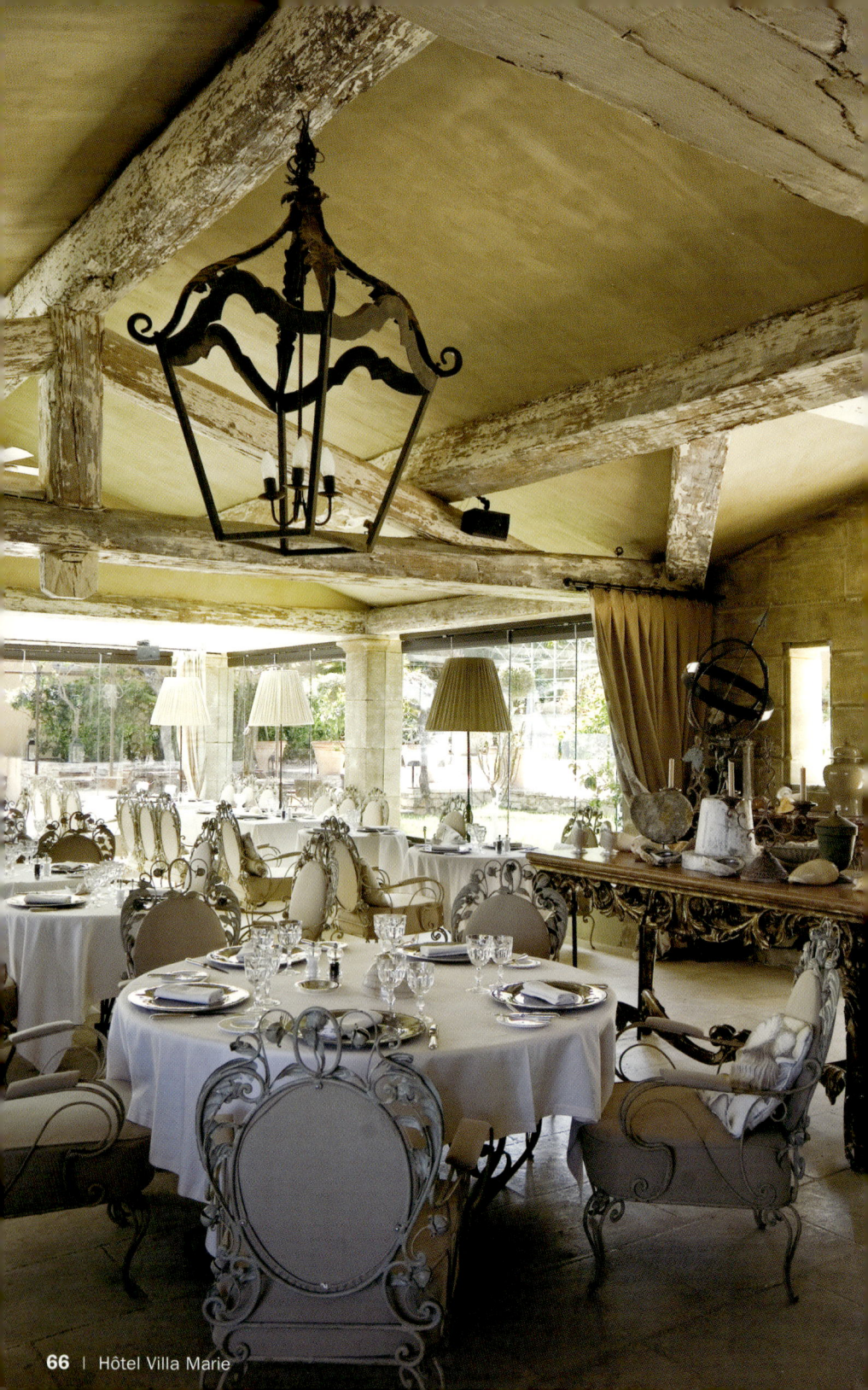

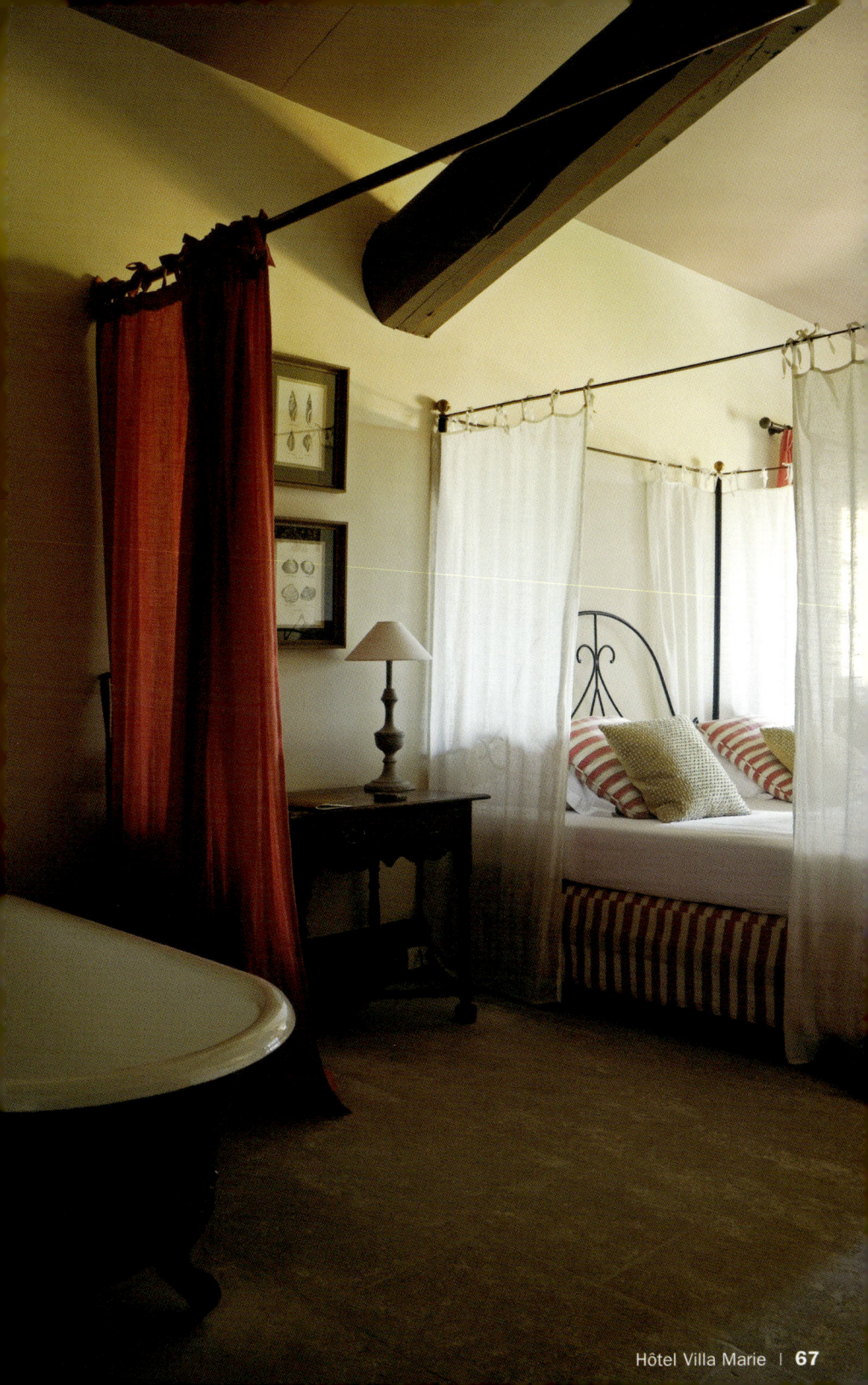

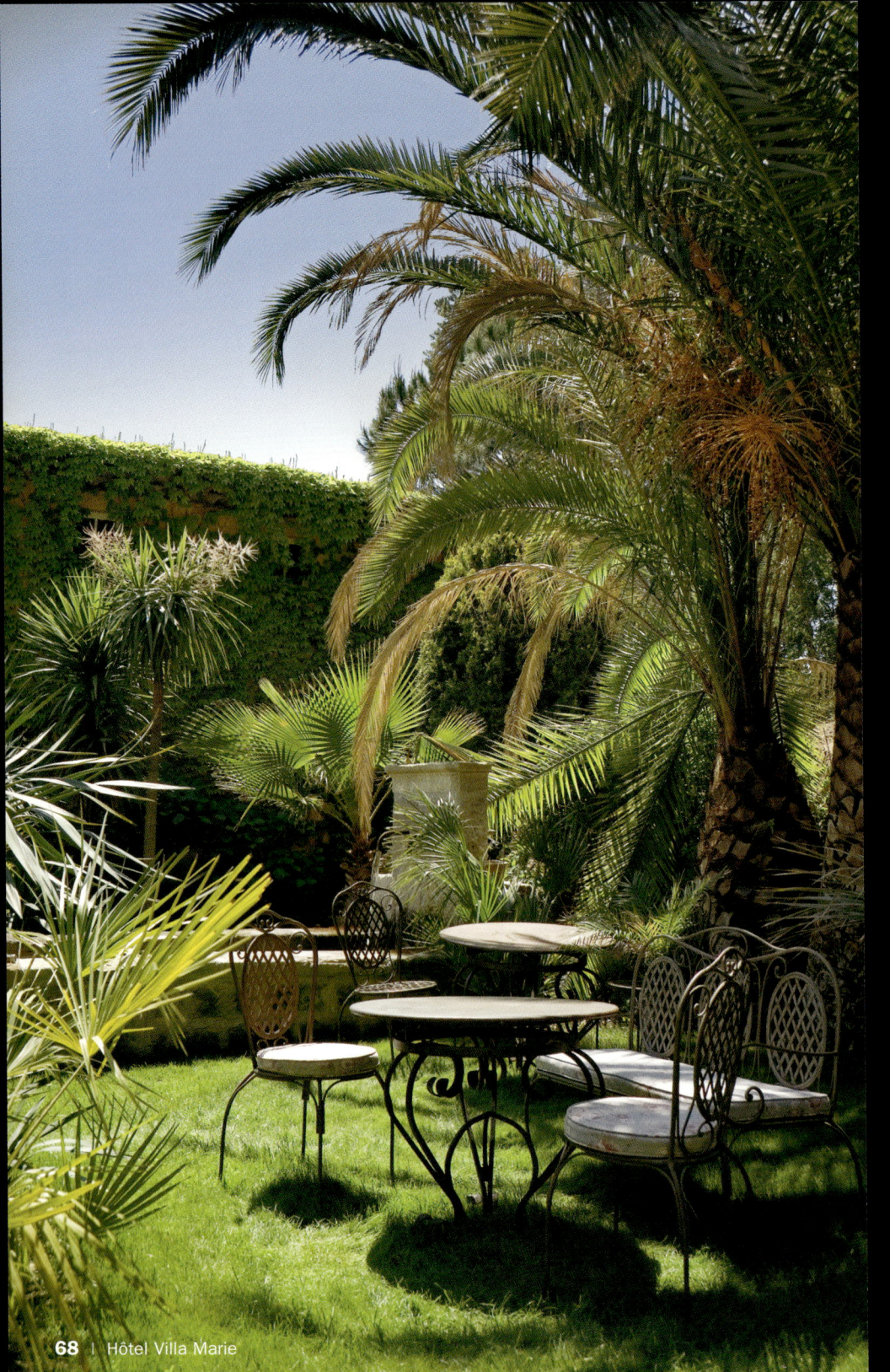

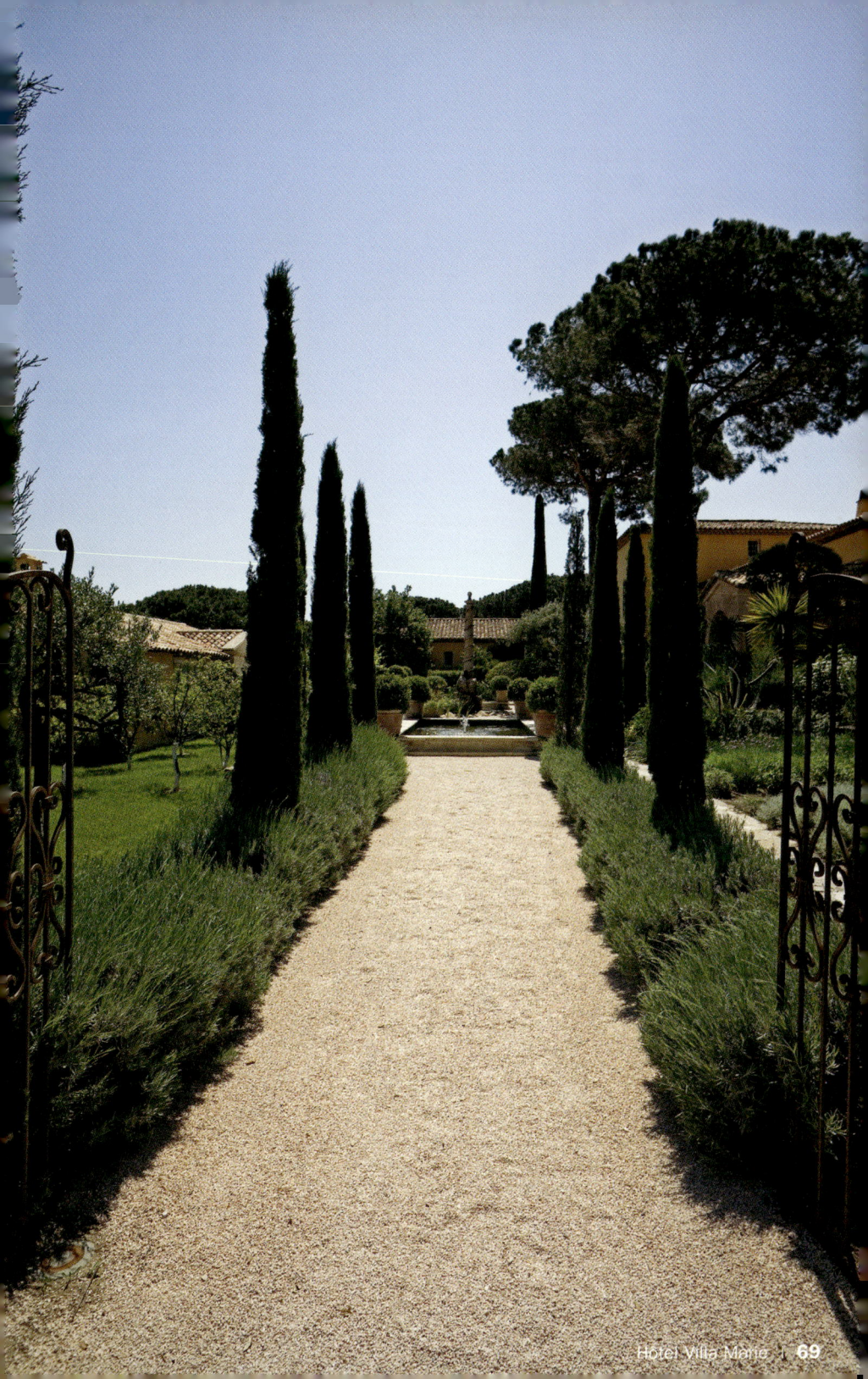

Jouni

Design: By the owner, Giuseppe Serena

10 Rue Lascaris | 06000 Nice
Phone: +33 4 97 08 14 80
www.jouni.fr
Opening hours: Tues–Sat from noon to 2 am and from 7:30 pm to 10 pm
Special features: A 19th century building hosts this elegant bistro with an exquisite and ever-changing menu

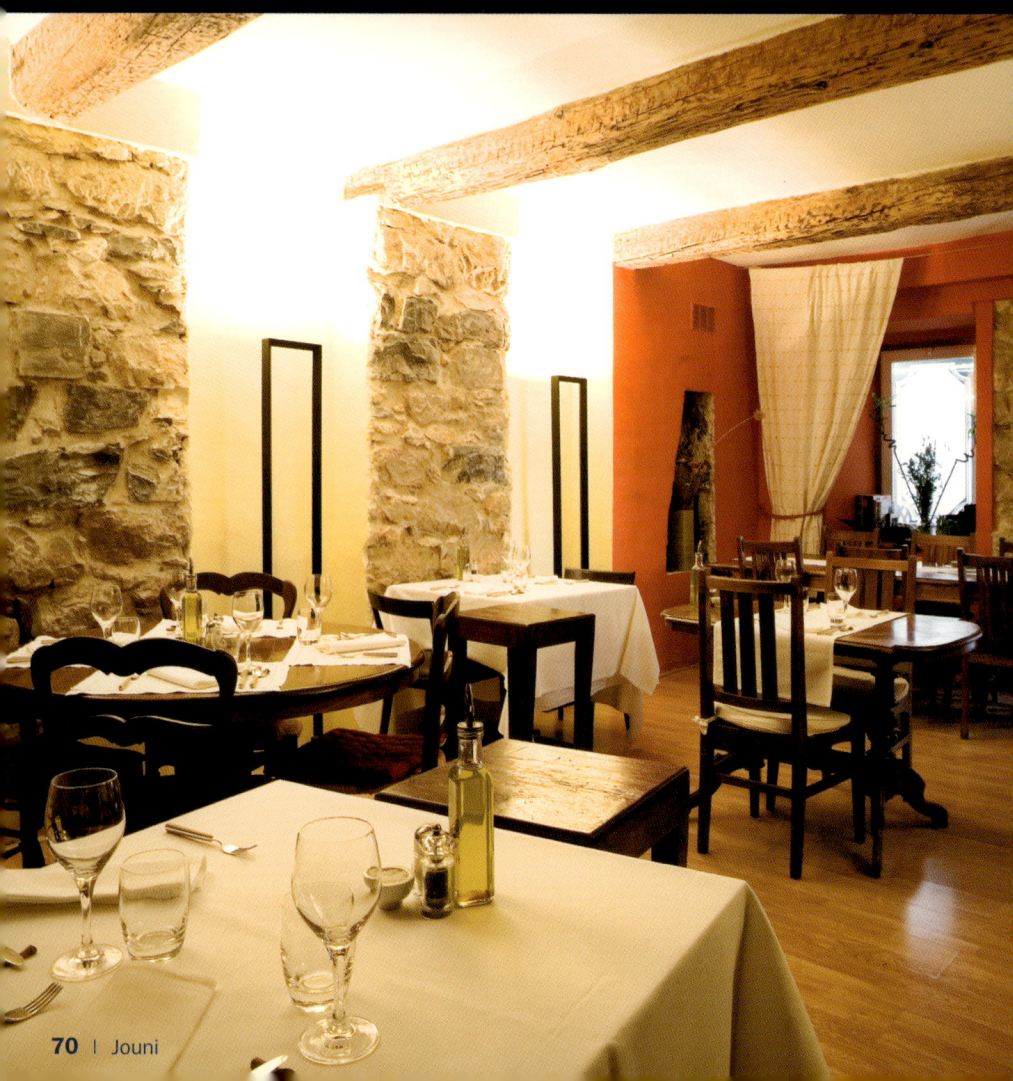

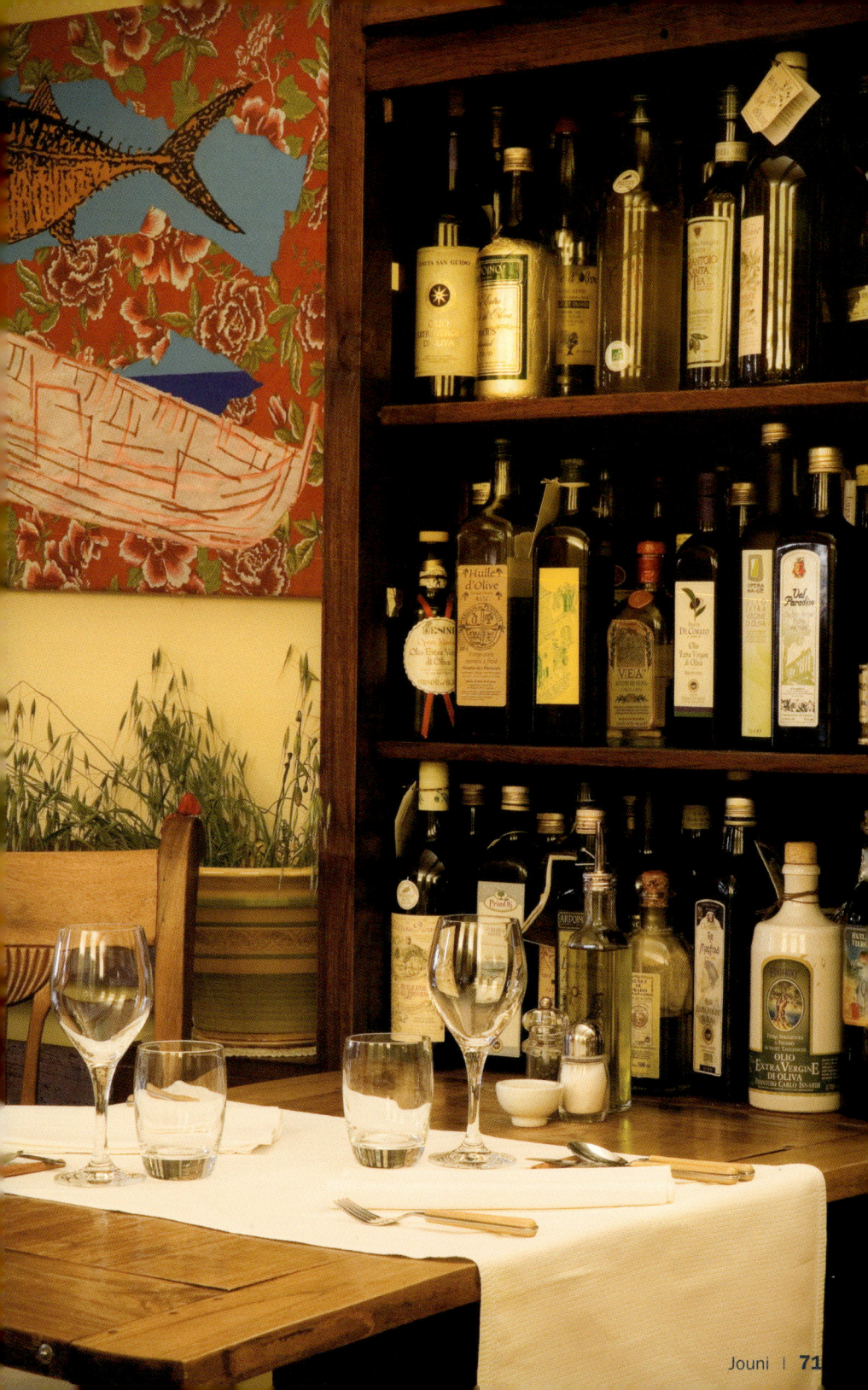

Karé(ment)

Design: By the owner, Francis Poidevin

10 Avenue Princesse Grace | Grimaldi Forum | 98000 Monte-Carlo
Phone: +377 99 99 20 20
www.karement.com
Opening hours: Thu–Sat from 6 pm to 4:30 am
Special features: This cool bar and disco offers breakfast, lunch, drinks and tapas
and a wonderful sea view lounge

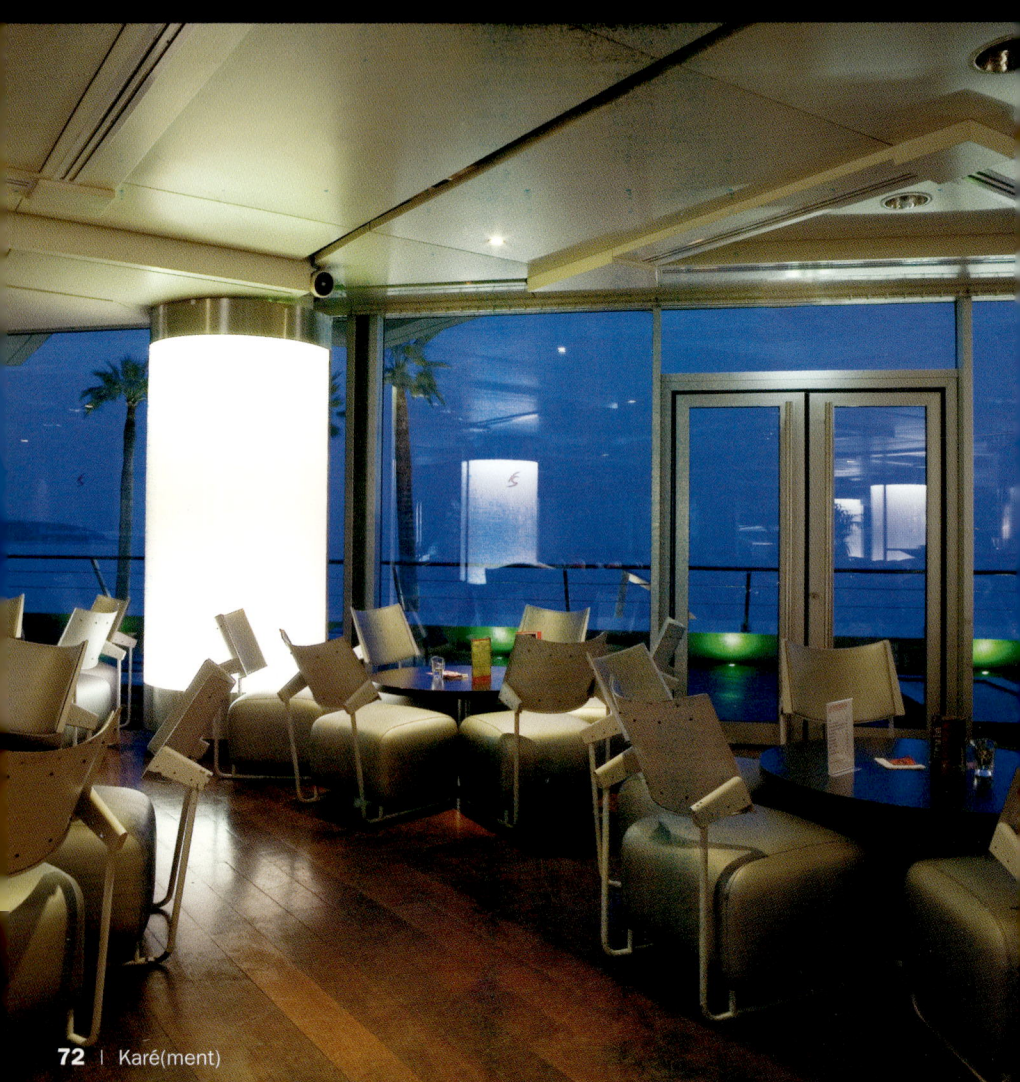

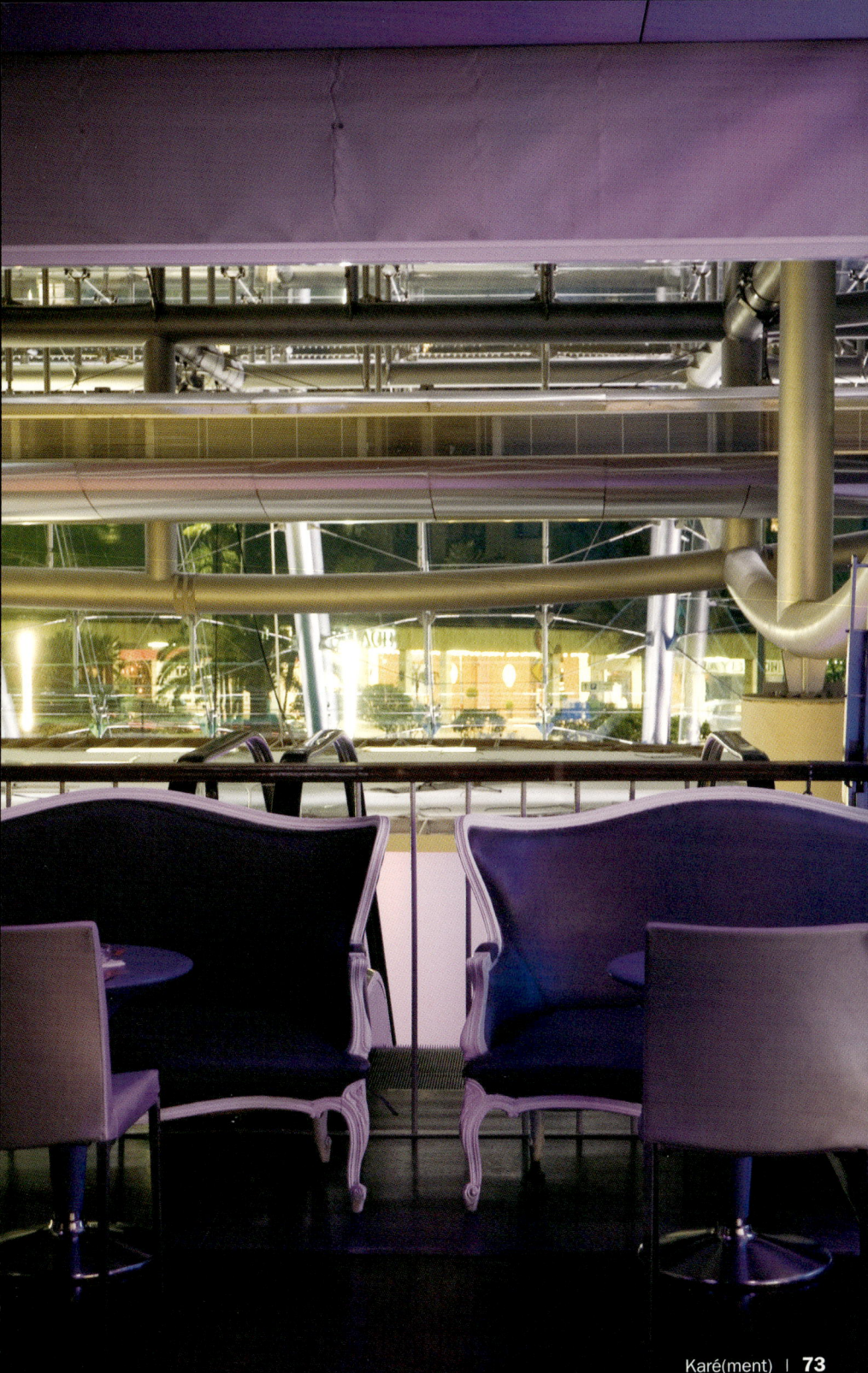

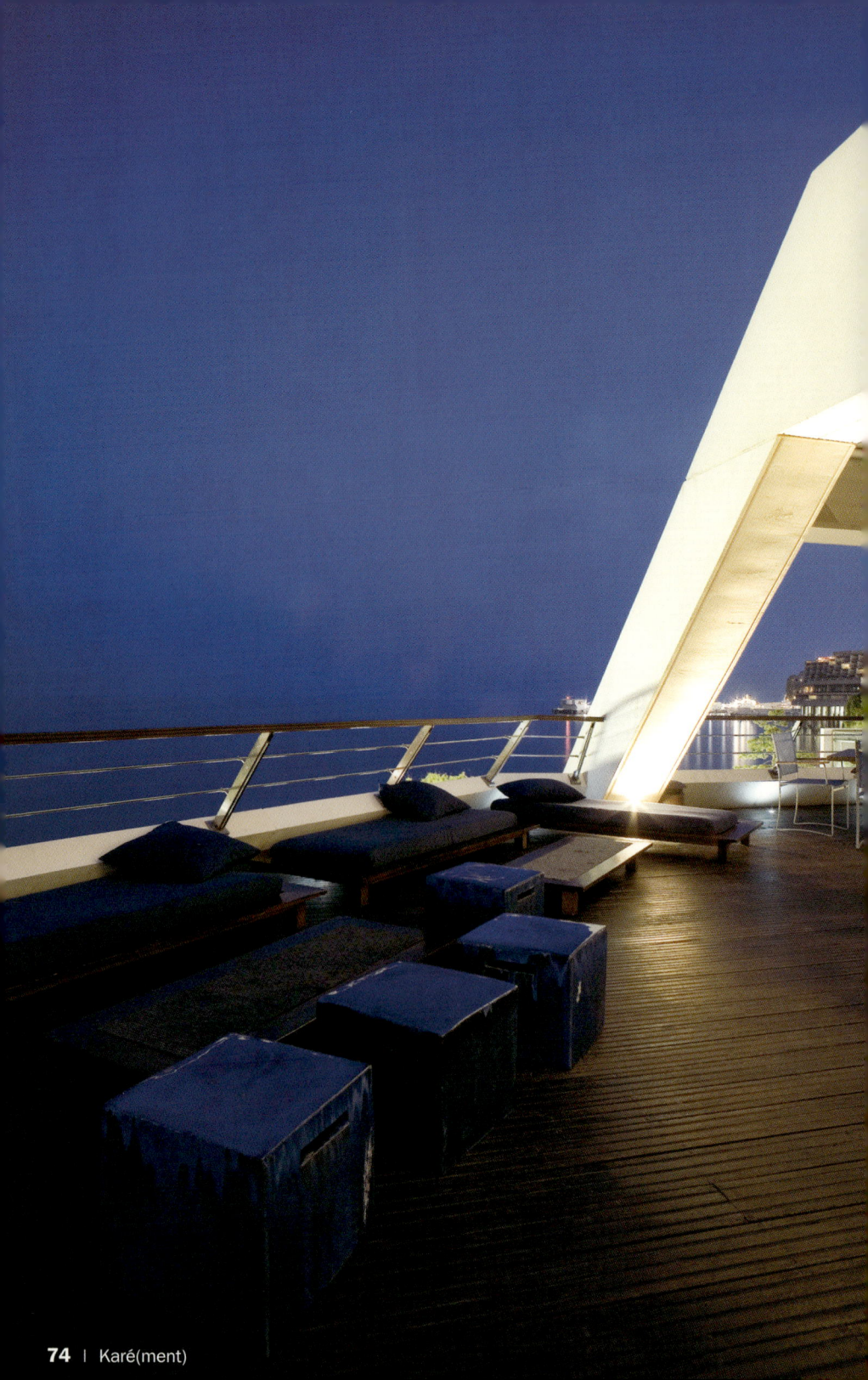

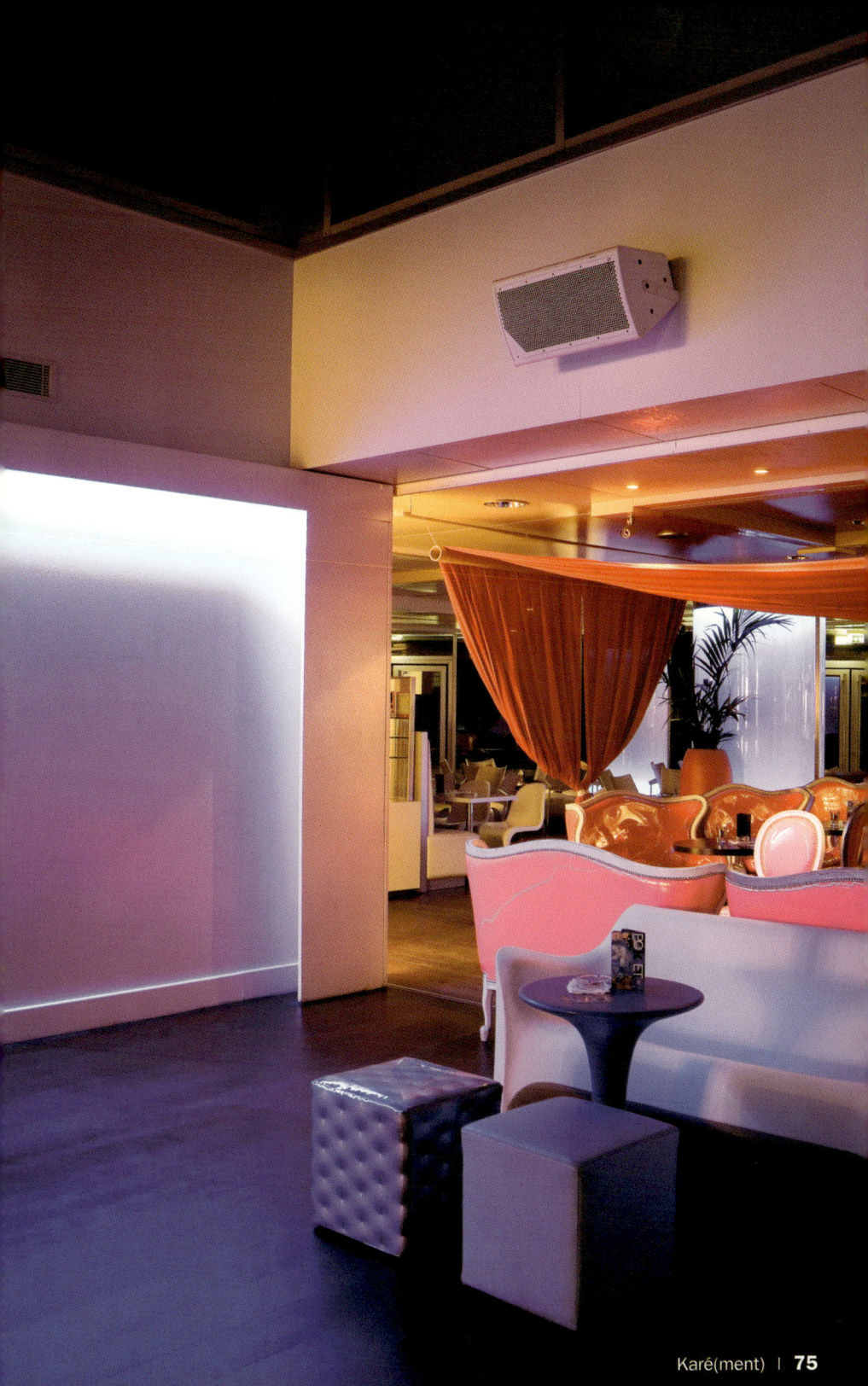

La Colombe d'Or

Design: Paul Roux, Jacques Couelle

Place du Général de Gaulle | 06570 Saint-Paul de Vence
Phone: +33 4 93 32 80 02
www.la-colombe-dor.com
Opening hours: Open 24 hours, closed from November until Christmas
Special features: Situated in Saint-Paul de Vence, place of refuge for impressionist painters during the late 19th century, the hotel's restaurant and pool are adorned with a number of original artworks that testify to its illustrious visitors

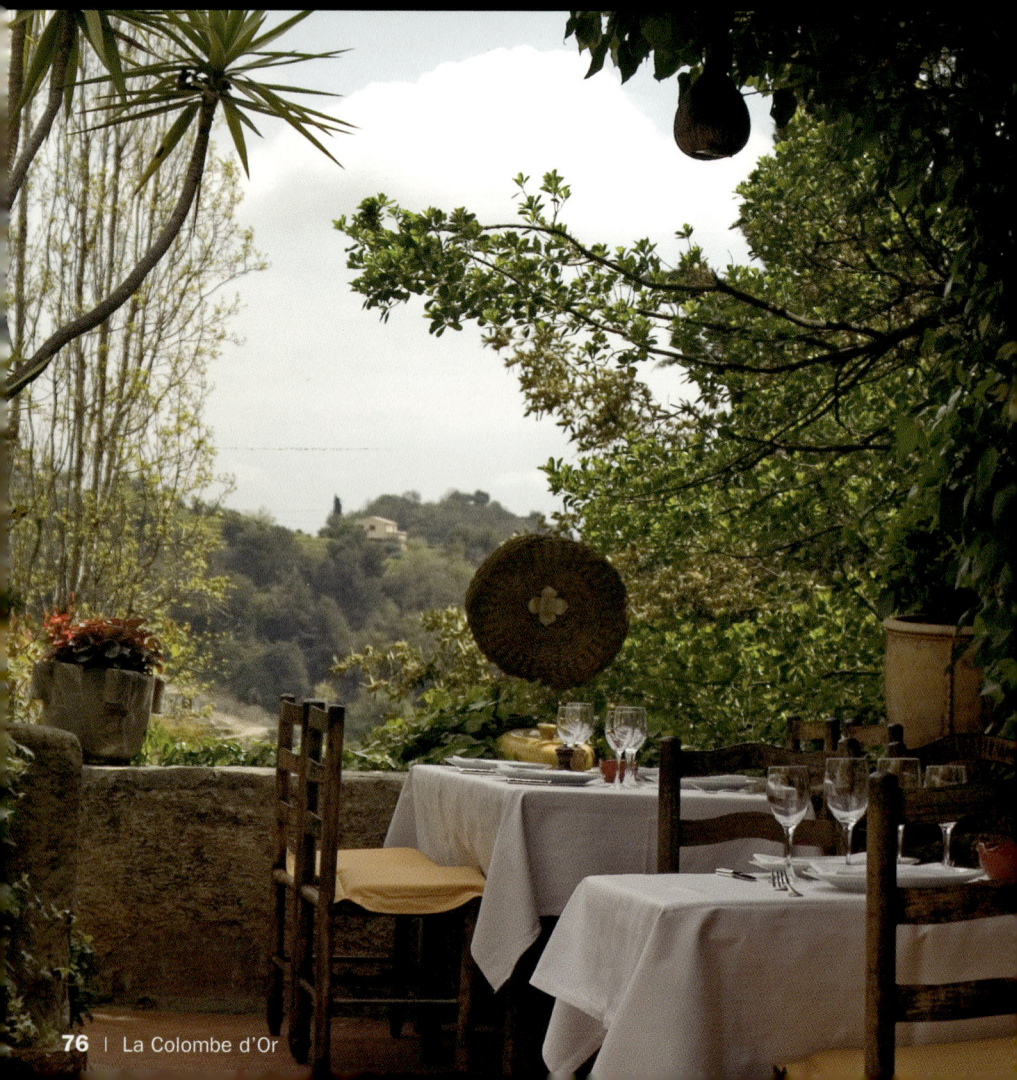

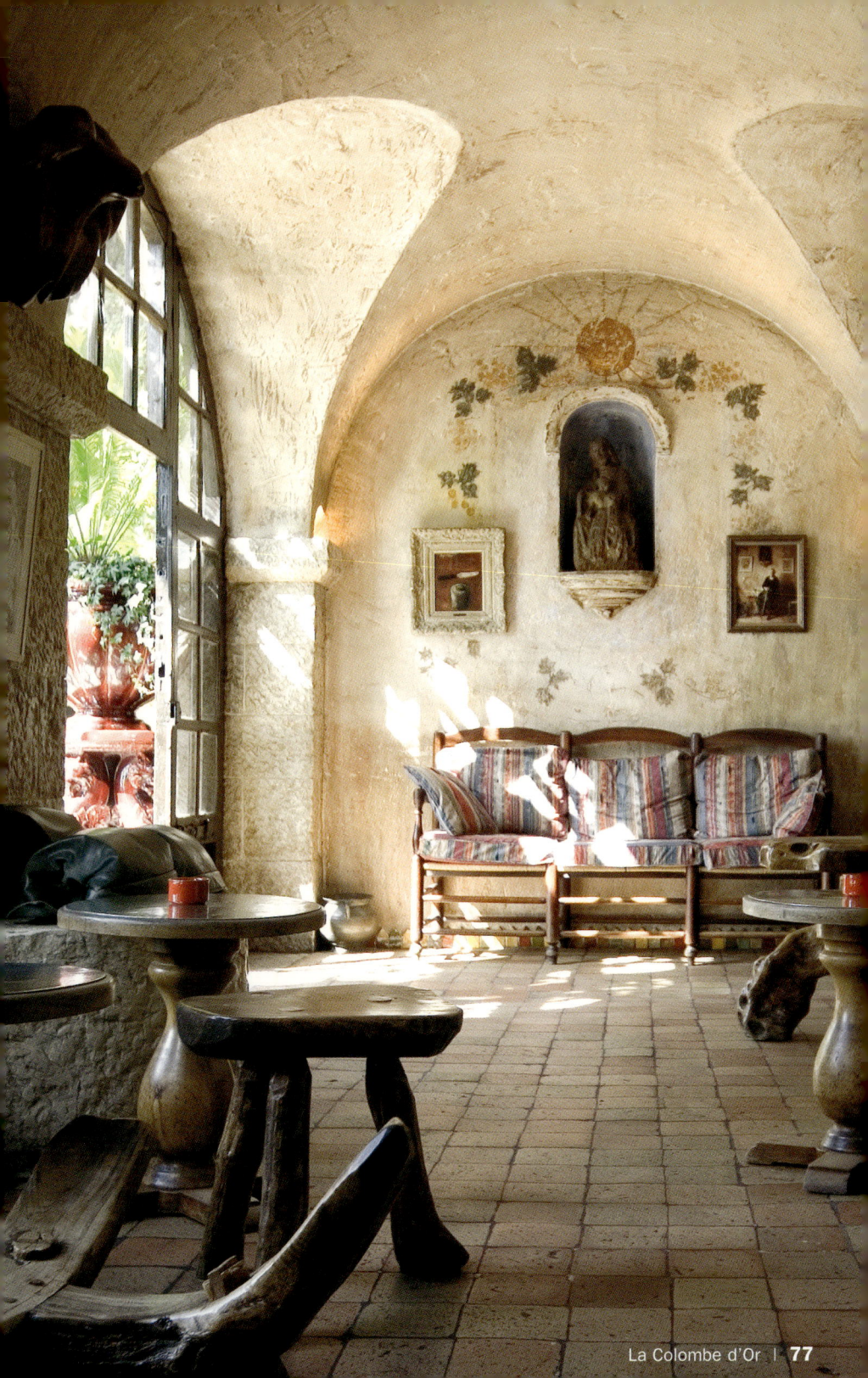

La Maison Blanche

Design: Fabienne Villacres

Places des Lices | 83990 Saint-Tropez
Phone: +33 4 94 97 52 66
www.hotellamaisonblanche.com
Opening hours: Every day, open 24 hours. Closed in February
Special features: A beautiful mansion redecorated in a minimal romantic spirit. A
champagne bar is open from April to September

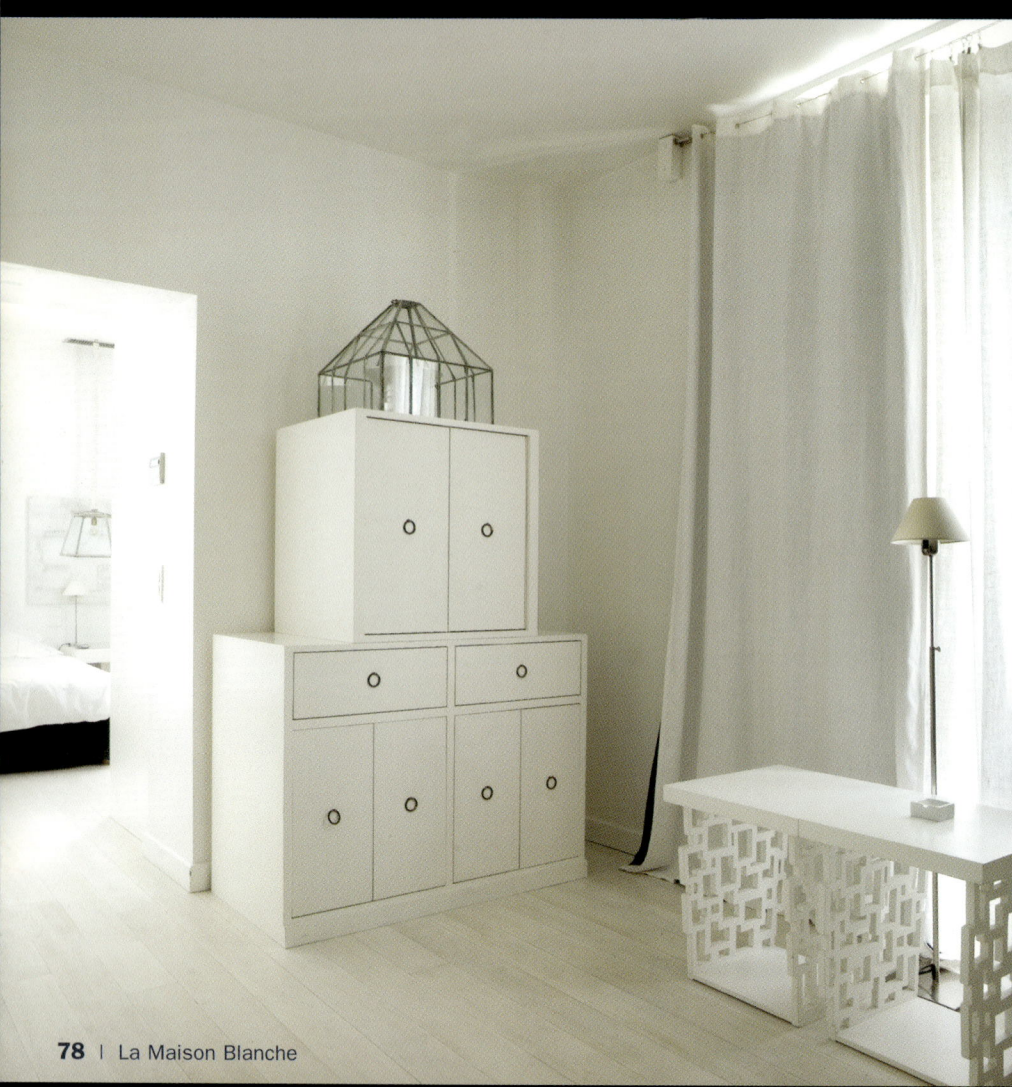

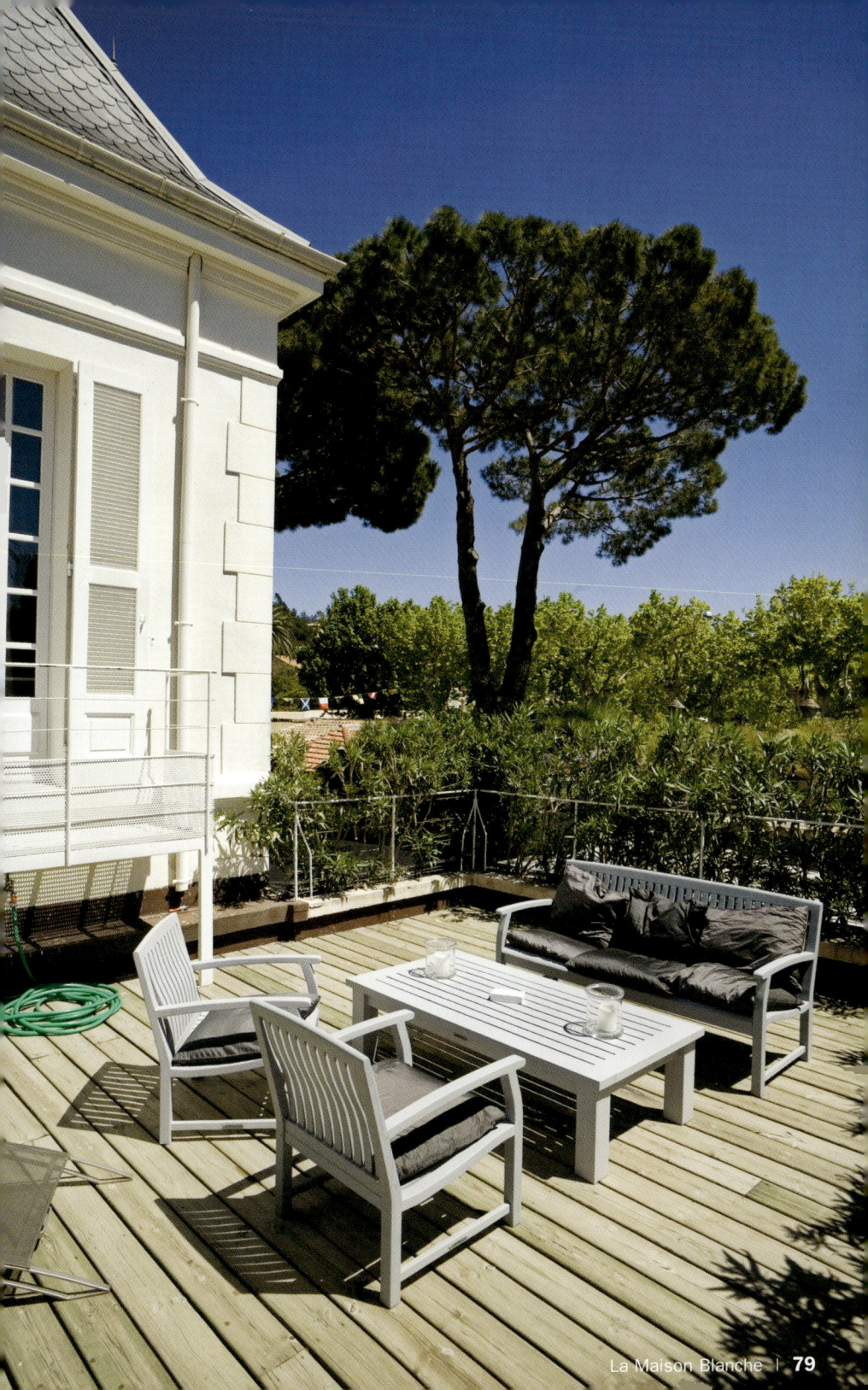

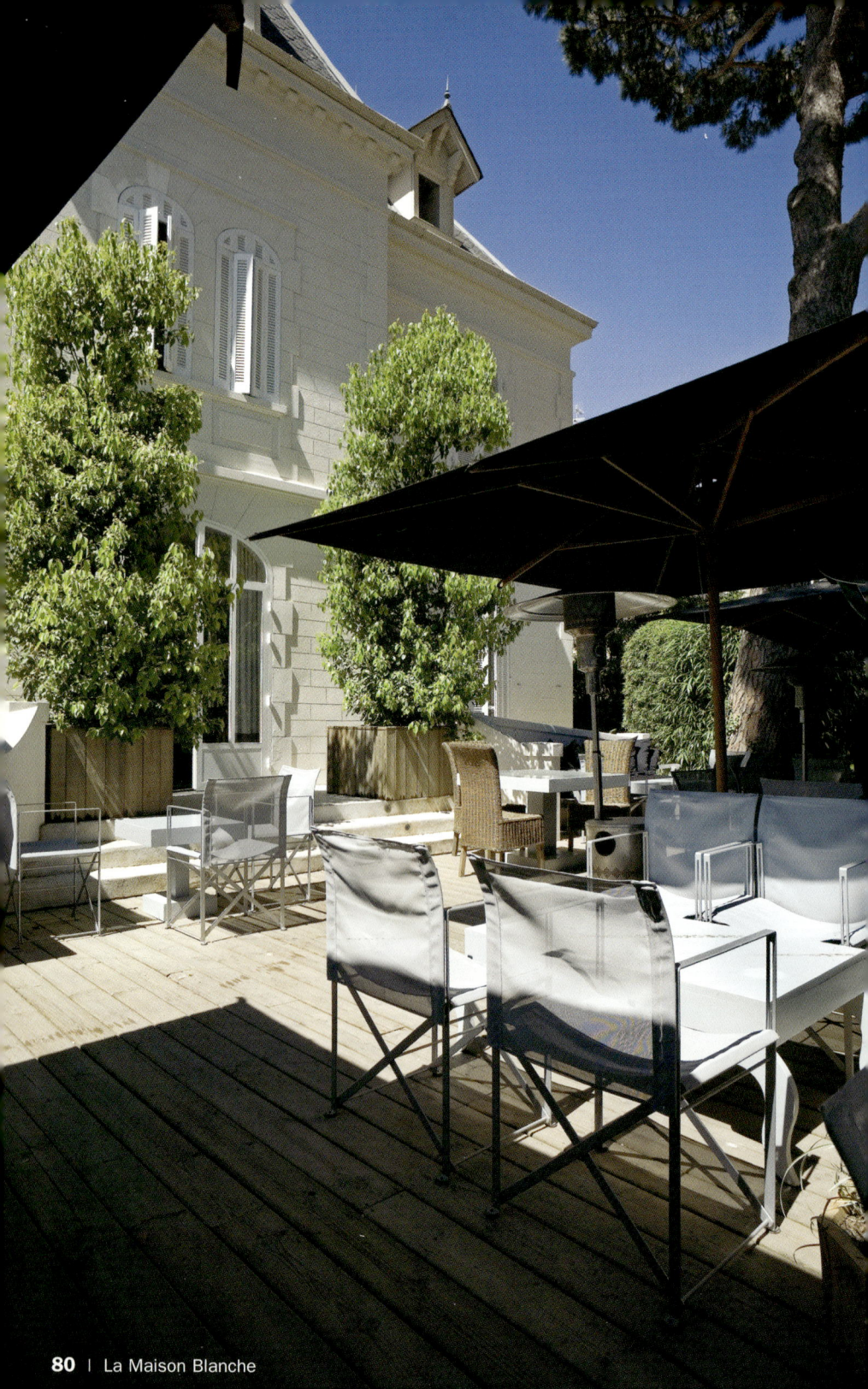

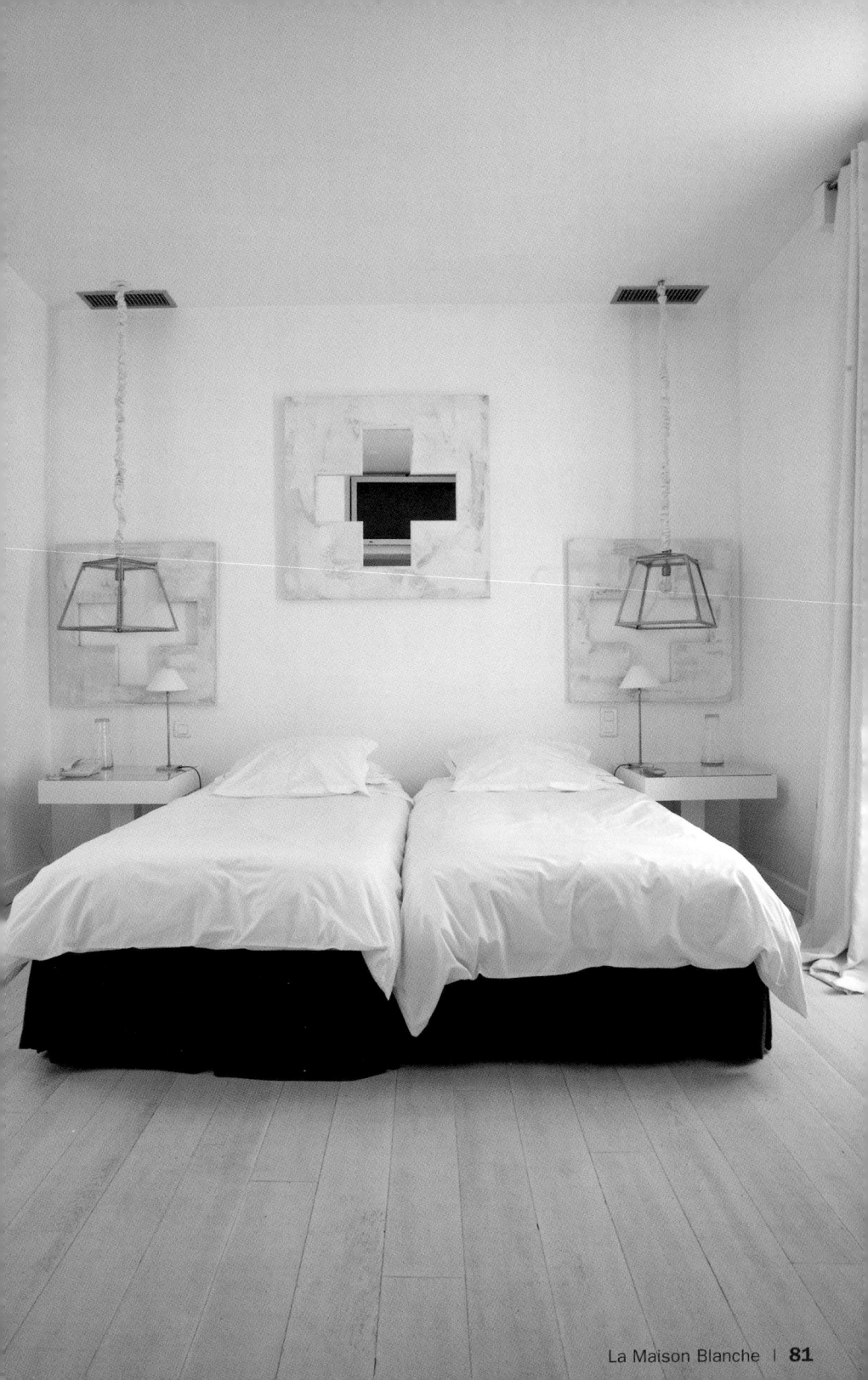

1 Quai Antoine 1er | 98000 Monte-Carlo
Phone: +377 93 25 56 90
www.larascasse.mc
Opening hours: Every day from 9 pm to 4:45 am
Special features: An exciting cocktail bar located in the famous "La Rascasse" curve in Monaco's Formula 1 racing circuit

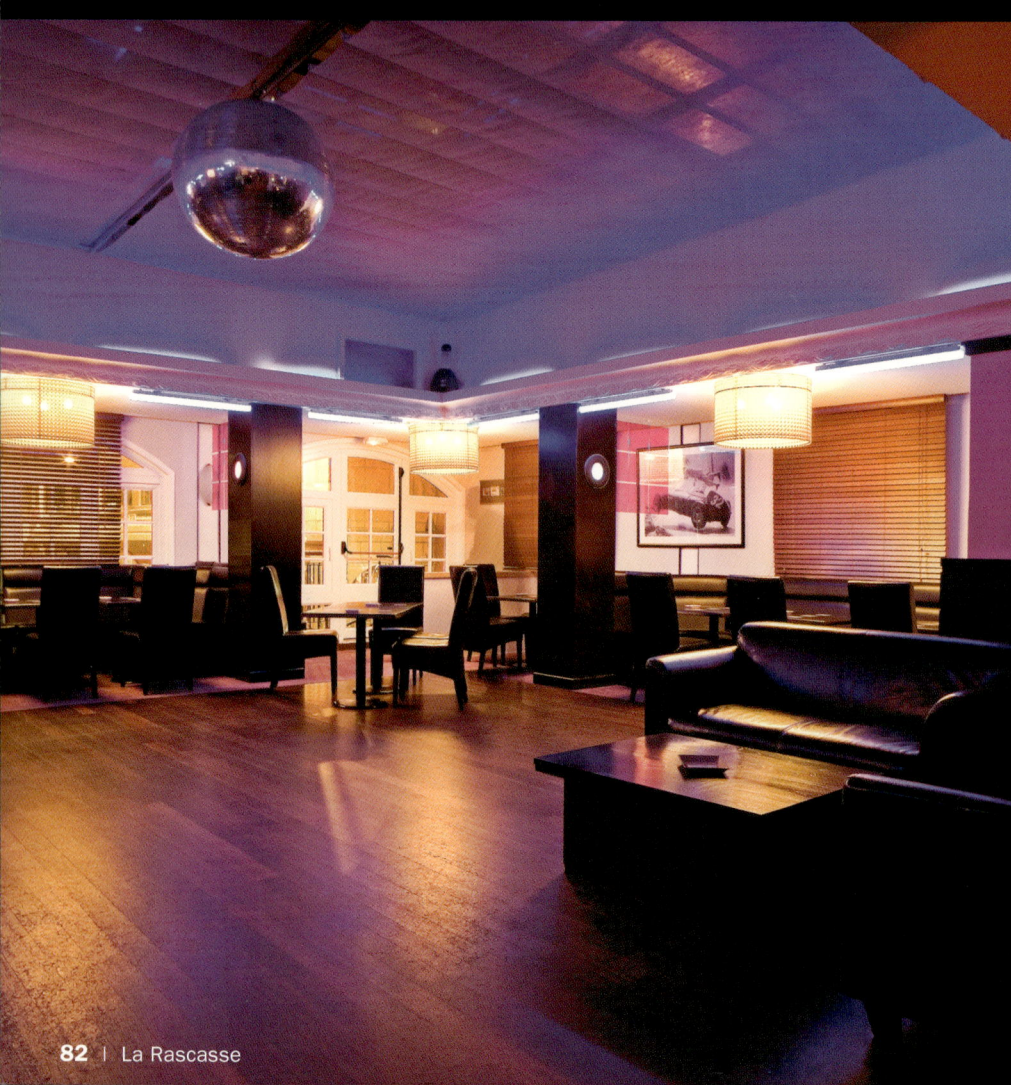

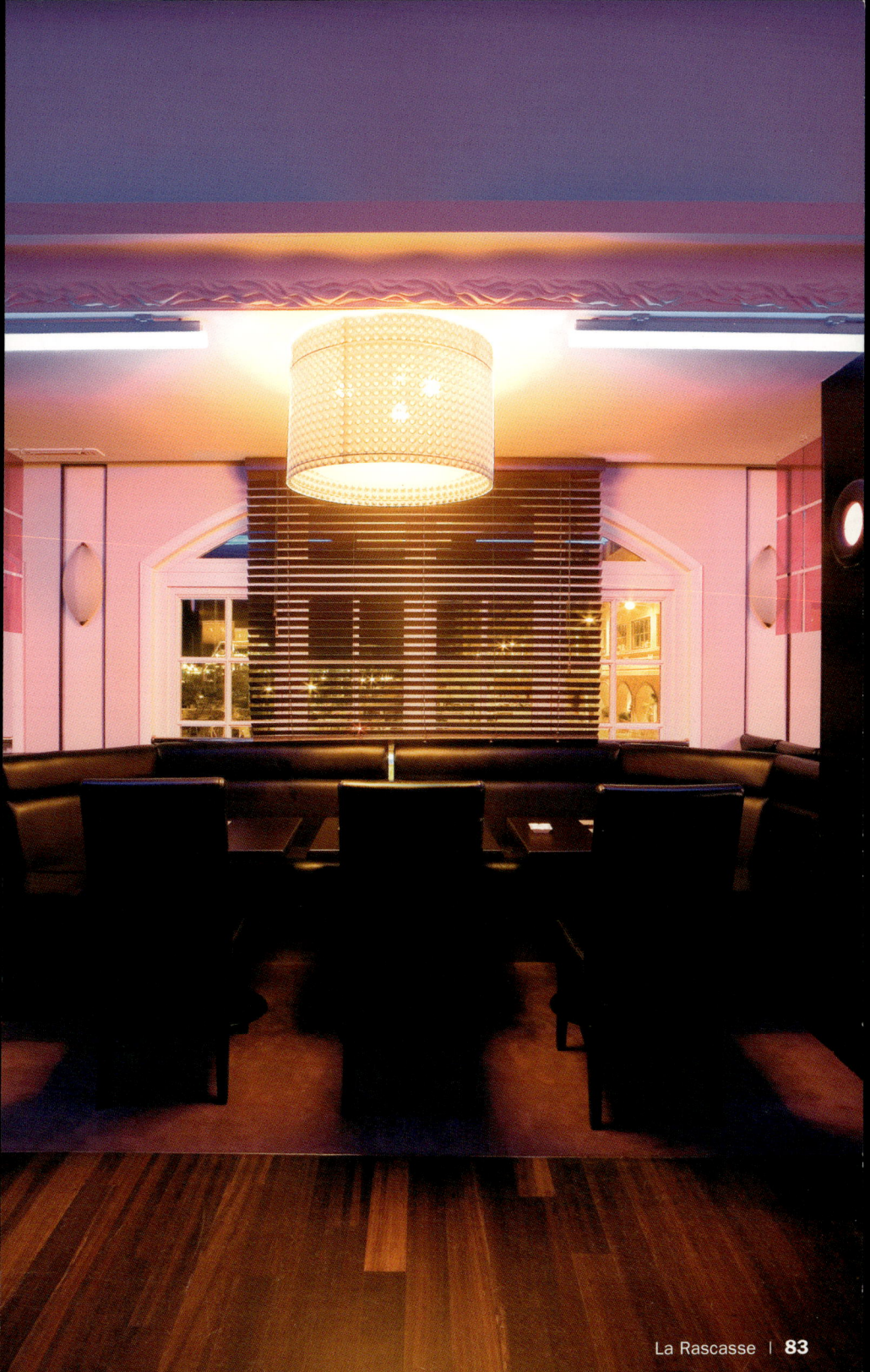

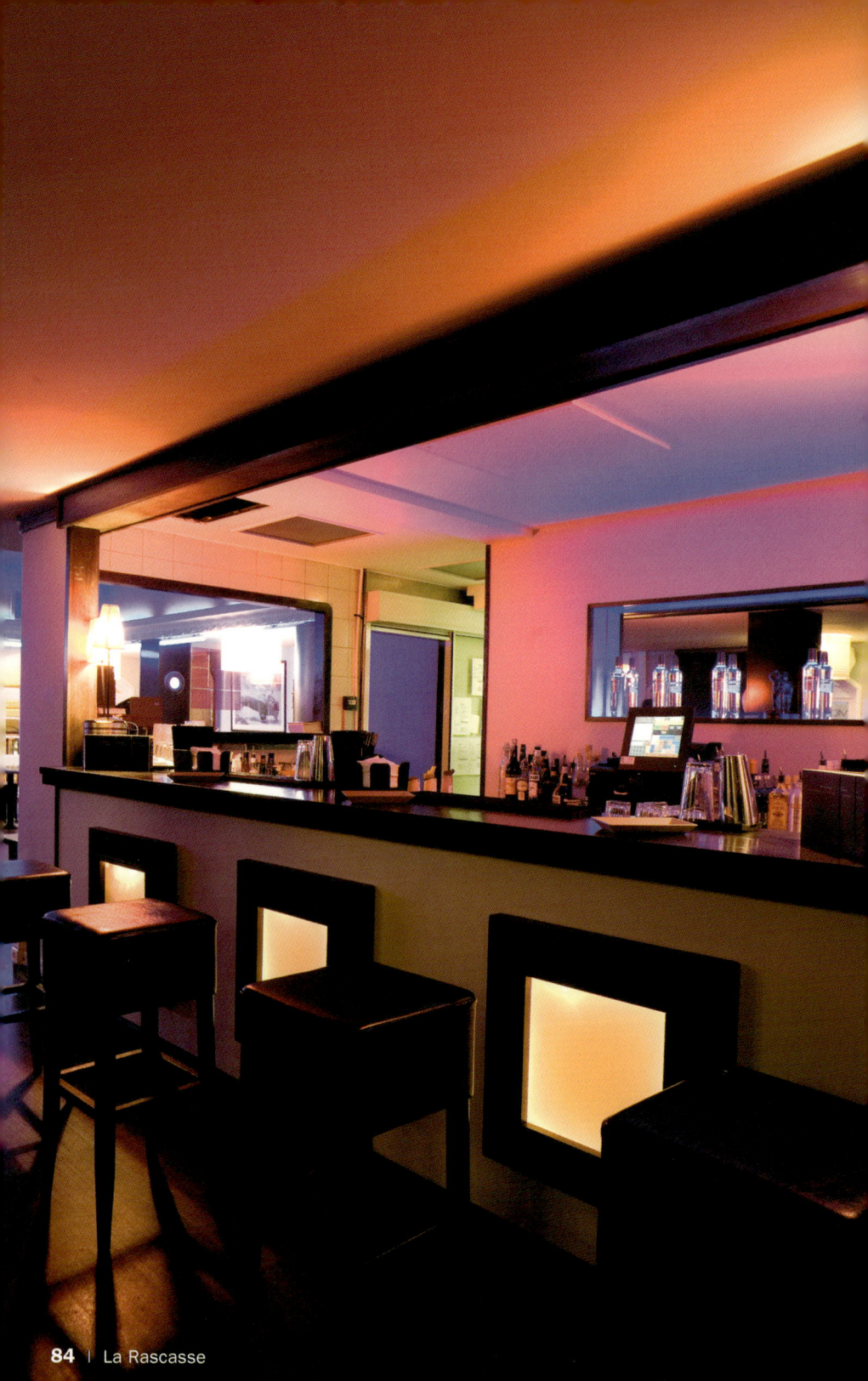

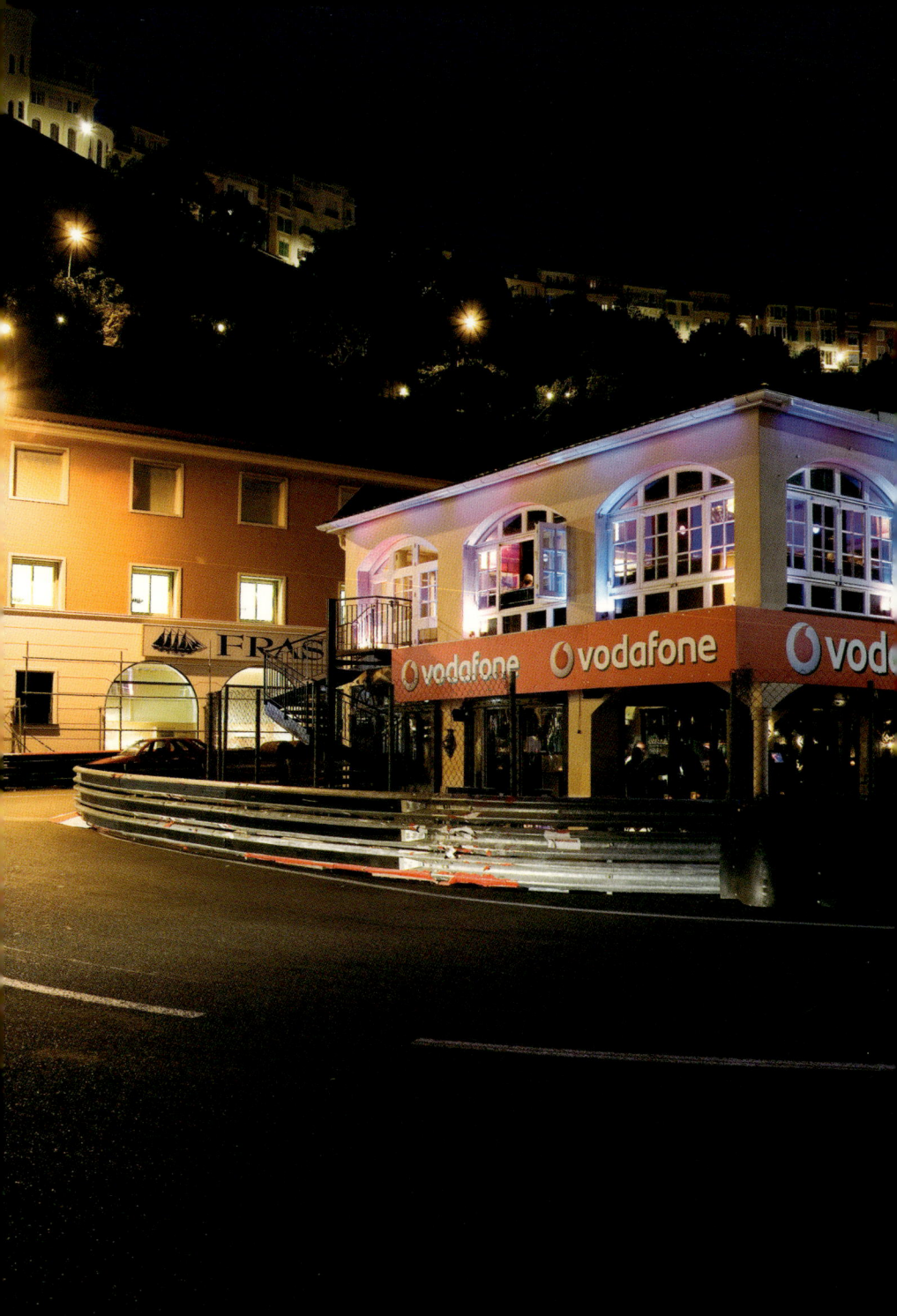

La Tarte Tropezienne
Traiteur

Design: Georges Tal-Fournier

Place des Lices | 83990 Saint-Tropez
Phone: +33 4 94 97 04 69
www.tarte-tropezienne-traiteur.com
Opening hours: Every day from 6:30 am to 10 pm
Special features: Retro bakery and pastry shop for gourmets, tasting directly at the home of the famous tropezienne cake

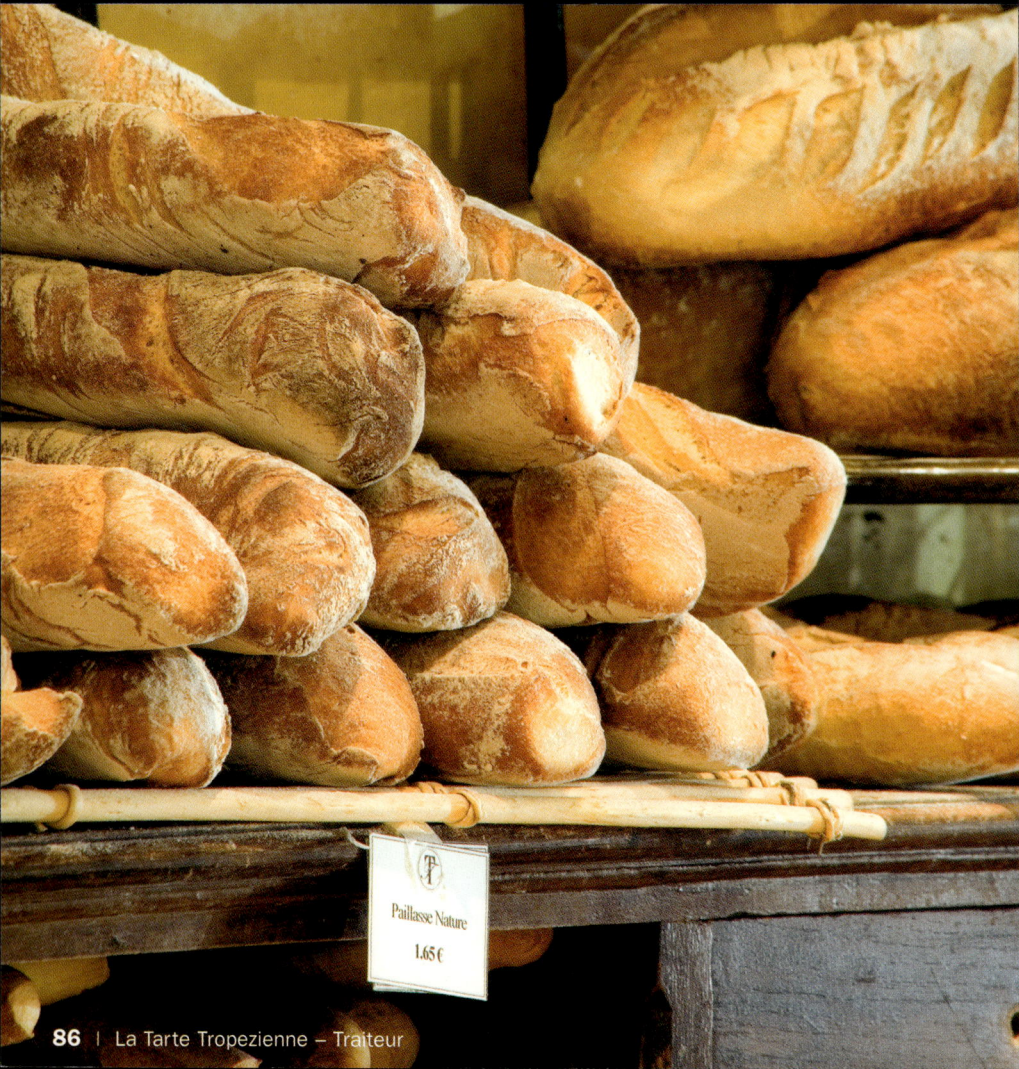

Paillasse Nature
1.65 €

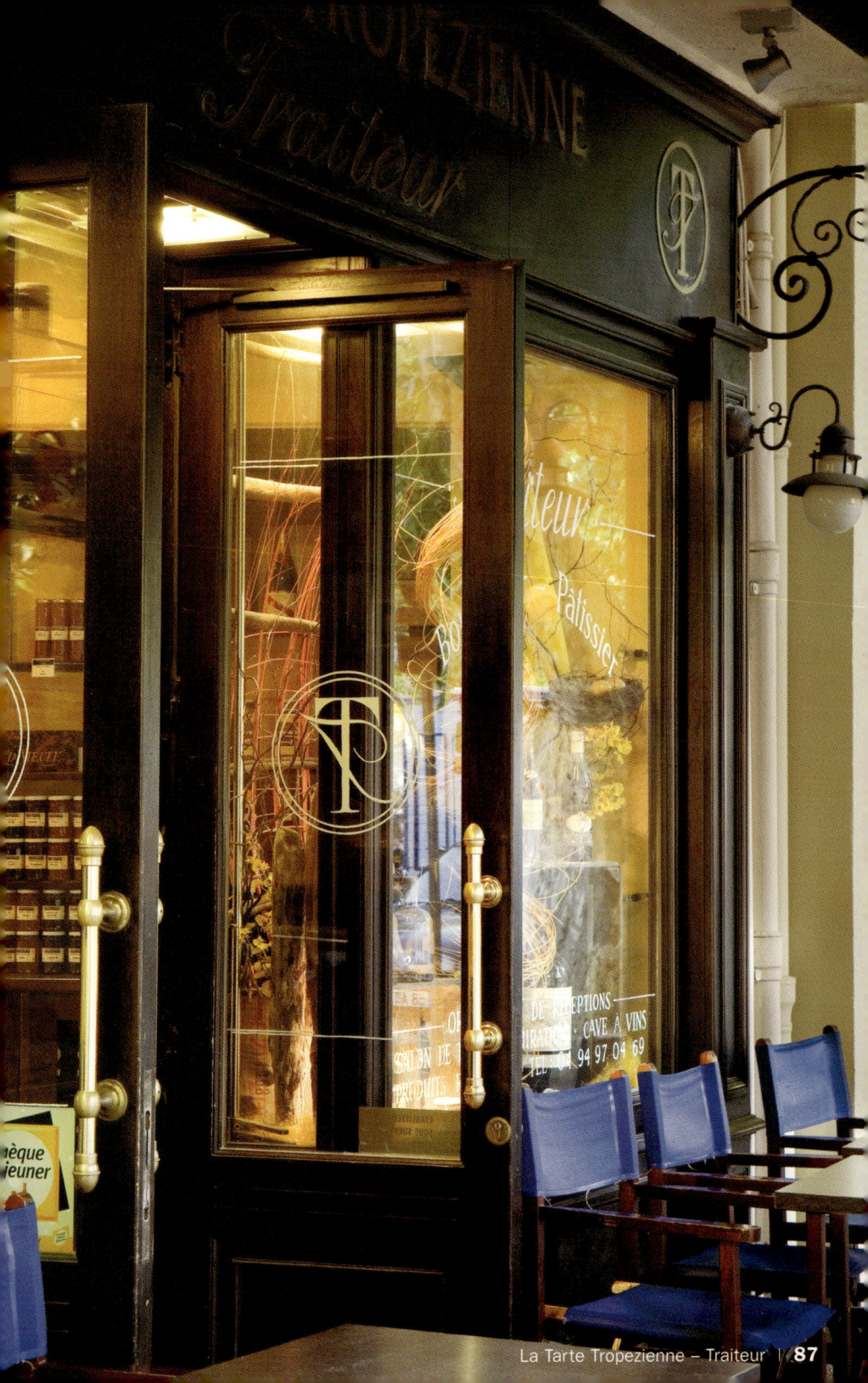

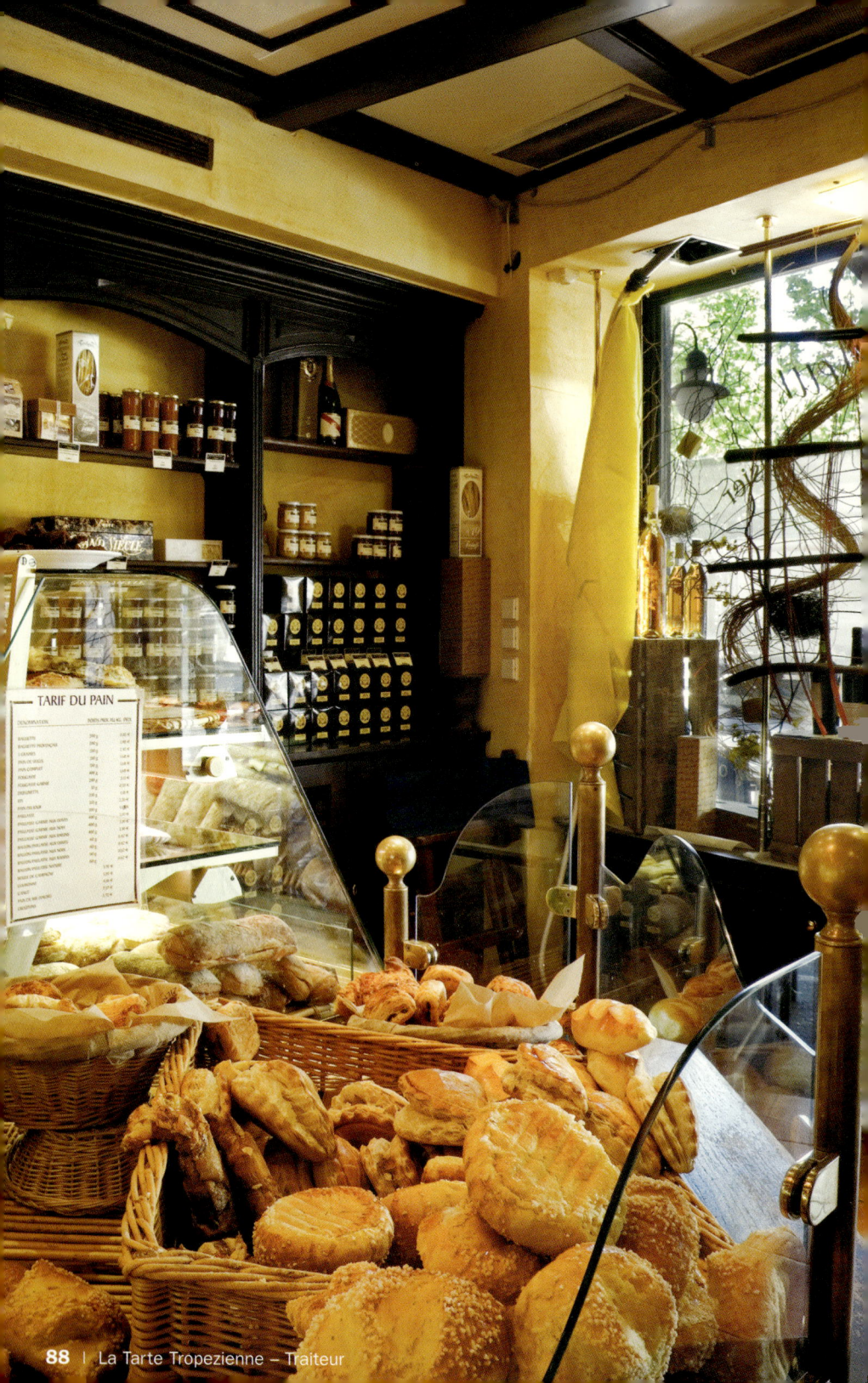

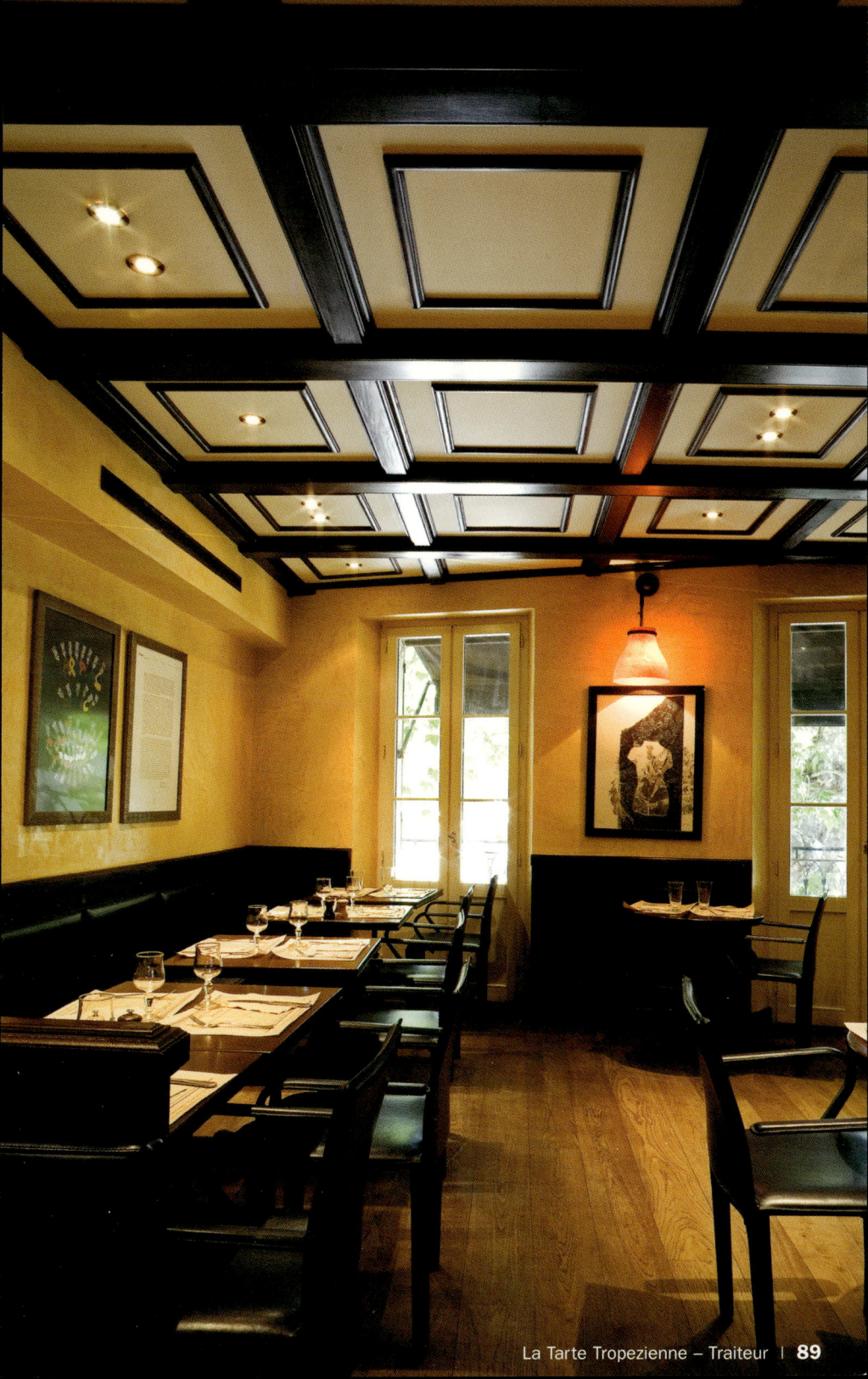

Le Club 55

Design: Patrice de Colmont

Plage de Pampelonne, Boulevard Patch | 83350 Ramatuelle
Phone: +33 4 94 55 55 55
Opening hours: From 8 pm to 12:30 am
Special features: A real cult restaurant not far from Saint-Tropez and a must for any jet-setter

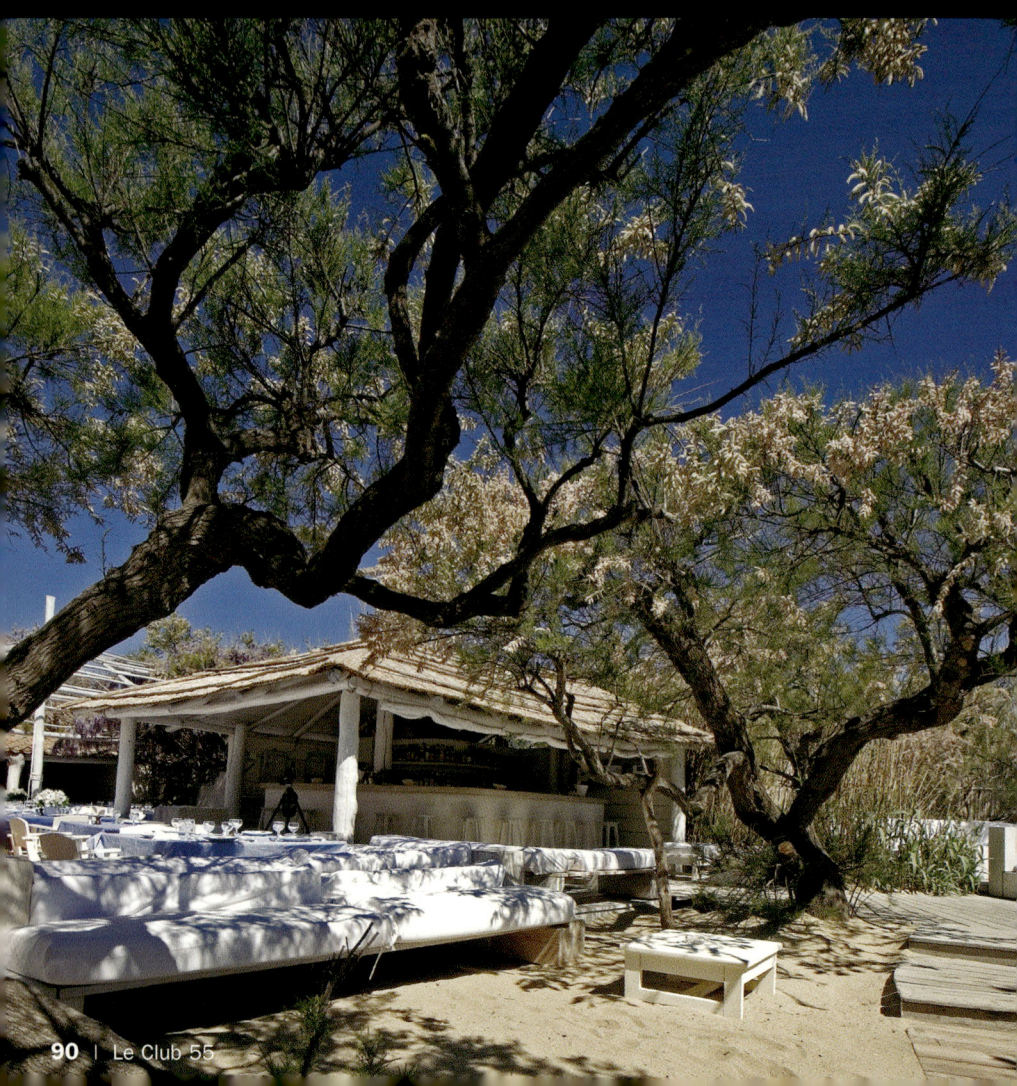

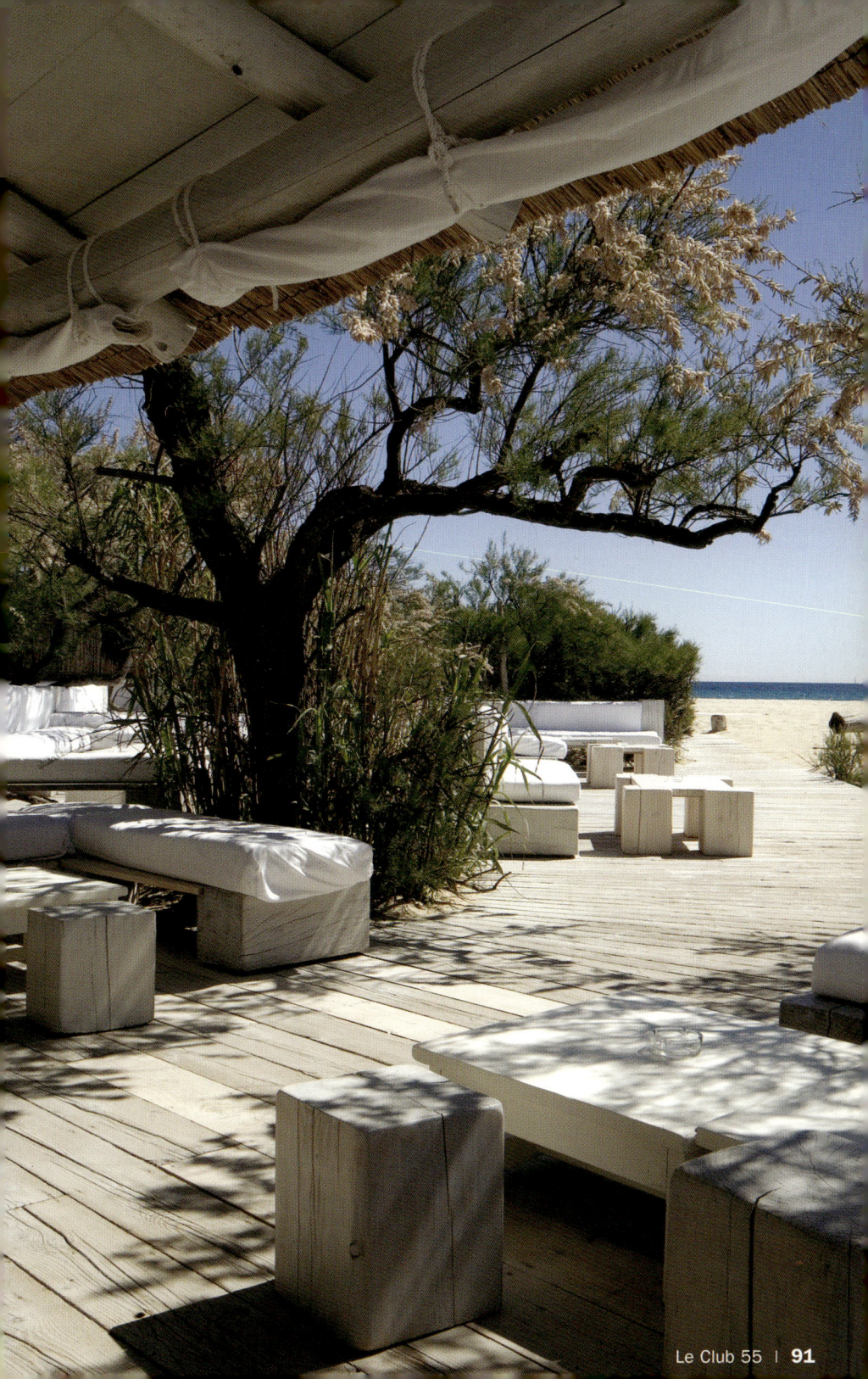

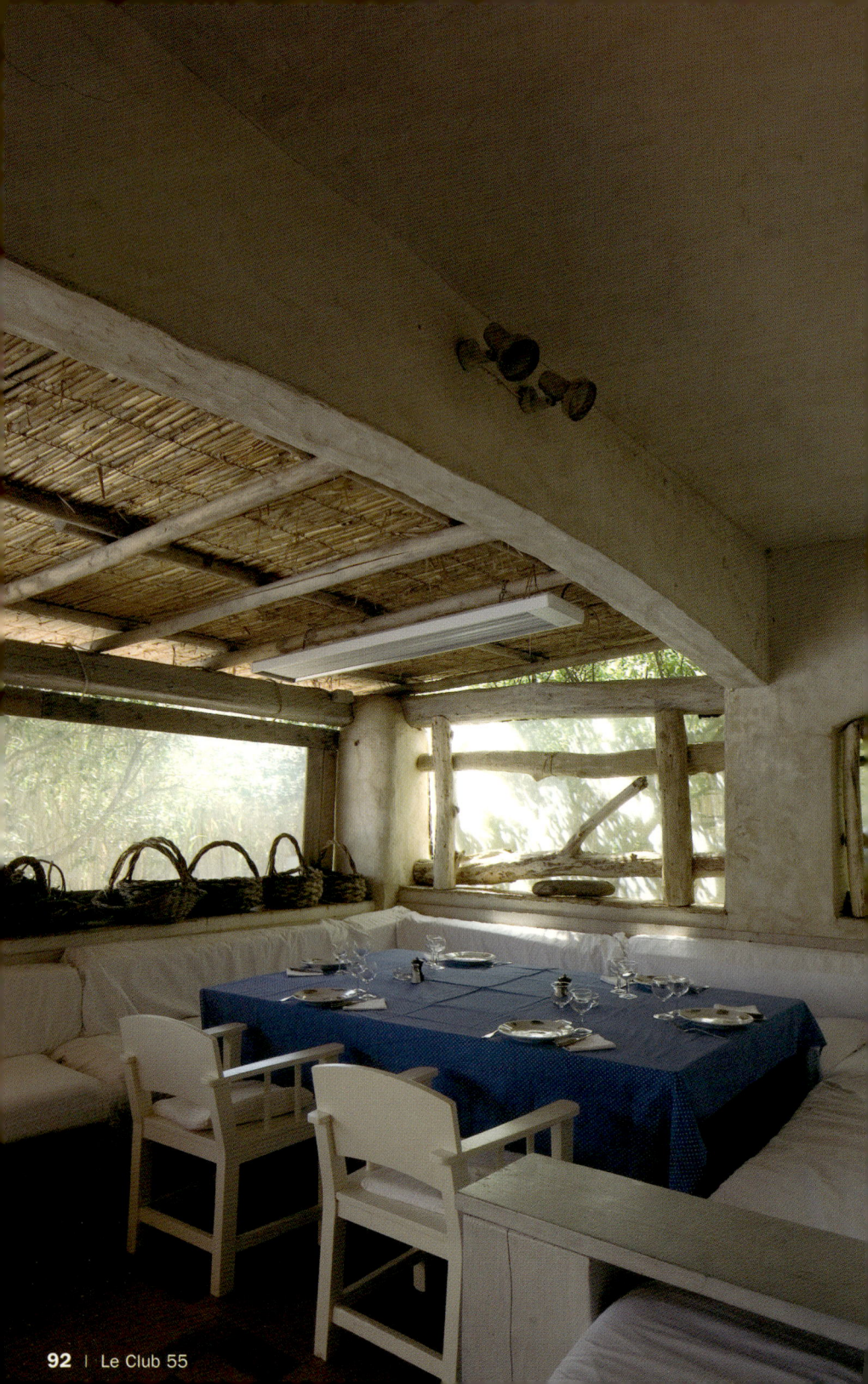

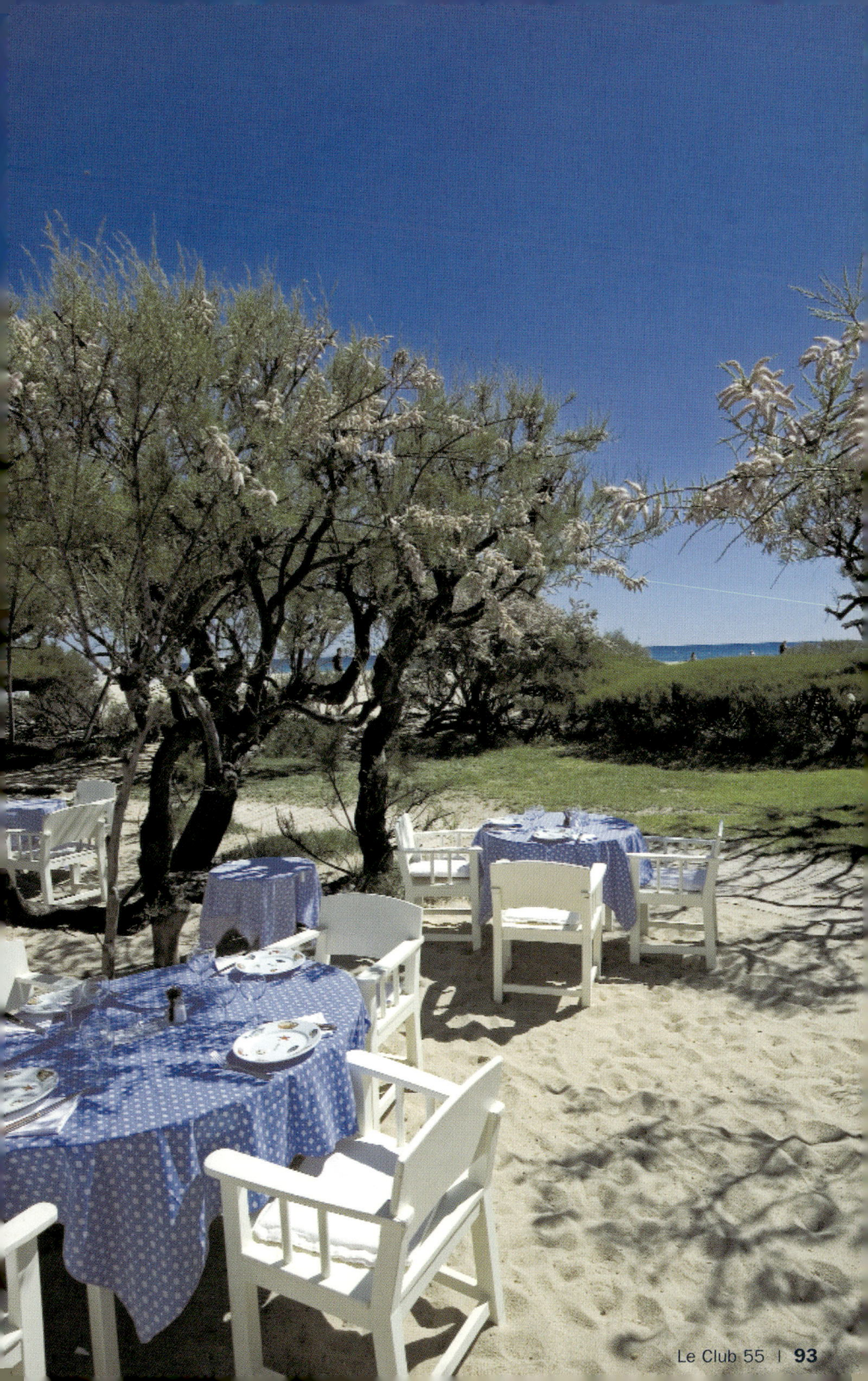

Les Caves du Roy

Design: Serge Sassouni

Avenue Paul Signac | 83990 Saint-Tropez
Phone: +33 4 94 56 68 00
www.lescavesduroy.com
Opening hours: From 11:45 pm to 5 am, closed weekdays from September to June
Special features: The most glamorous and fancy night club on the Côte d'Azur.
Celebrities, champagne and astonishing djs

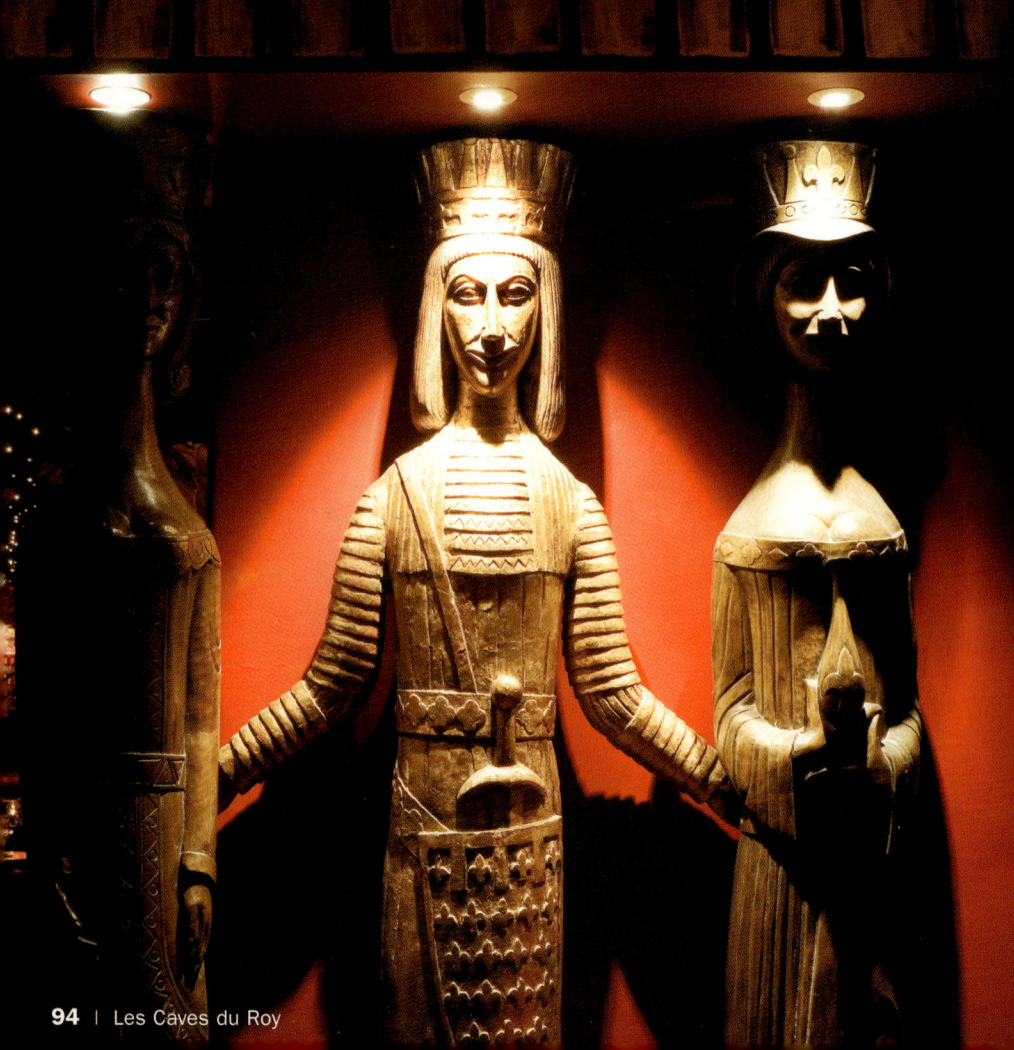

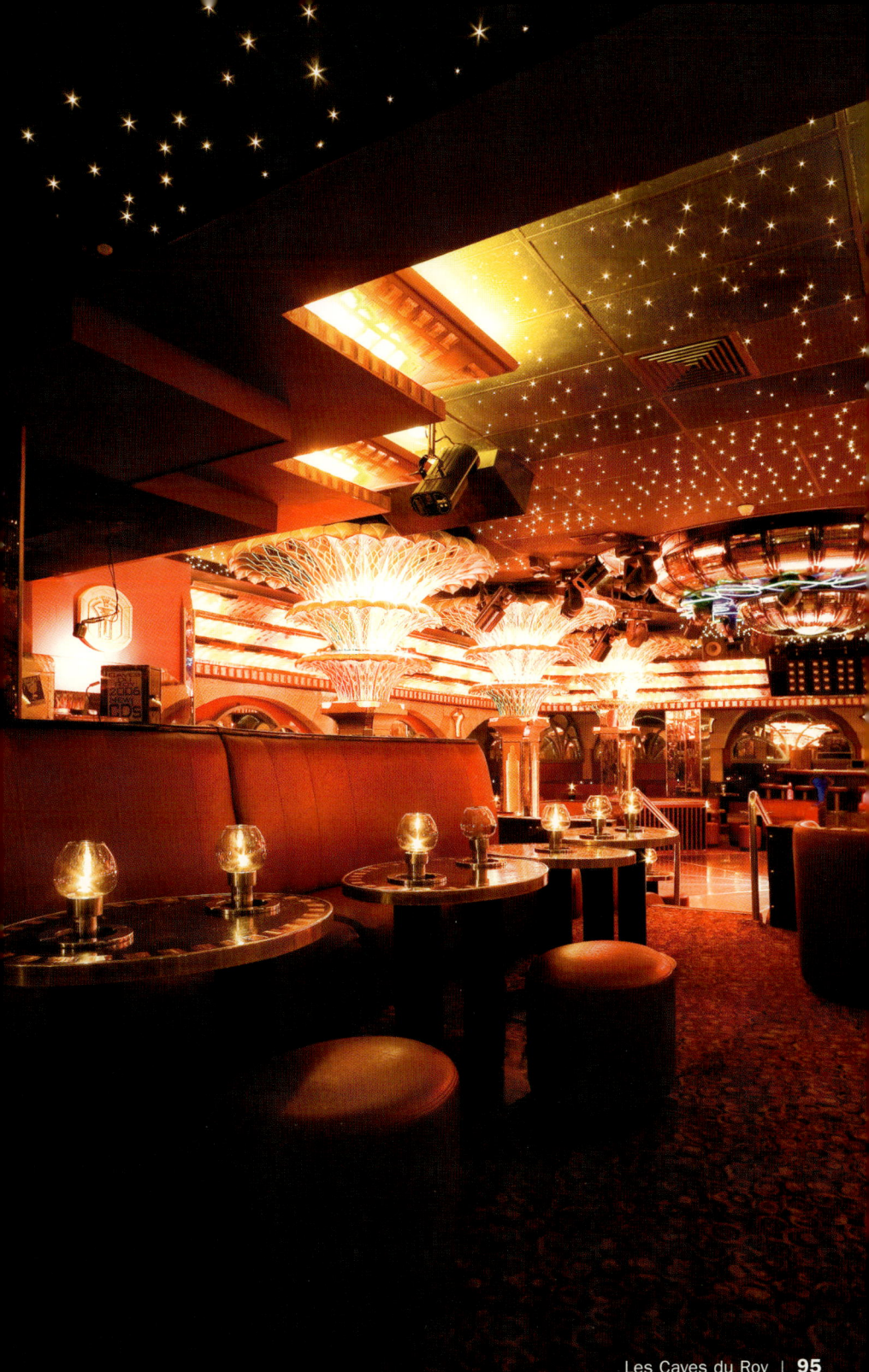

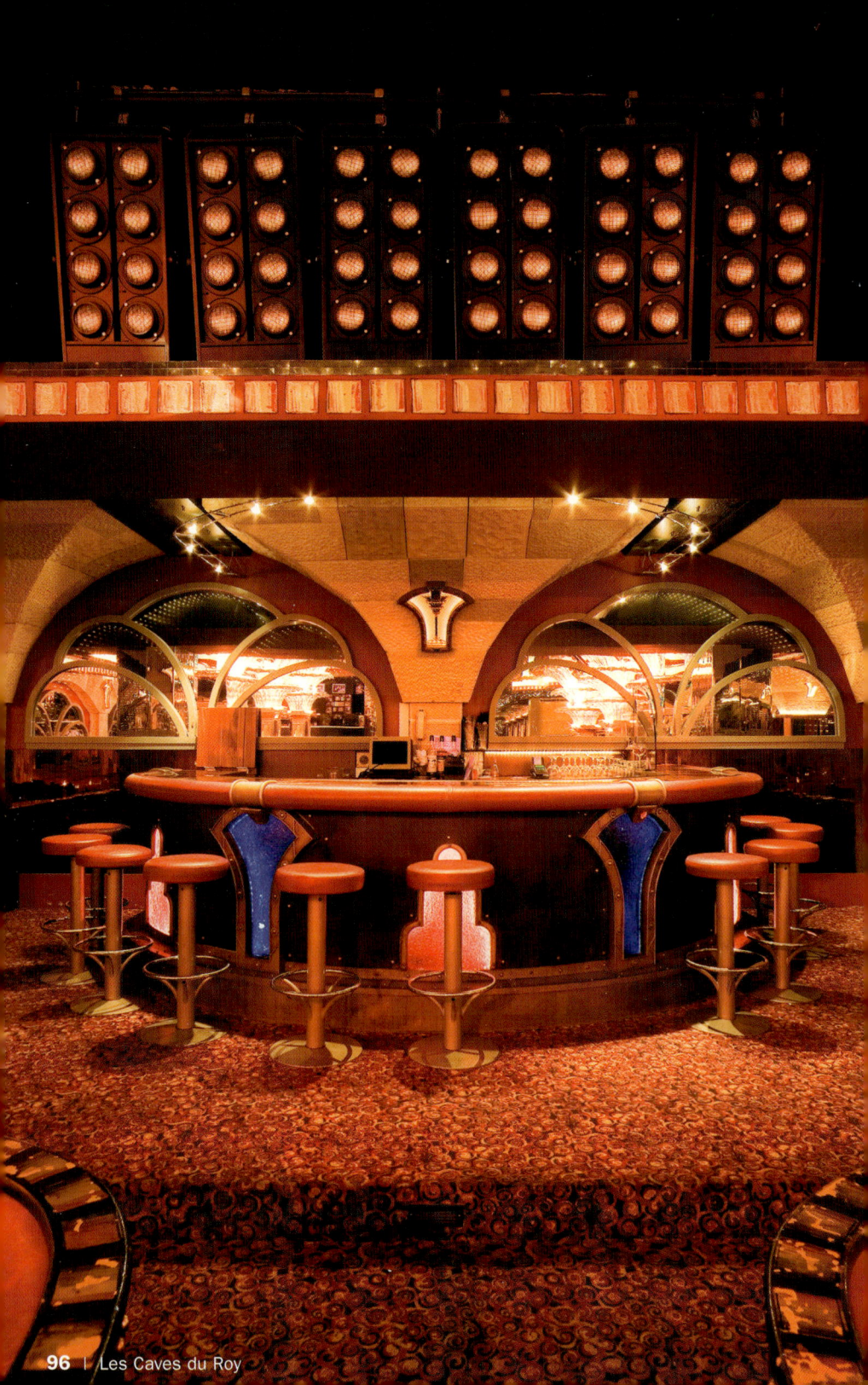

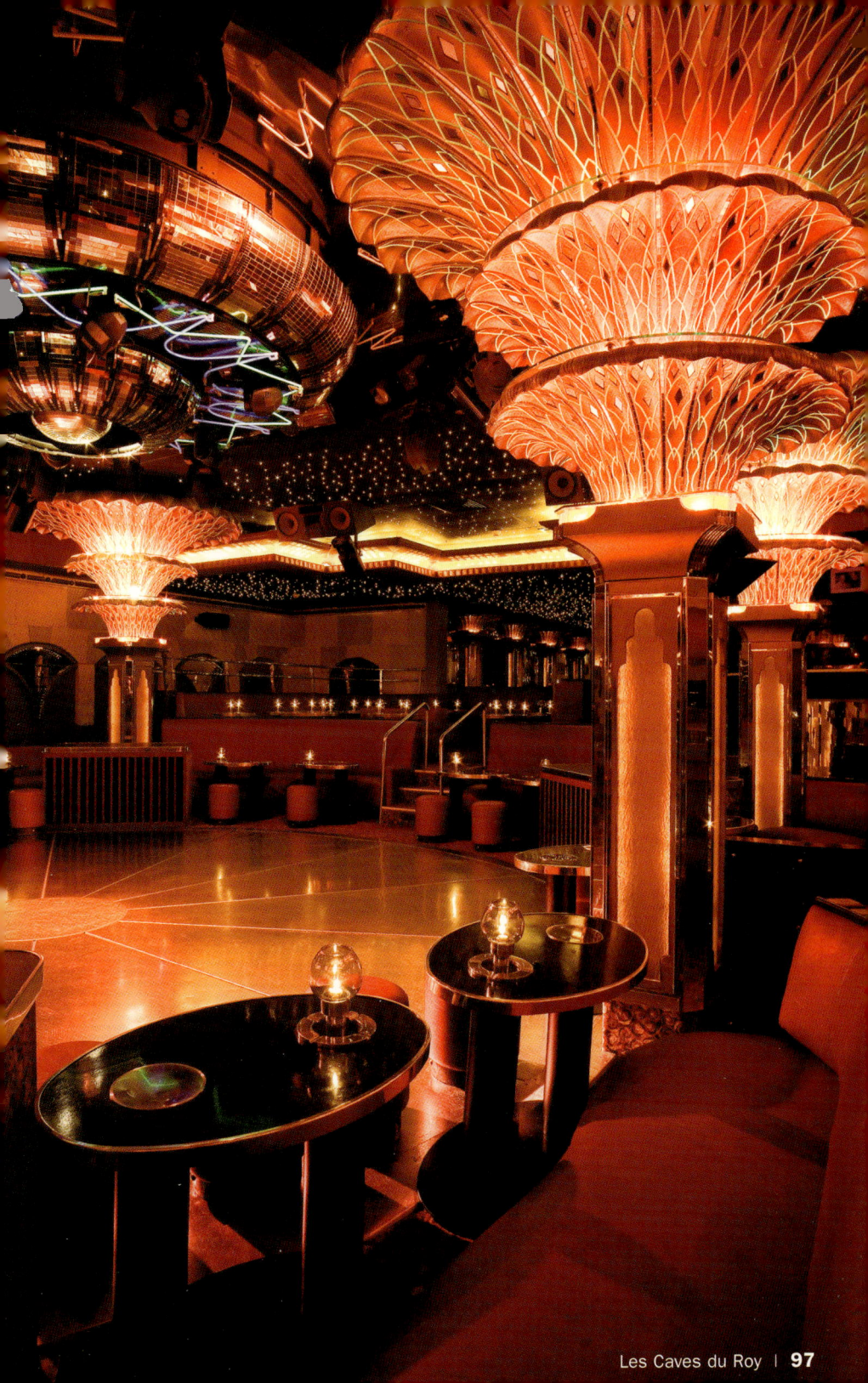

Li Li Boheme

Design: By the owners, Awatef and Angelo Marino

17 Rue Bivouac Napoleón | 06400 Cannes
Phone: +33 4 93 39 99 48
Opening hours: From 10:30 am to 7 pm
Special features: A jewelry shop looking more like an art gallery, less than 100 meters from the Palais de Festival

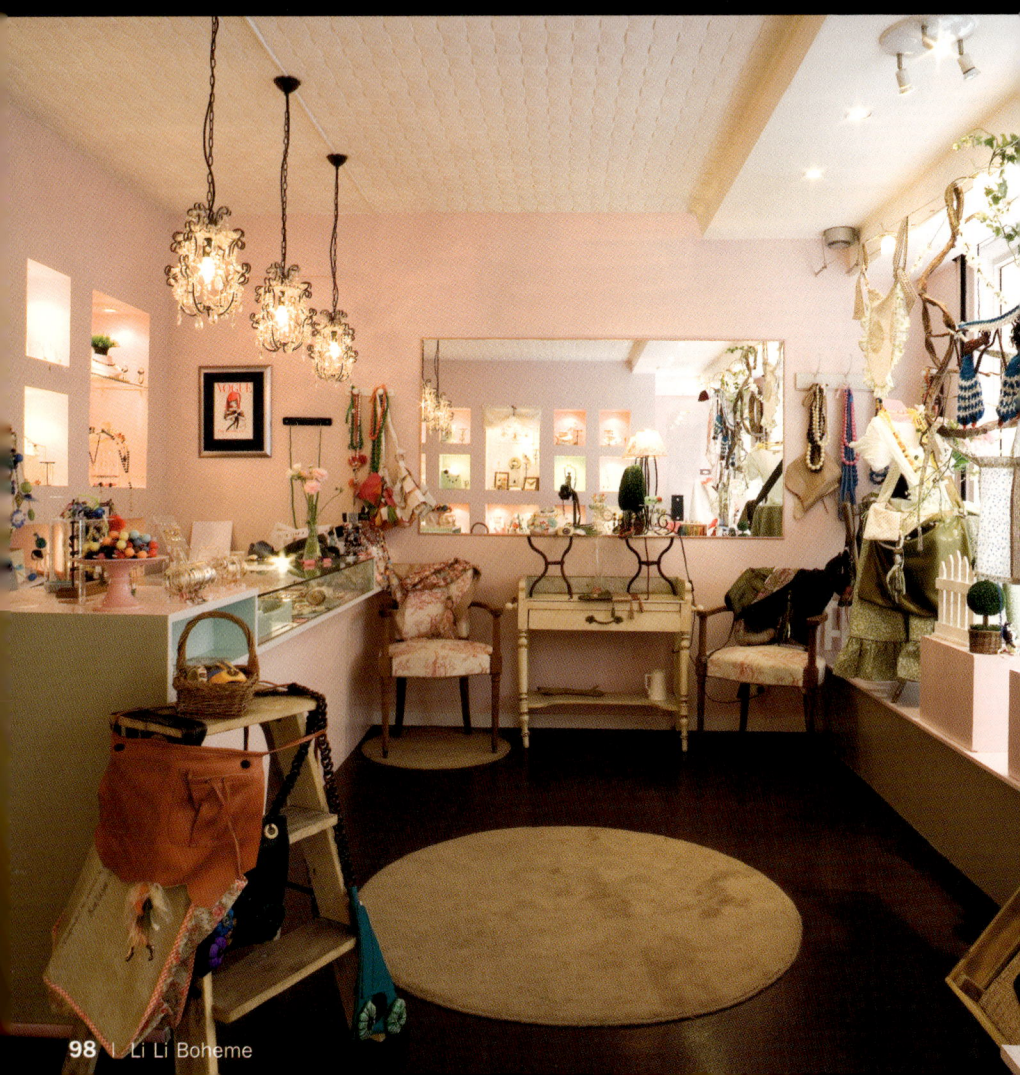

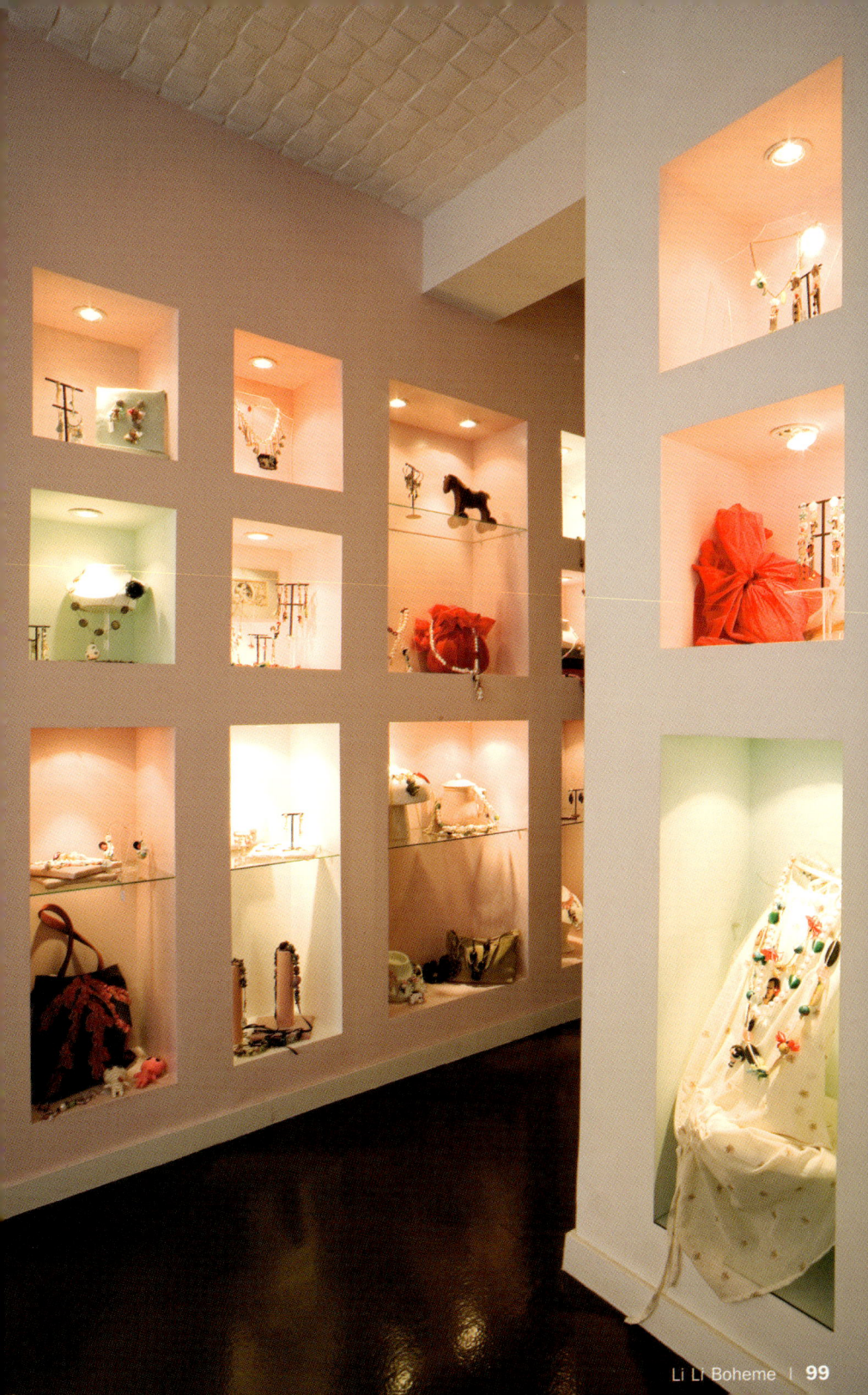

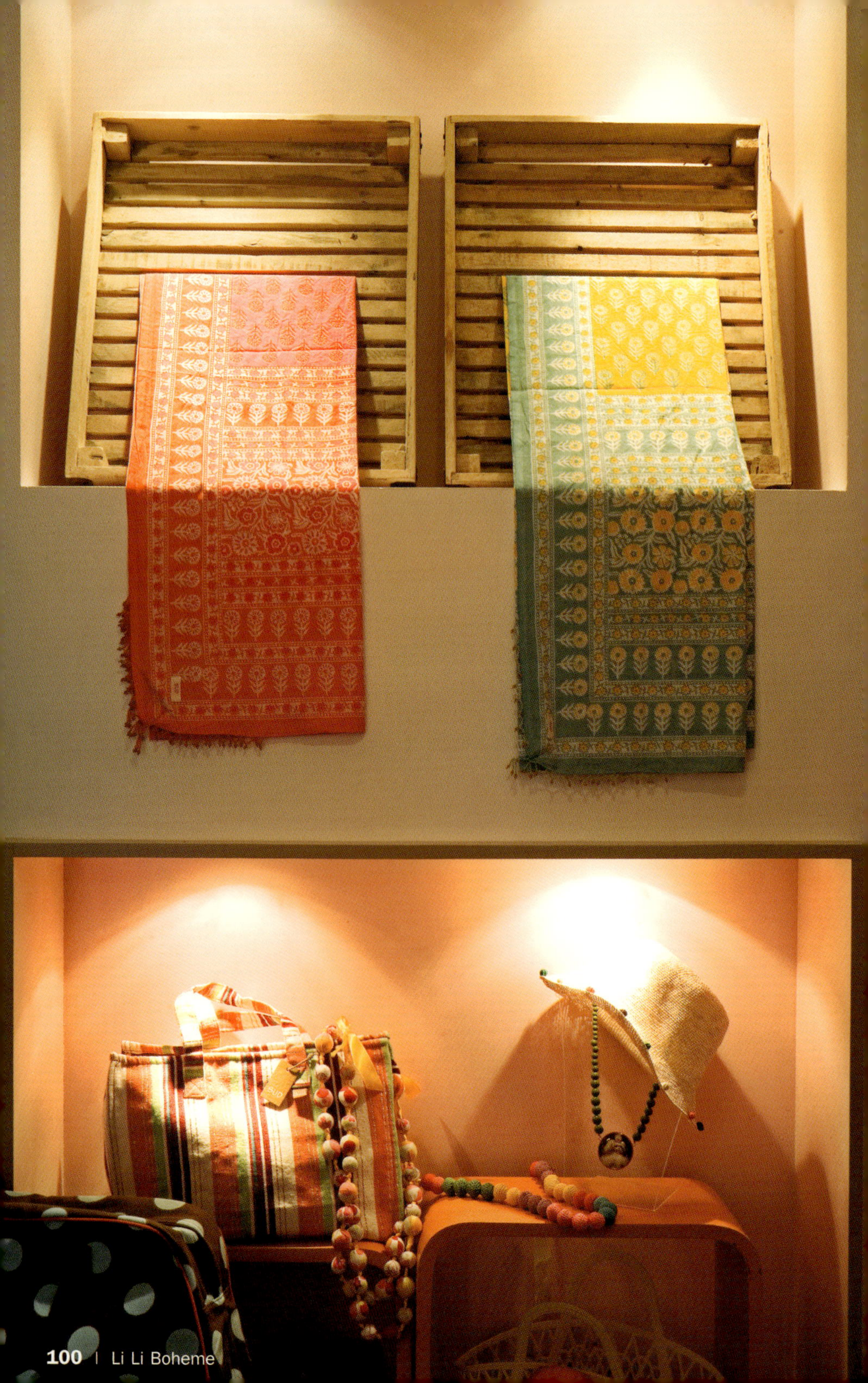

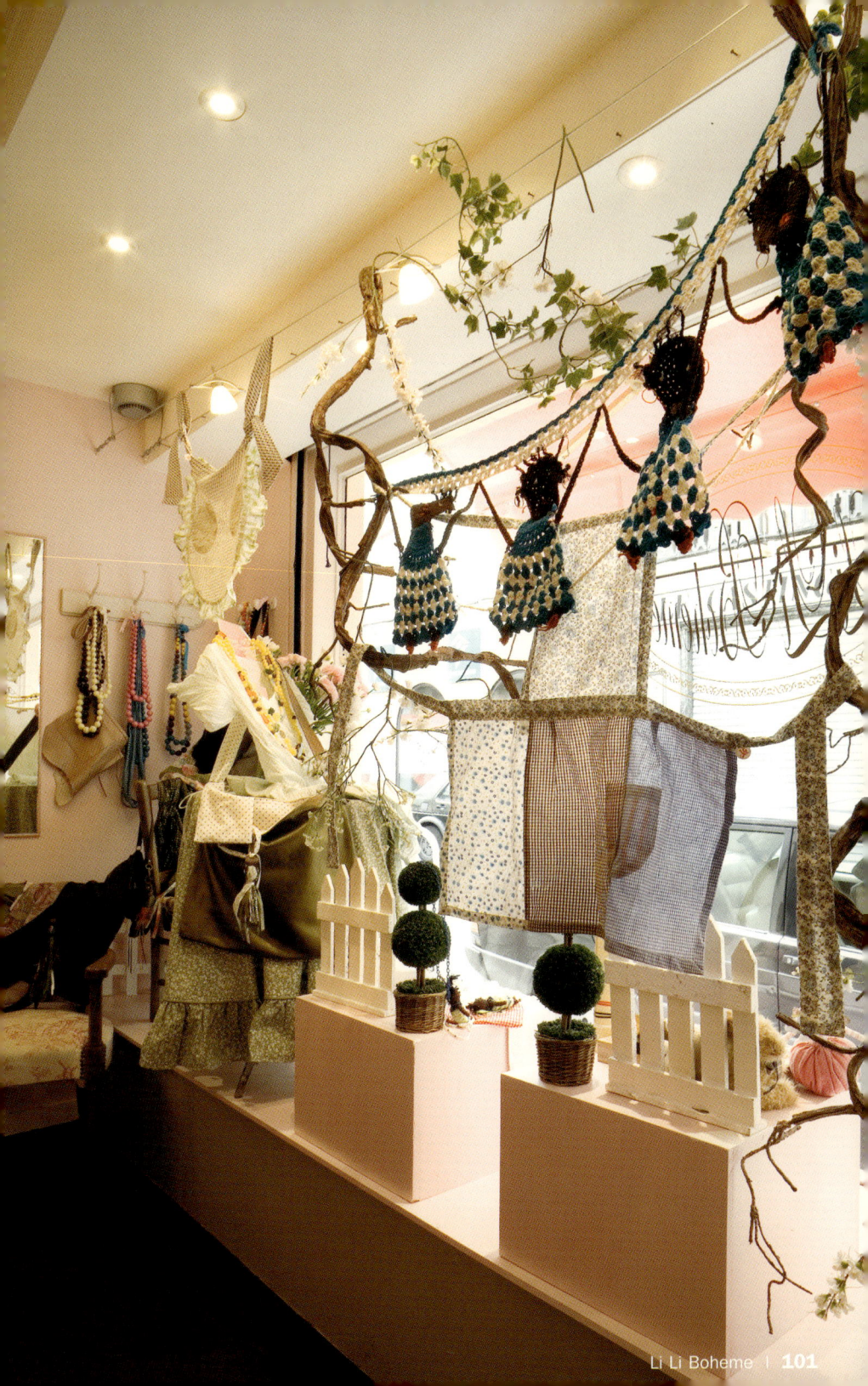

Liqwid

Design: Tony Phung

11 Rue Alexandre Mari | 06300 Nice
Phone: +33 4 93 76 14 28
www.liqwid-lounge.com
Opening hours: Bar from 6 pm to 5 am, restaurants from 7 pm to 12:30 am
Special features: The Resto-club and the Resto-lounge, restaurants with two
different atmospheres that create a mixture of styles inspired by the latest
tendencies in Miami, London and New York

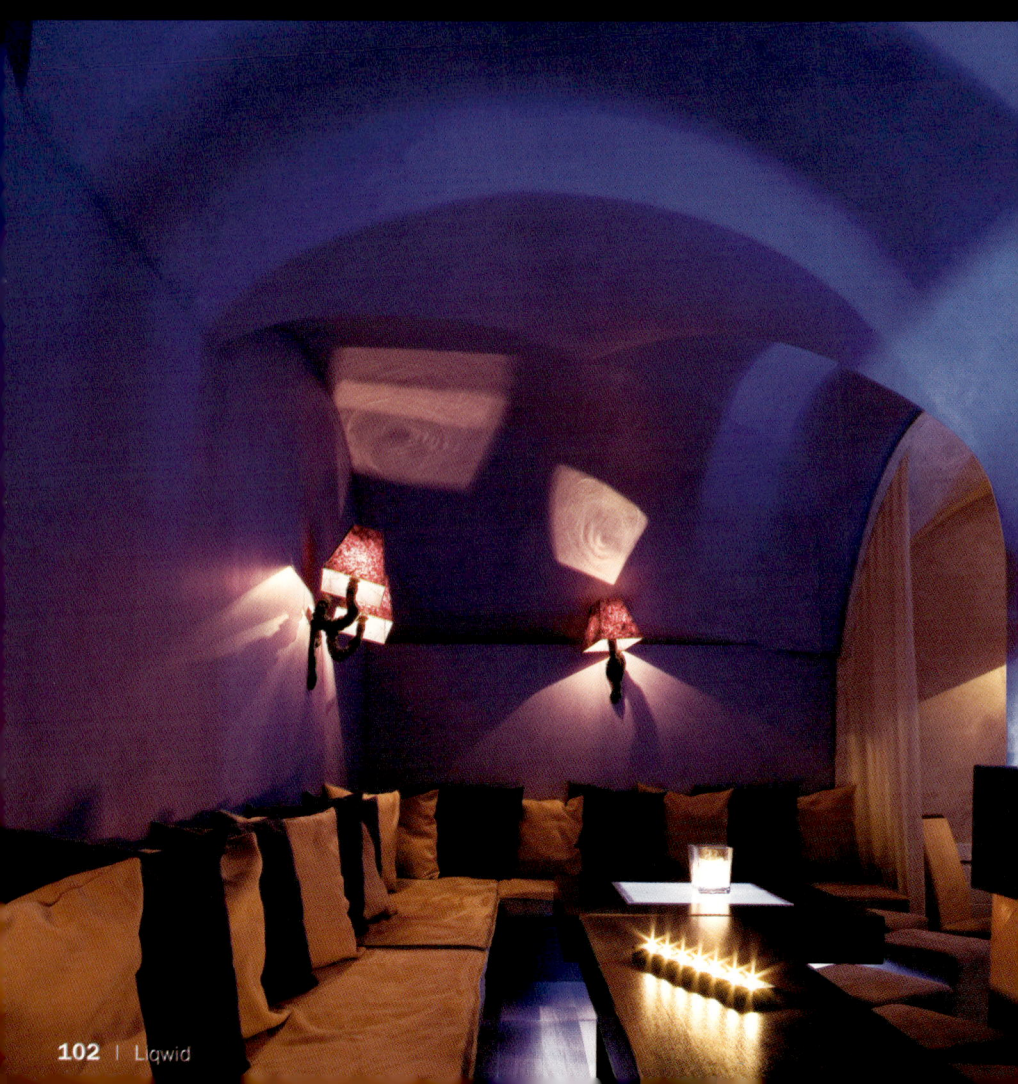

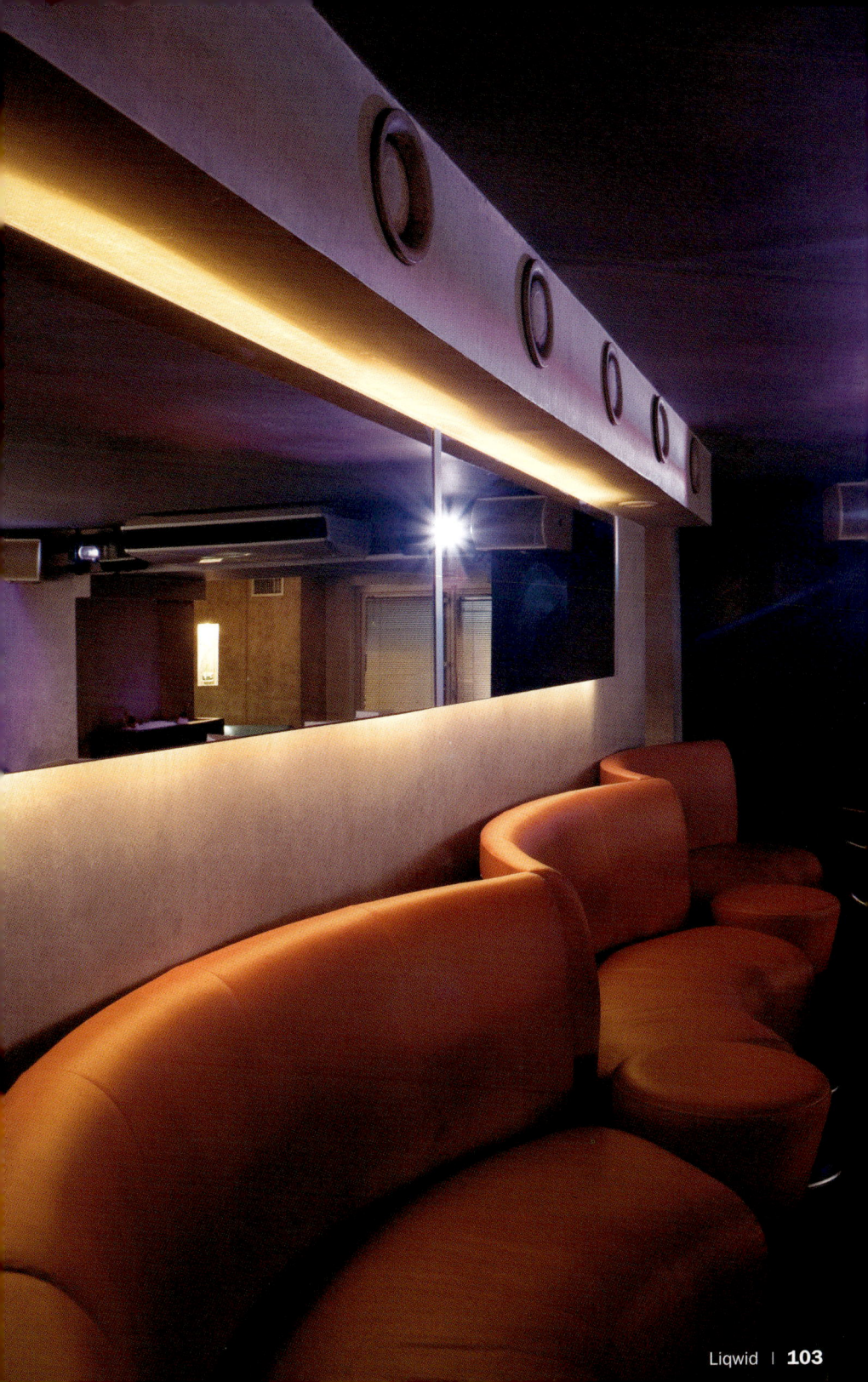

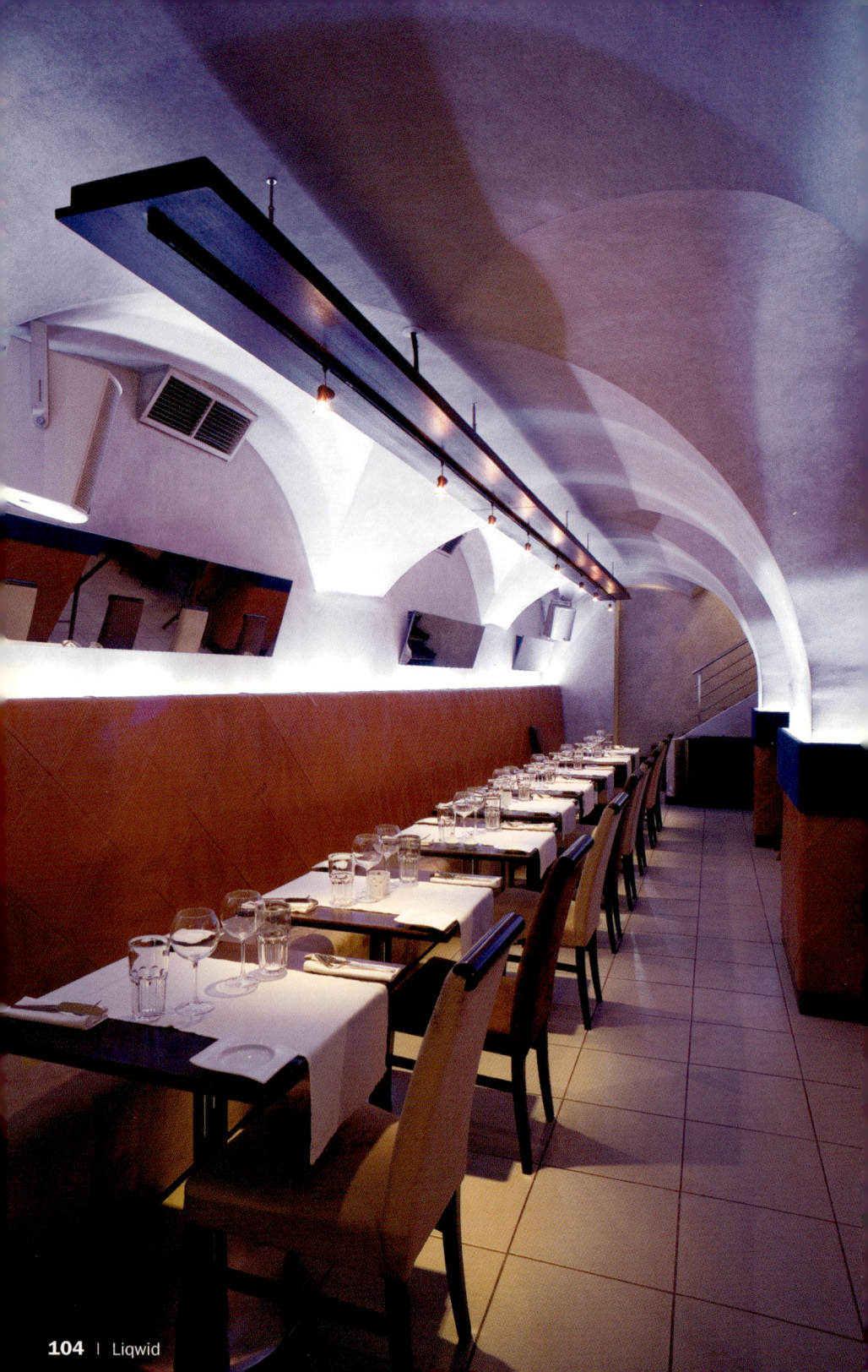

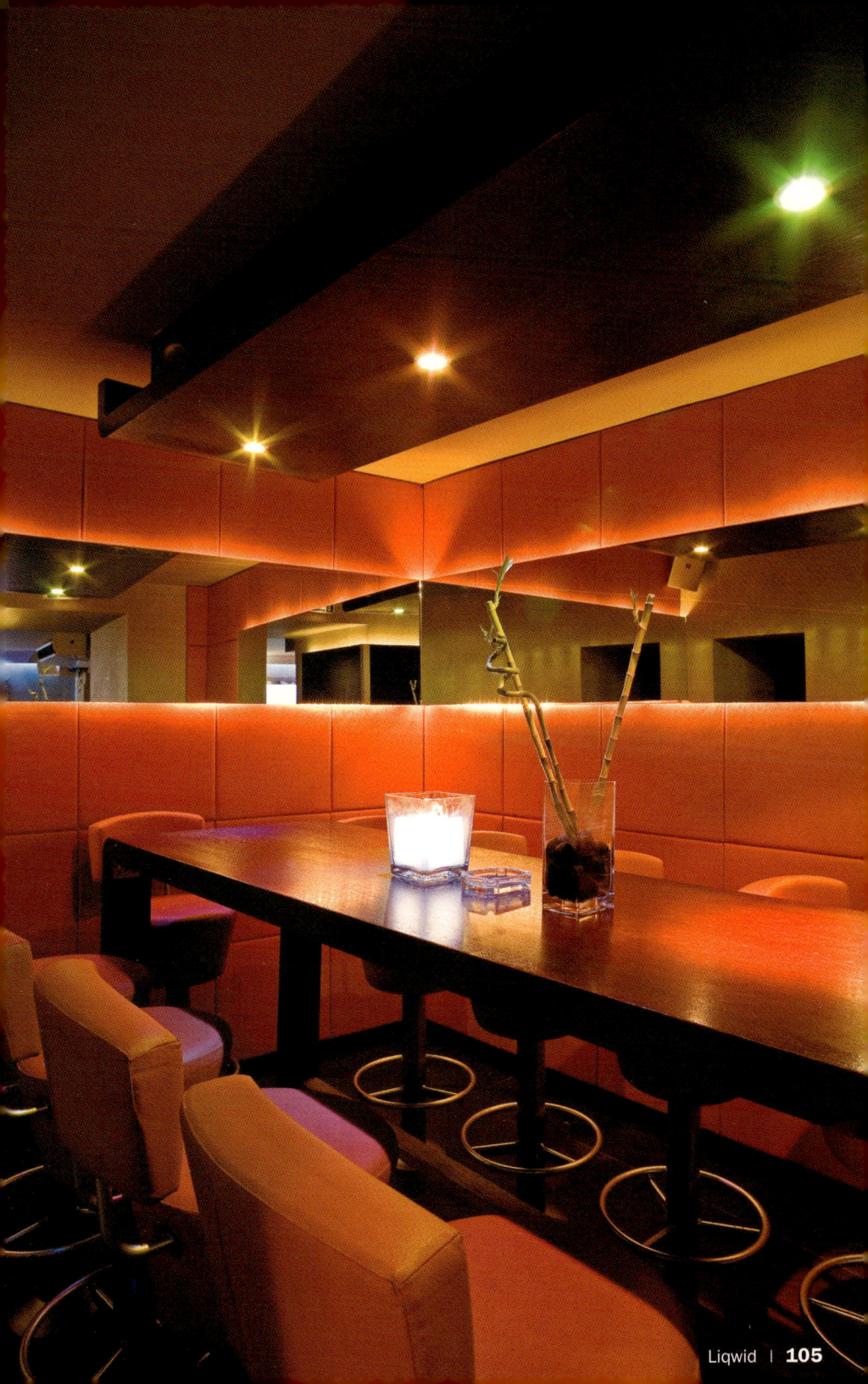

Maison Ocoa

Design: By the owner, Stephane Cantatore

Plage de Pampelonne, Boulevard Patch | 83350 Ramatuelle
Phone: +33 4 94 79 89 80
www.maison-ocoa.com
Opening hours: From 9 am to 7 pm all year long, to 2 am from July 1st to August 31st
Special features: A trendy spot in Saint-Tropez, perfect for a drink facing the sea during the summer, or to spend a romantic moment close to the chimney by bad weather

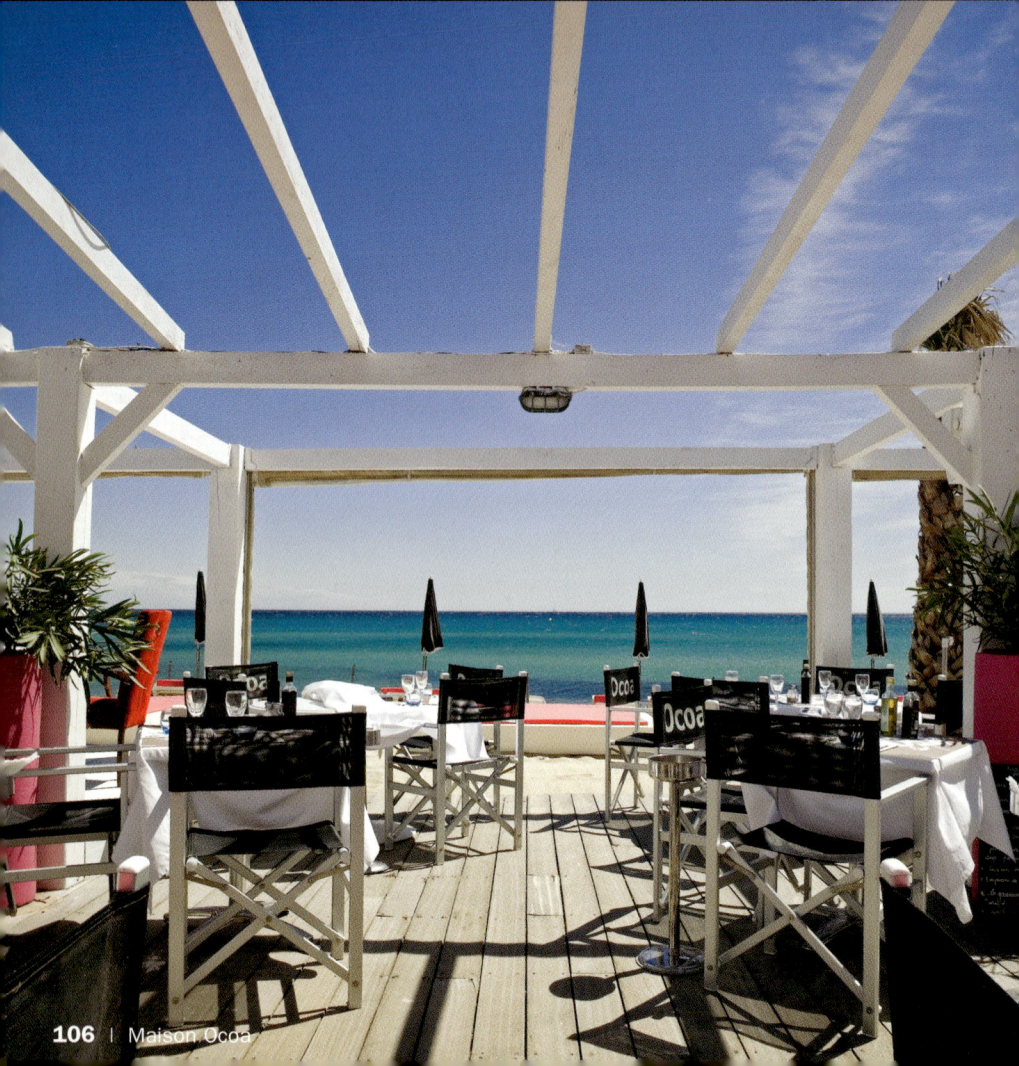

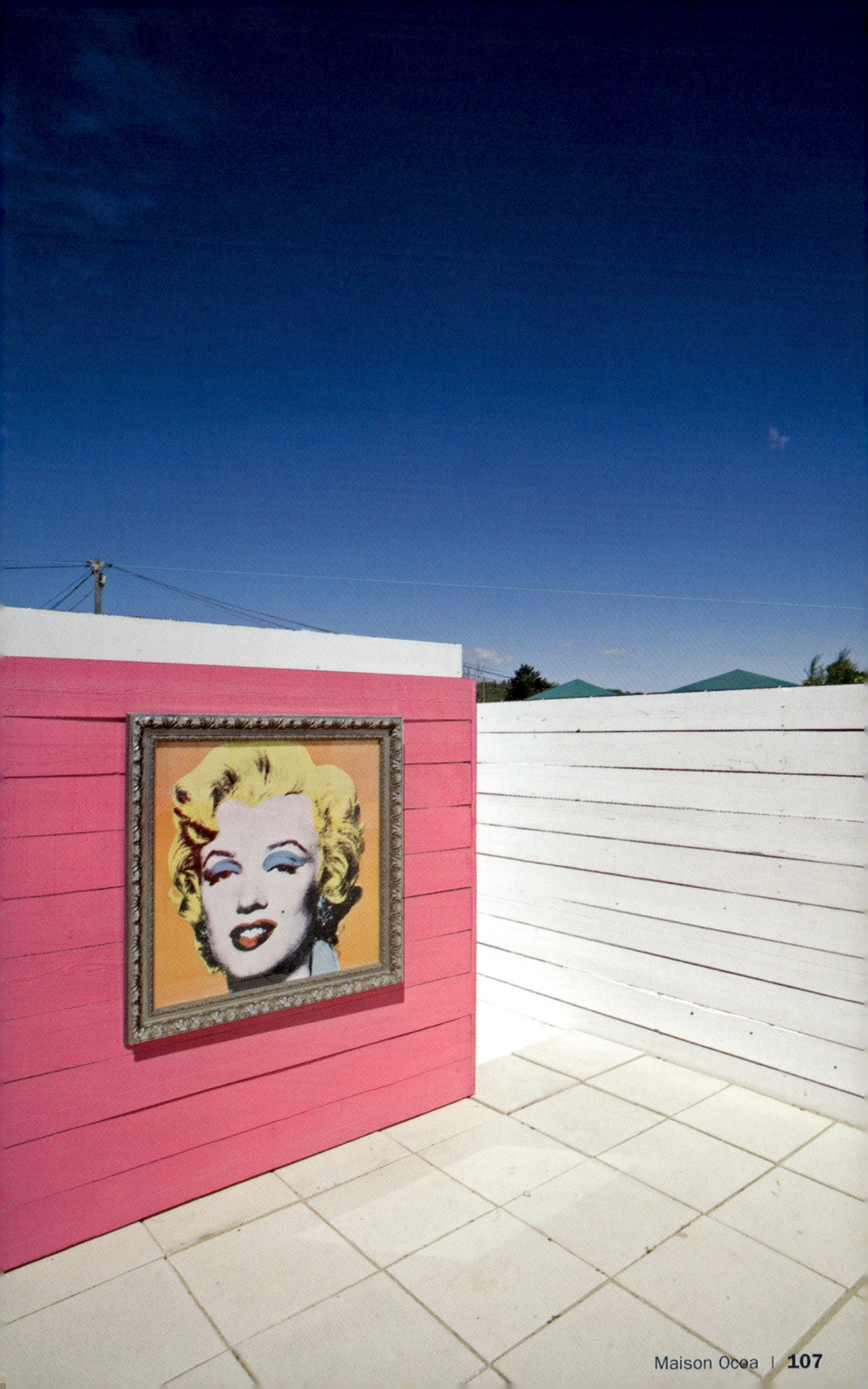

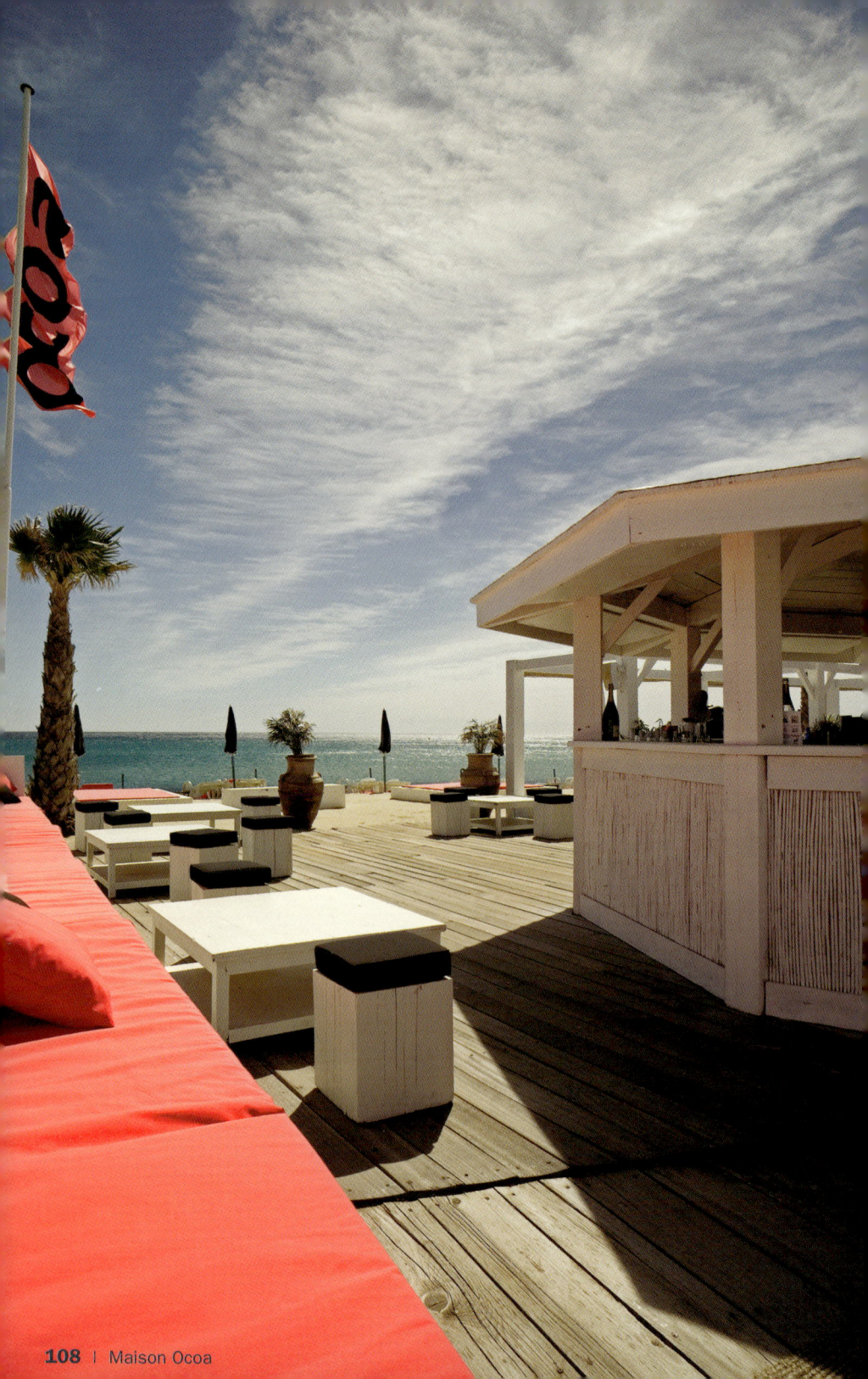

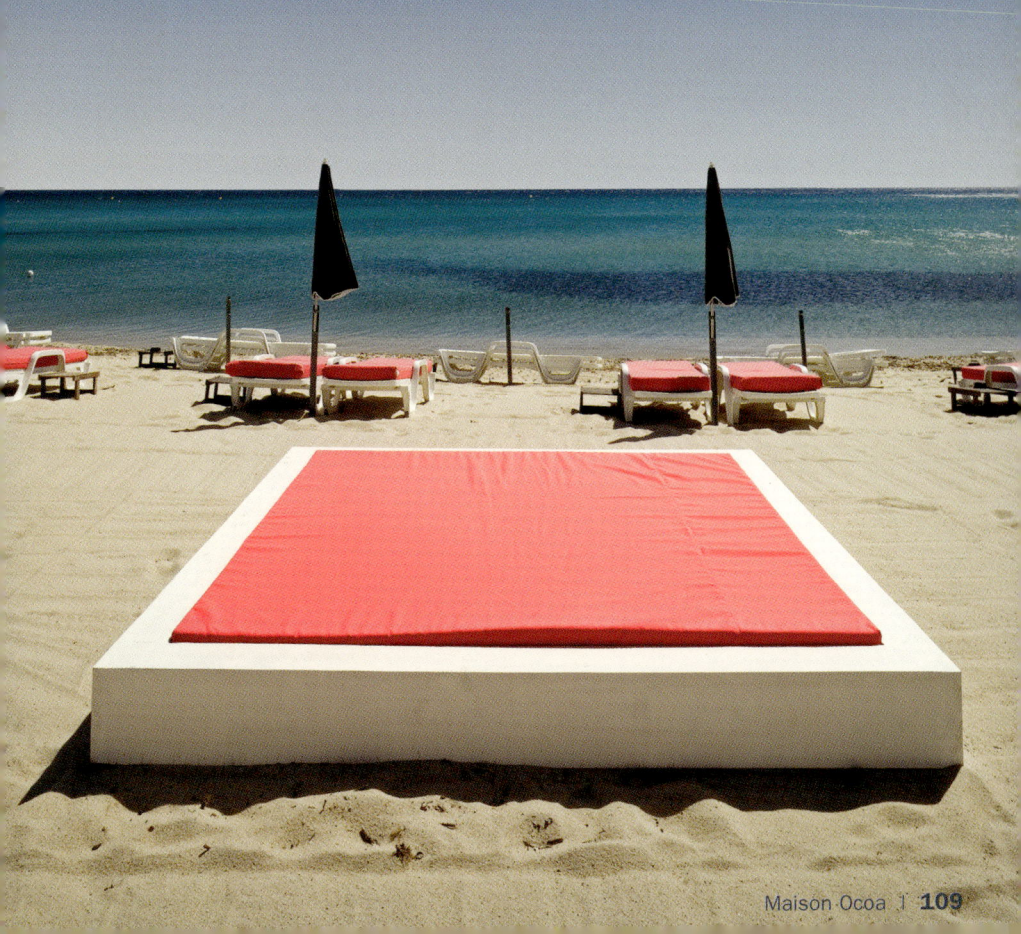

Manuréva

Design: By the owners, Hervé and Alexandra Langlet

Route de Tahiti | 83550 Ramatuelle
Phone: +33 4 94 94 97 24
www.plage-manureva.com
Opening hours: From April to October, from 9 am to midnight
Special features: Lounge bar, restaurant and rooms at one of the most beautiful
beaches of the Saint-Tropez area

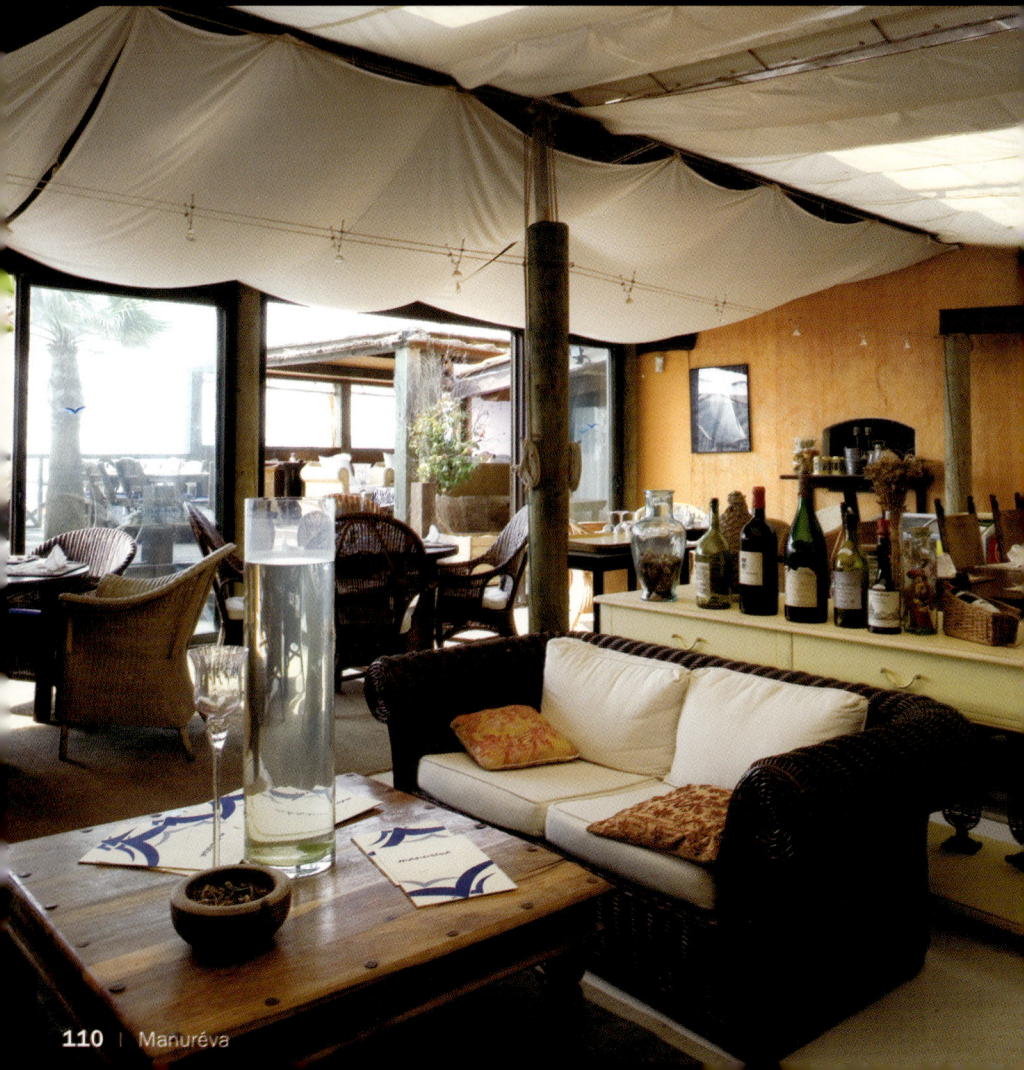

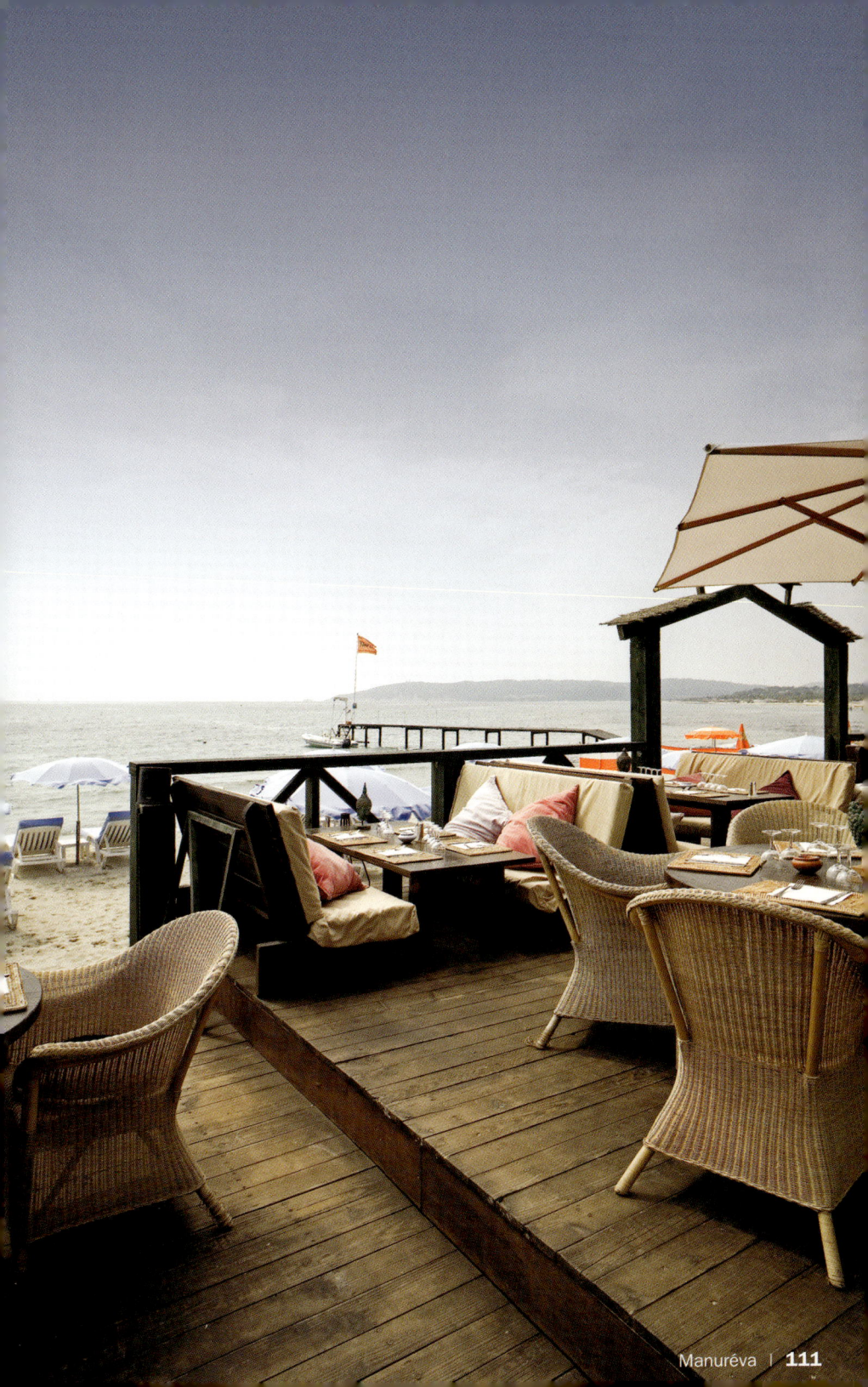

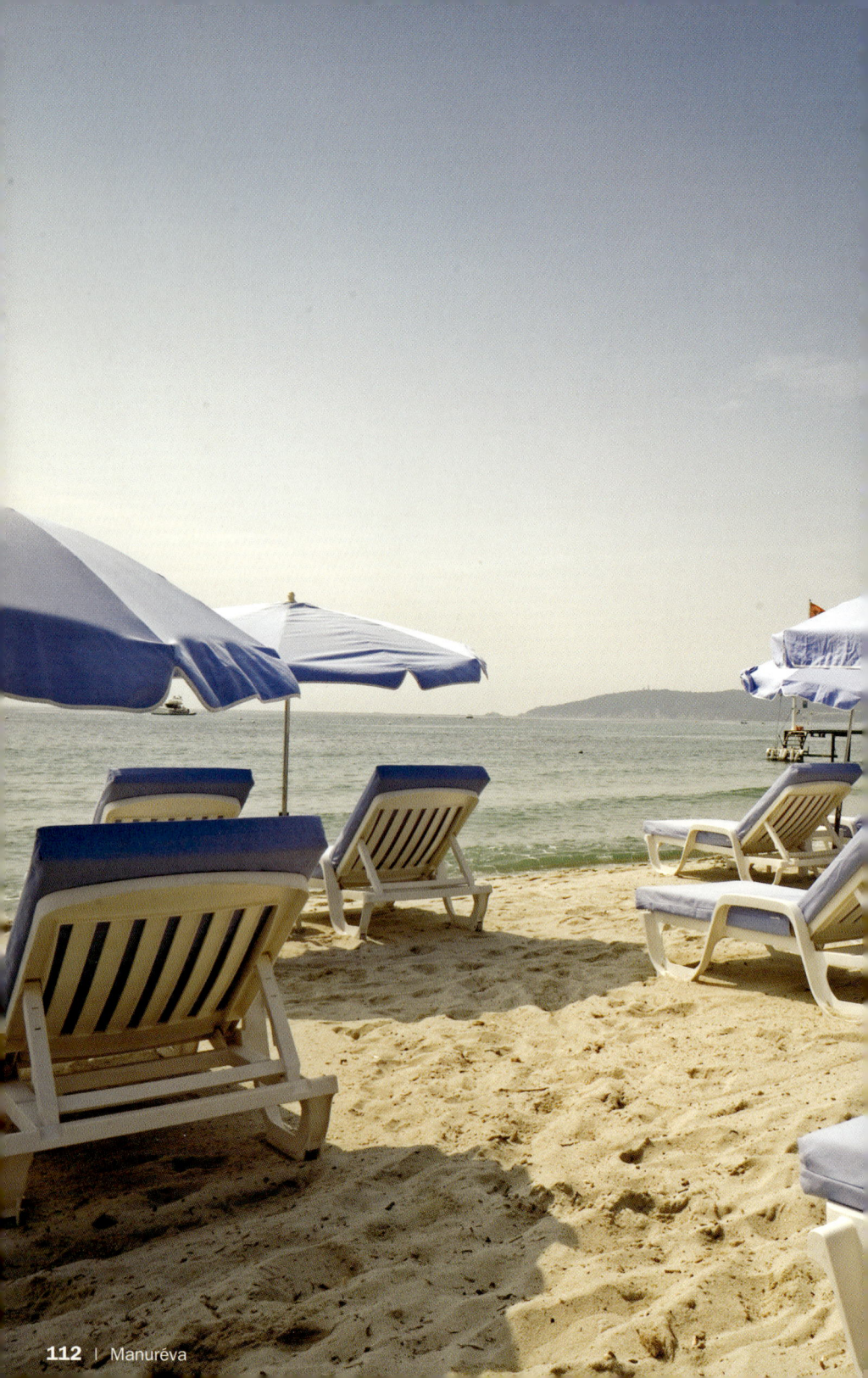

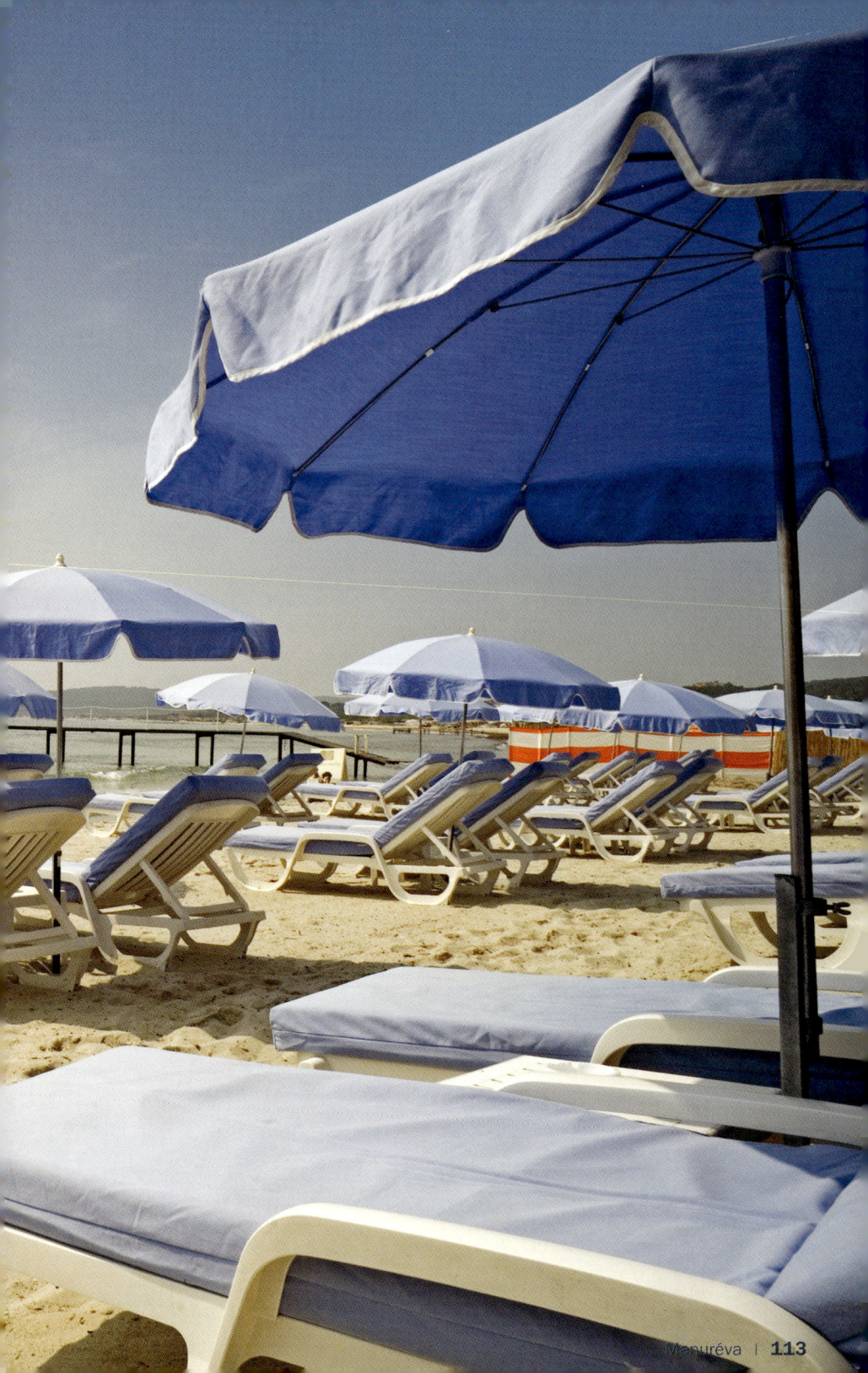

Mes Anges

Design: By the owner, Daniel Goubert

15 Rue Macé | 06400 Cannes
Phone: +33 4 92 99 11 43
Opening hours: Mon–Sat from 10 am to 7 pm
Special features: Two Englishmen and a Frenchman run this stylish boutique, which
they like to think of more like a dressing room than a shop

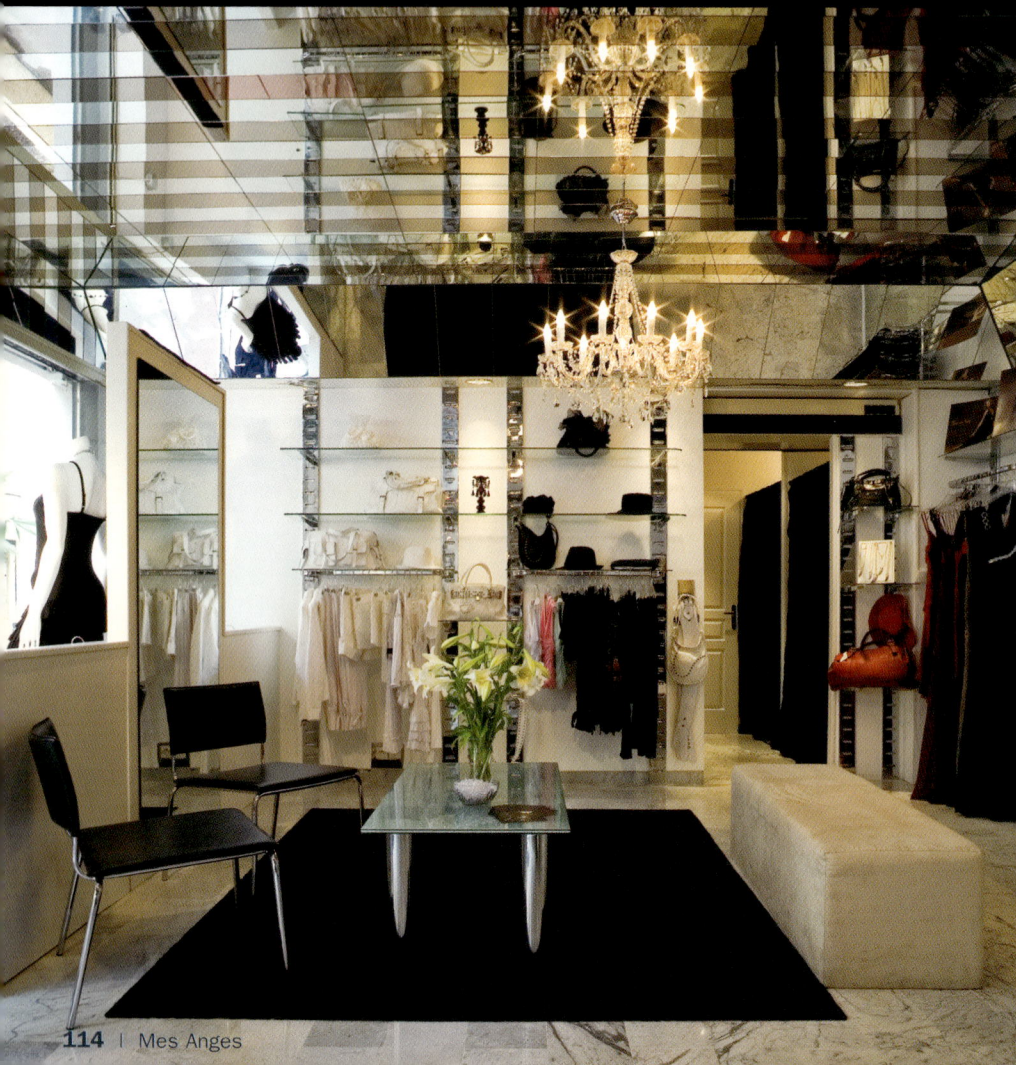

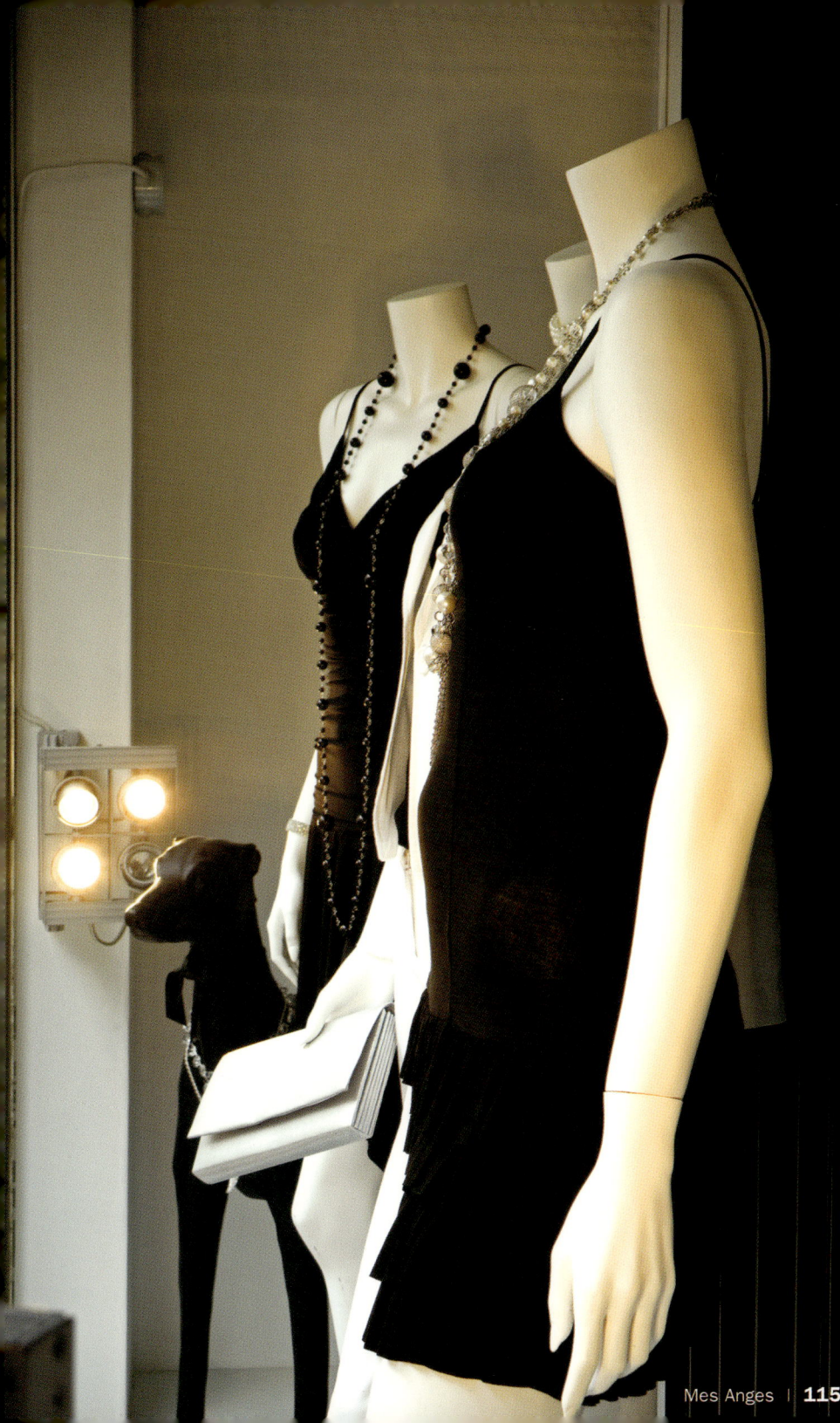

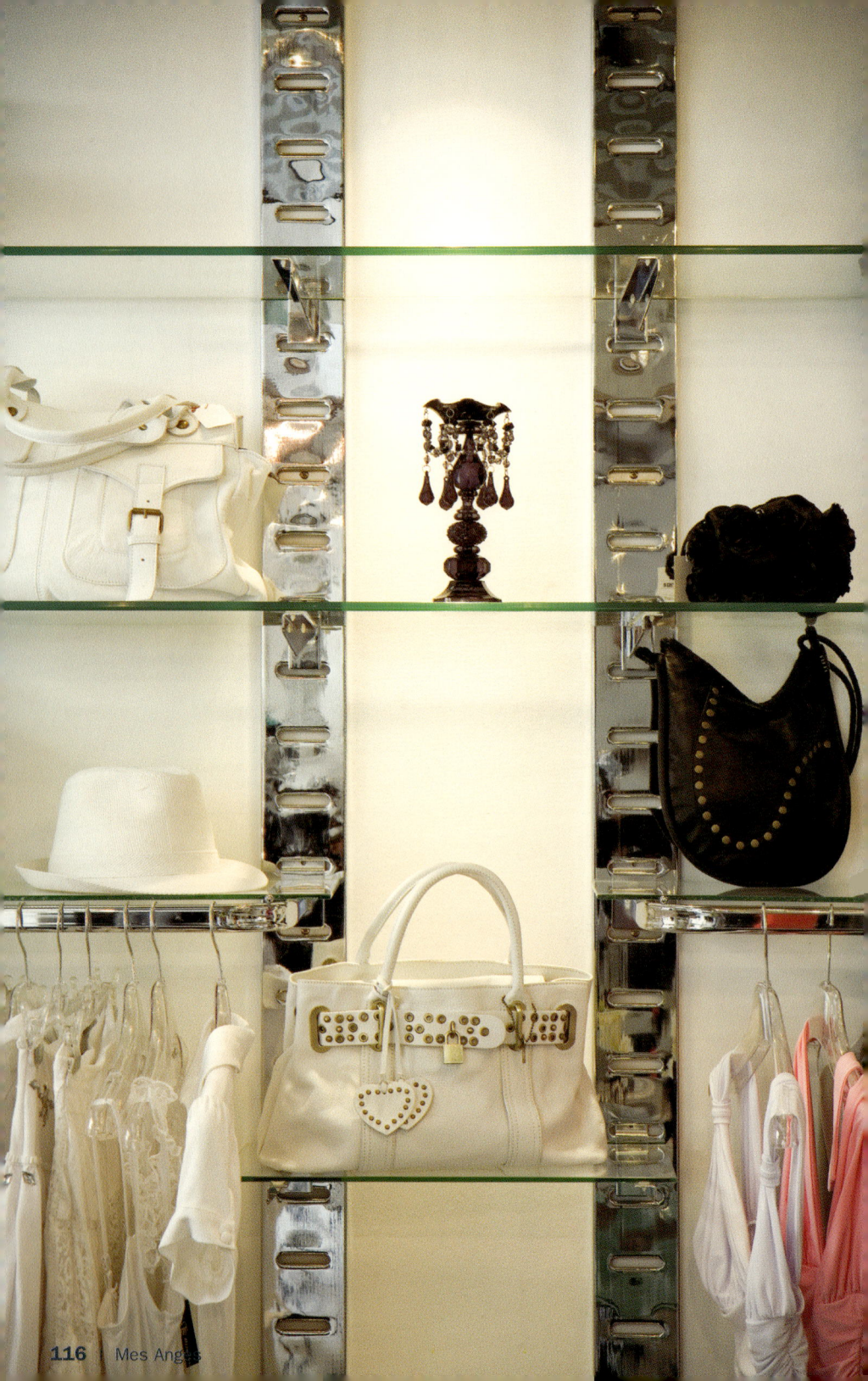

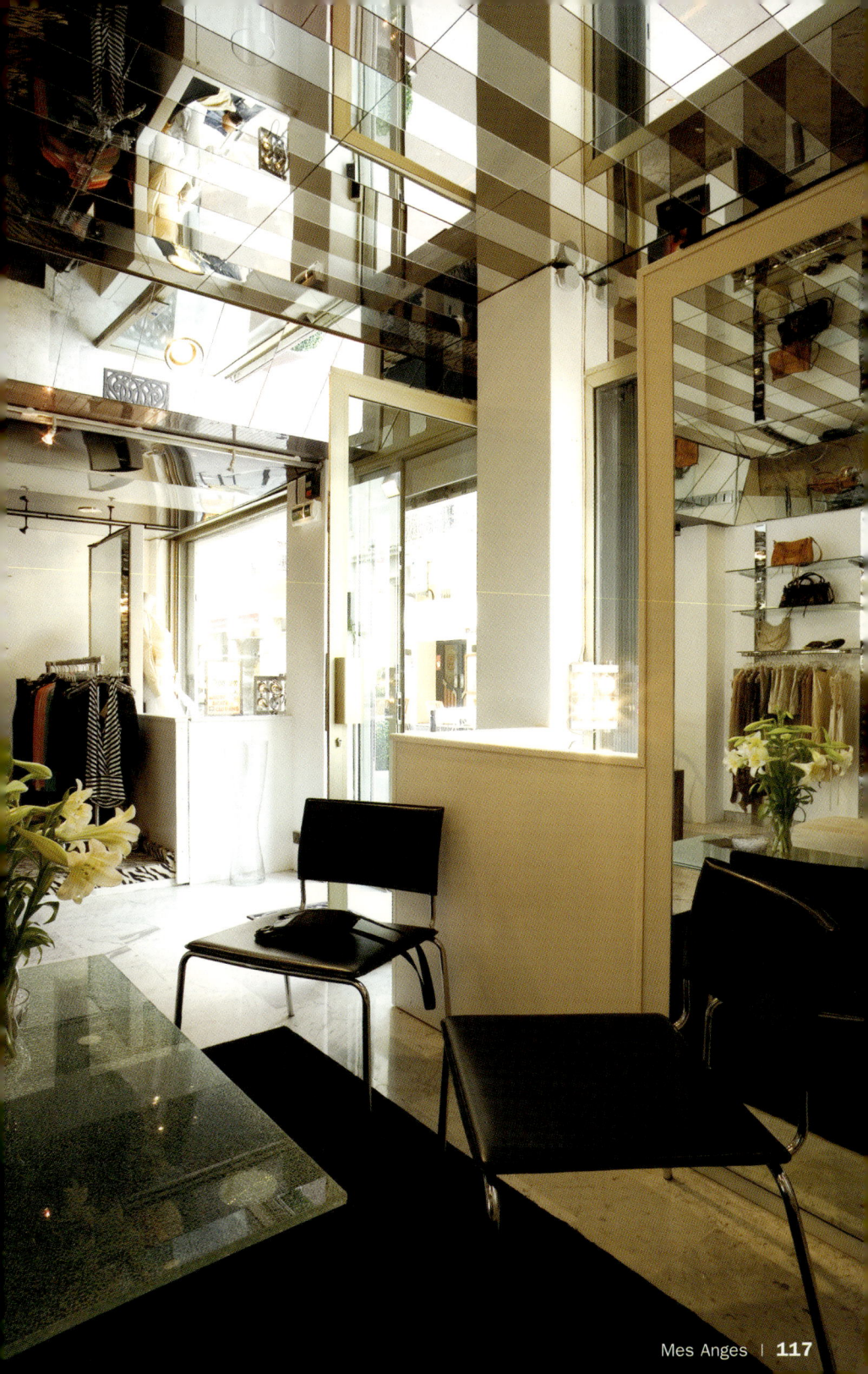

Millesim Beach Club

Design: By the owner, Frédérique Blanc

Route de Tahiti | 83950 Ramatuelle
Phone: +33 4 94 97 20 99
www.millesim.net
Opening hours: Every day from 9 am to 5 pm and from 7:30 pm to 11 pm
Special features: A fancy beach club offering lunch and dinner. The resort includes
a massage salon with special Shiatsu and relaxation sessions

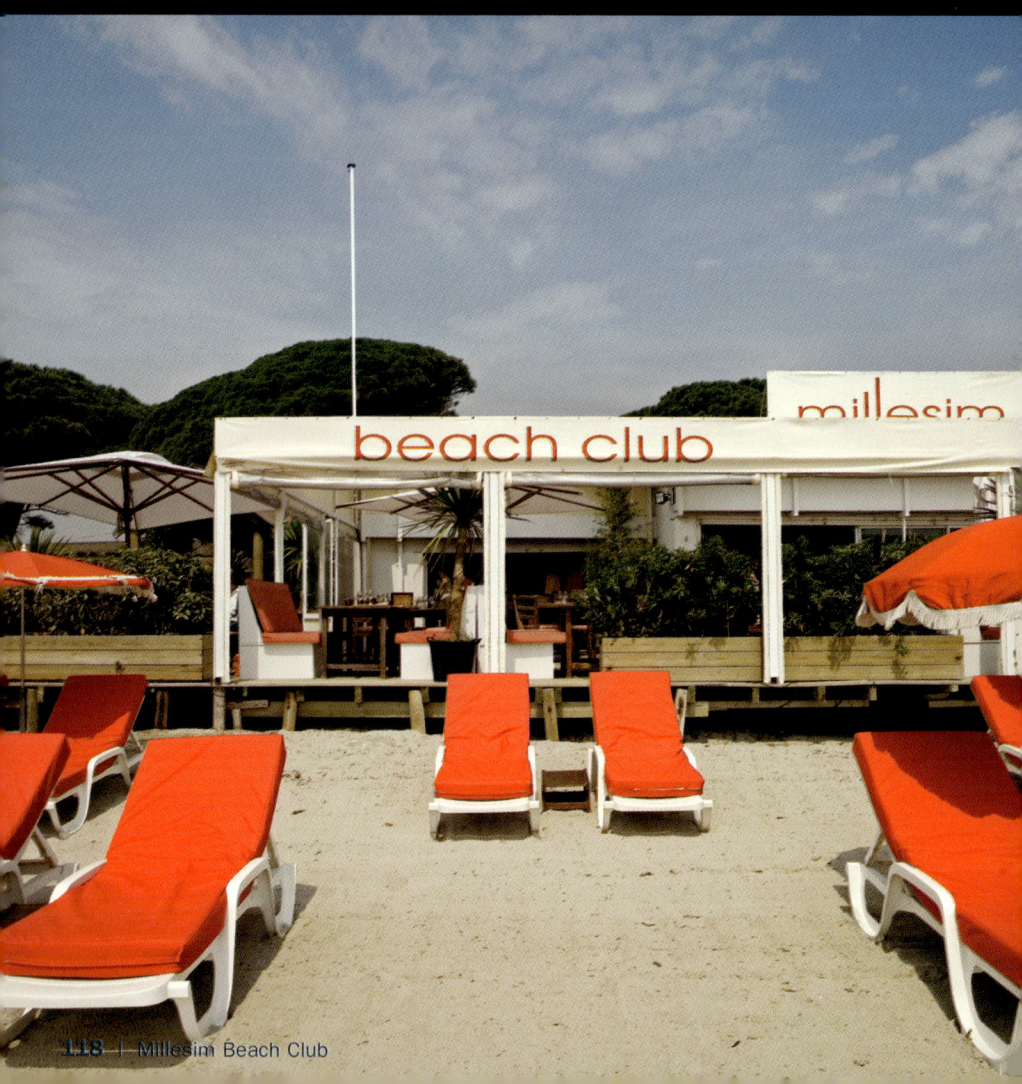

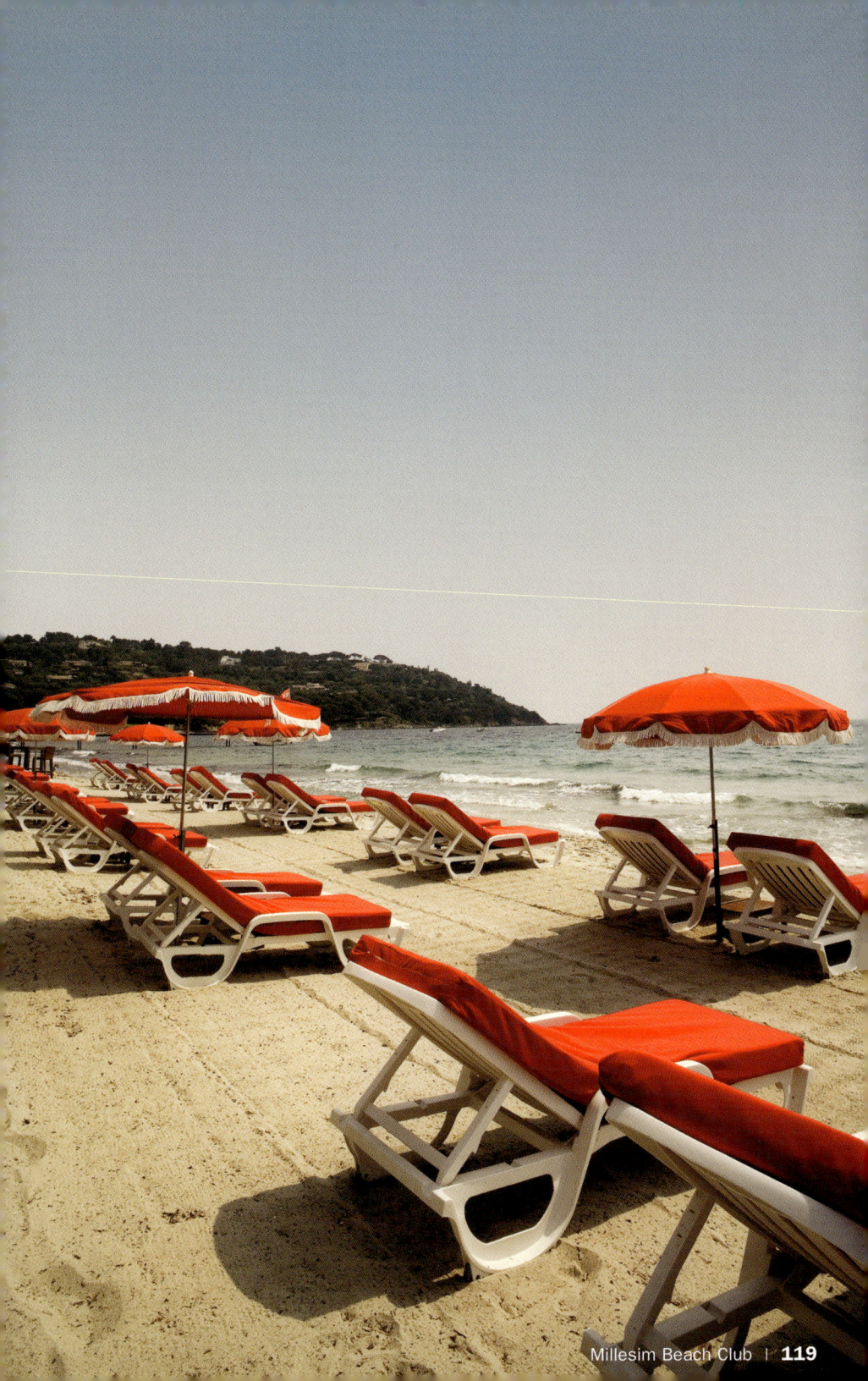

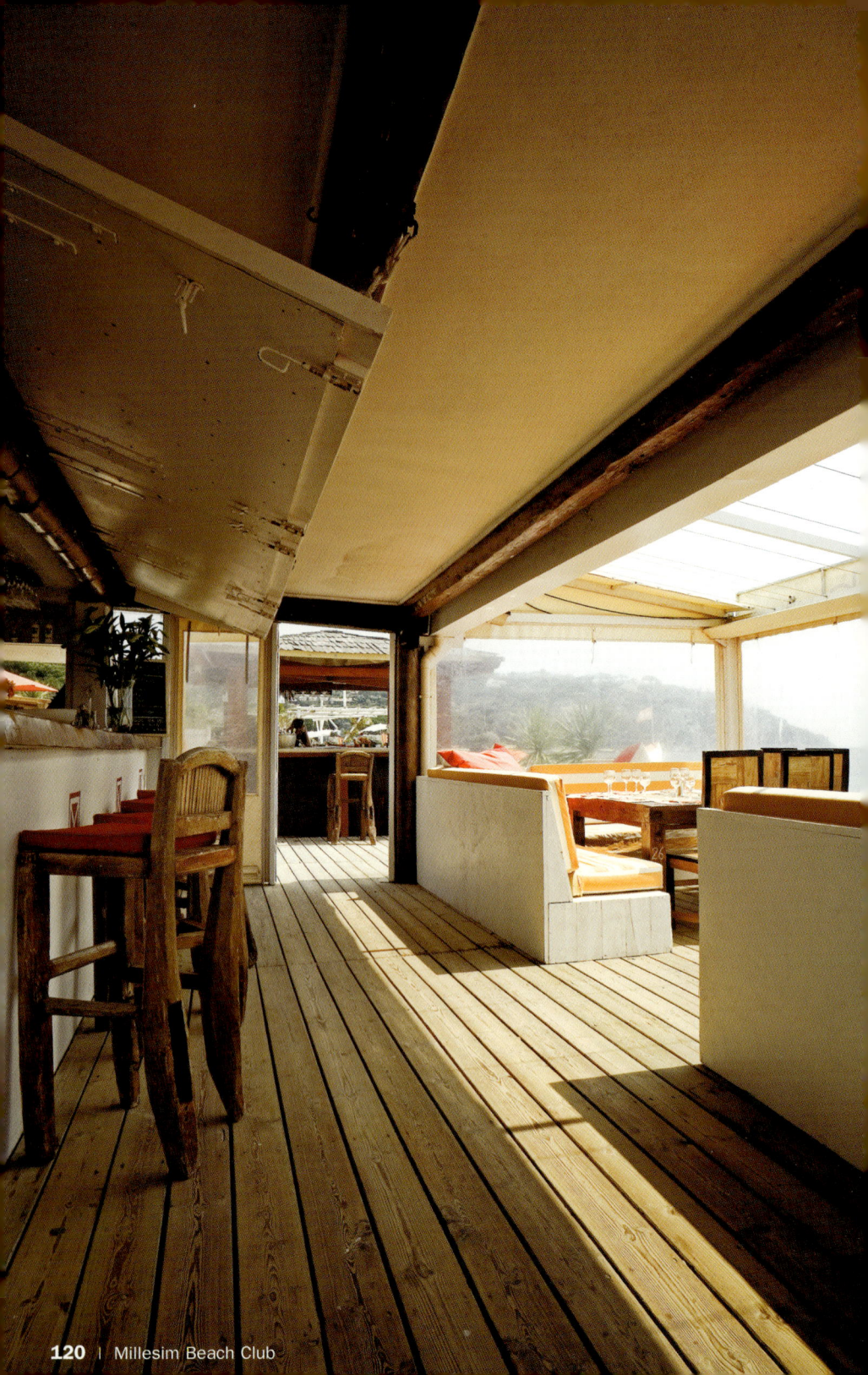

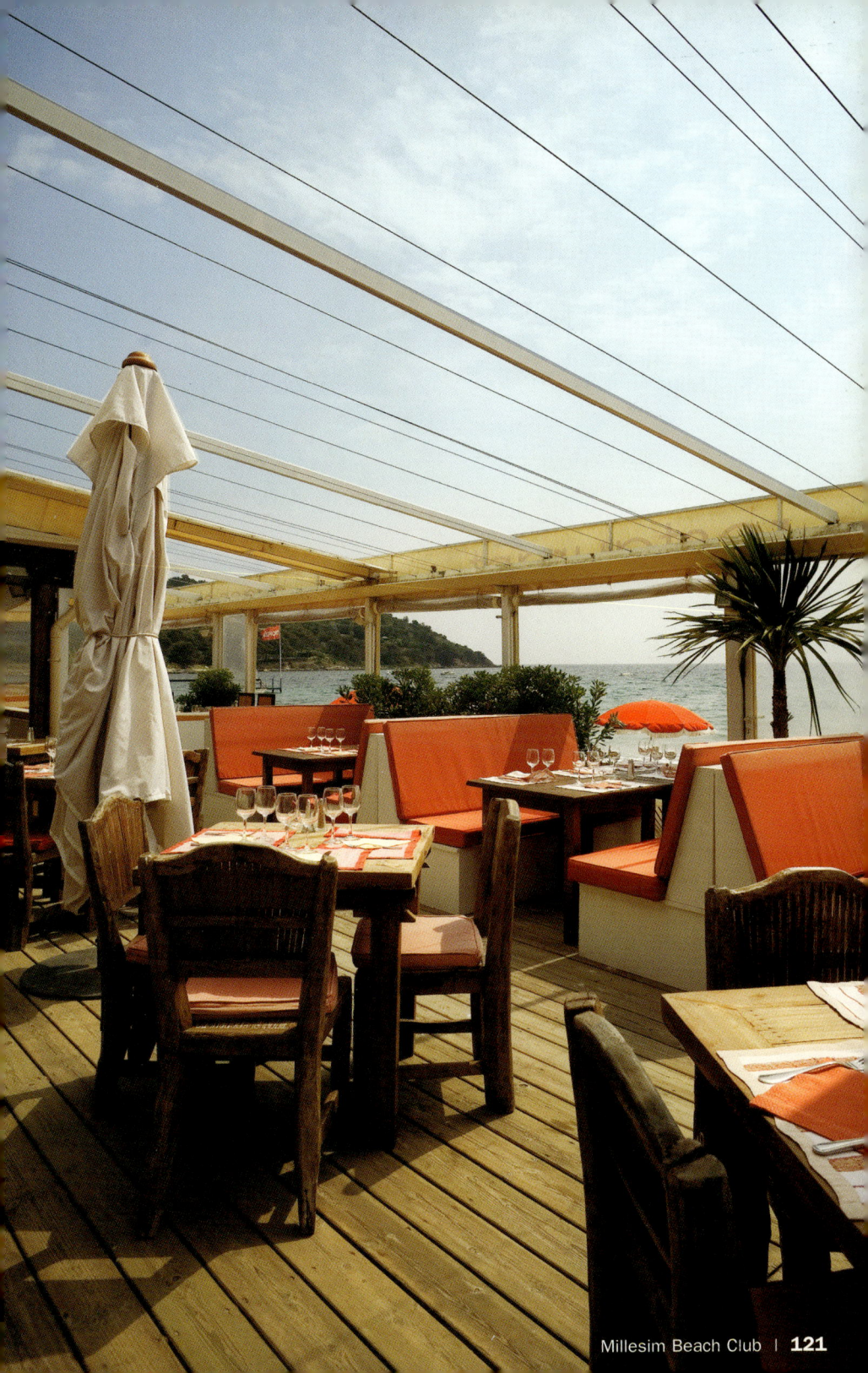

Mirazur

Design: R. Mather and J. Larsson

30 Avenue Aristide Briand | 06500 Menton
Phone: +33 4 92 41 86 86
www.mirazur.fr
Opening hours: From 12 pm to 2:30 pm and from 7:30 pm to 10:30 pm, closed
Tuesdays, Wednesday open only for dinner
Special features: Creative cooking and a magnificent view over the bay of Menton

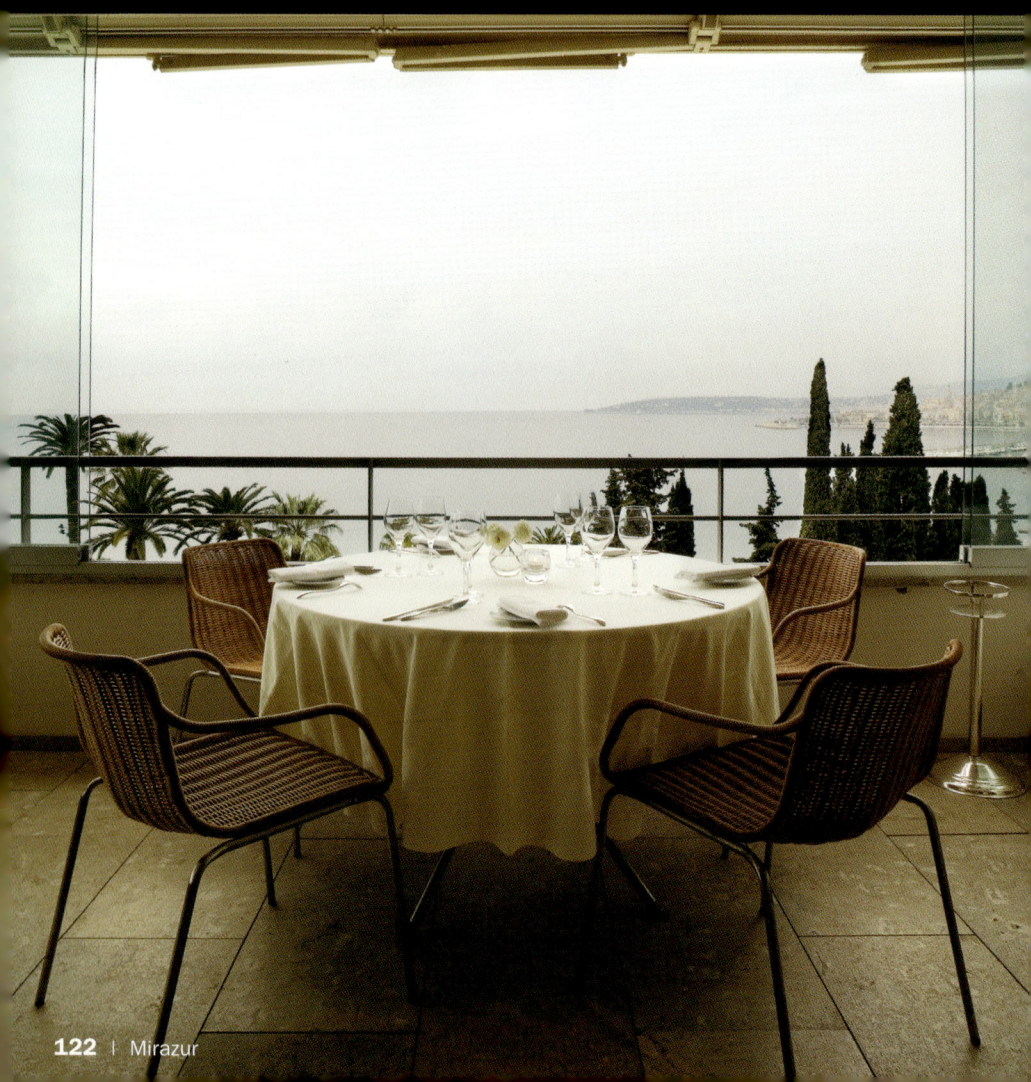

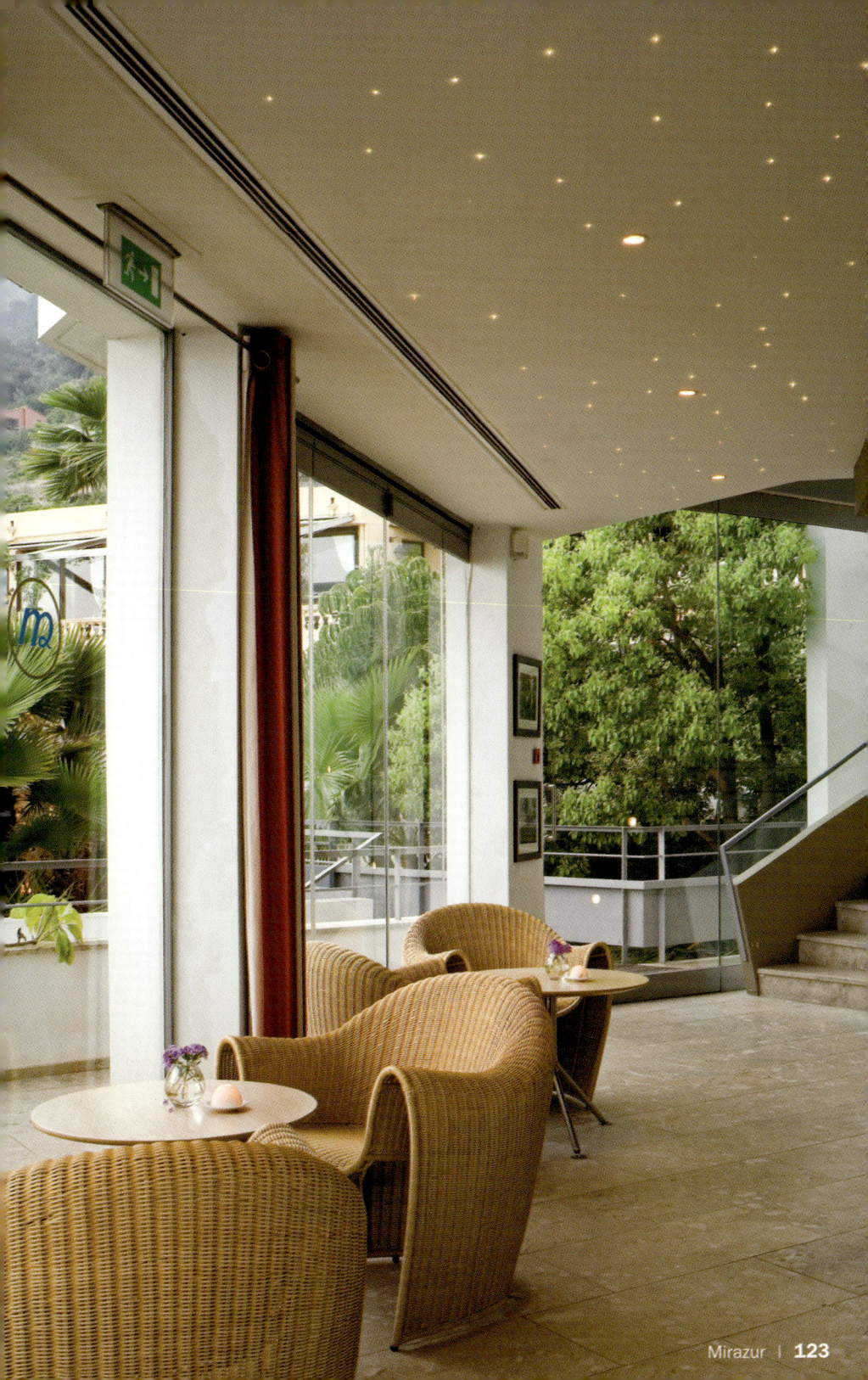

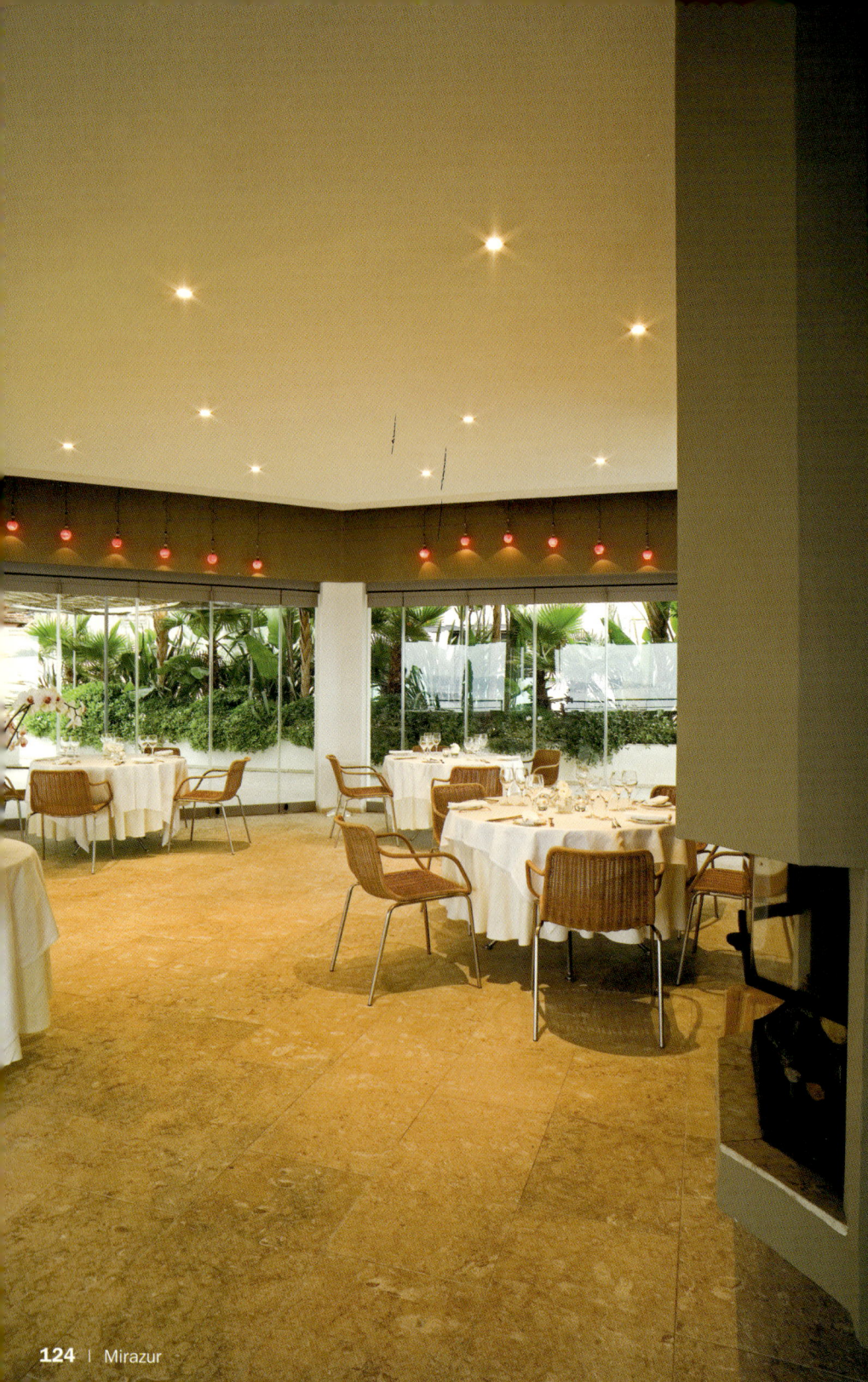

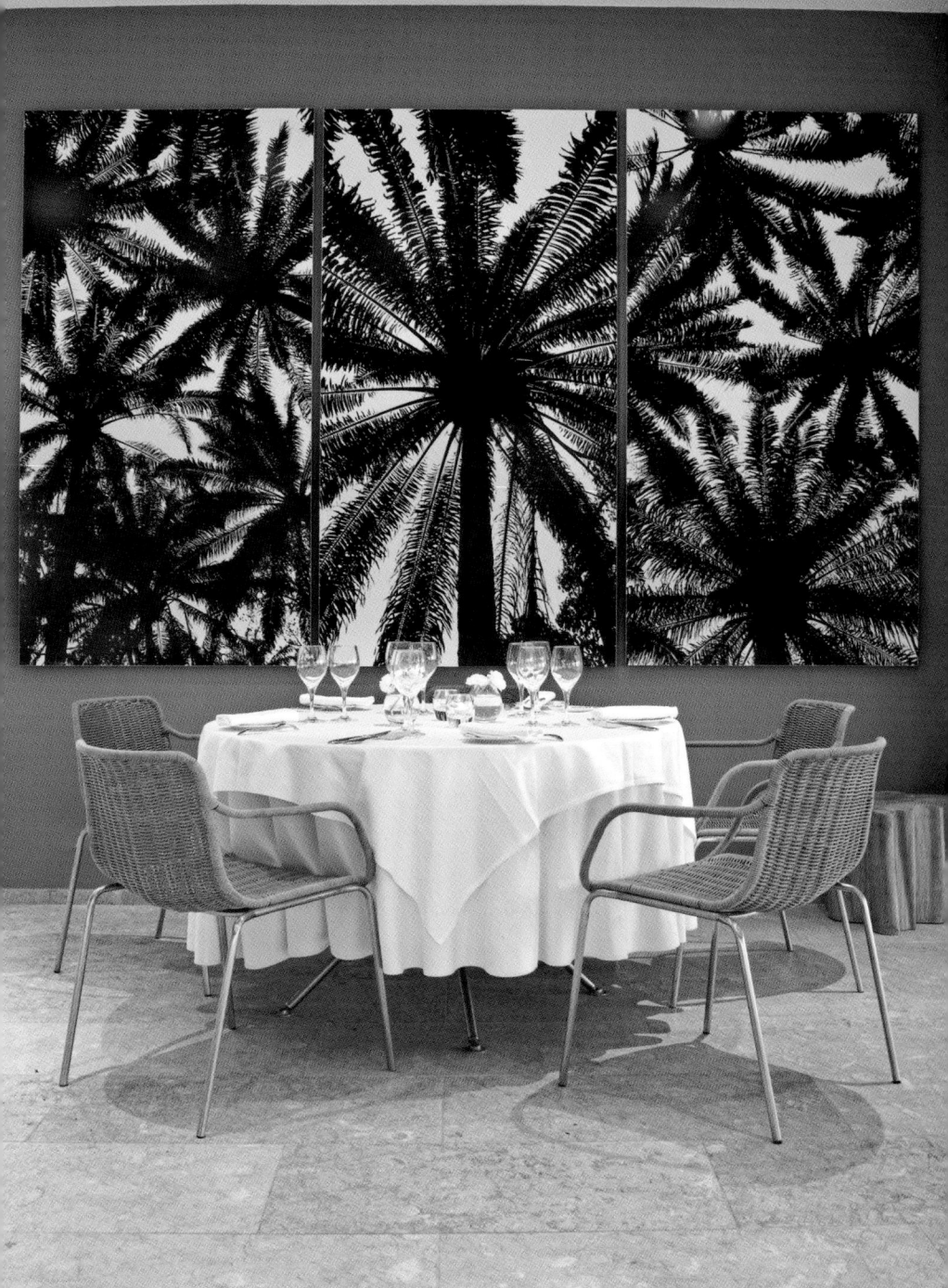

19 Rue Bonaparte | 06300 Nice
Phone: +33 4 92 04 22 09
Opening hours: Every day from 7:30 pm to 1 am, services at 8 pm or 10:30 pm
Special features: Young chef Anthony Riou was trained by some of France's best
chefs and proposes an innovative Mediterranean cuisine

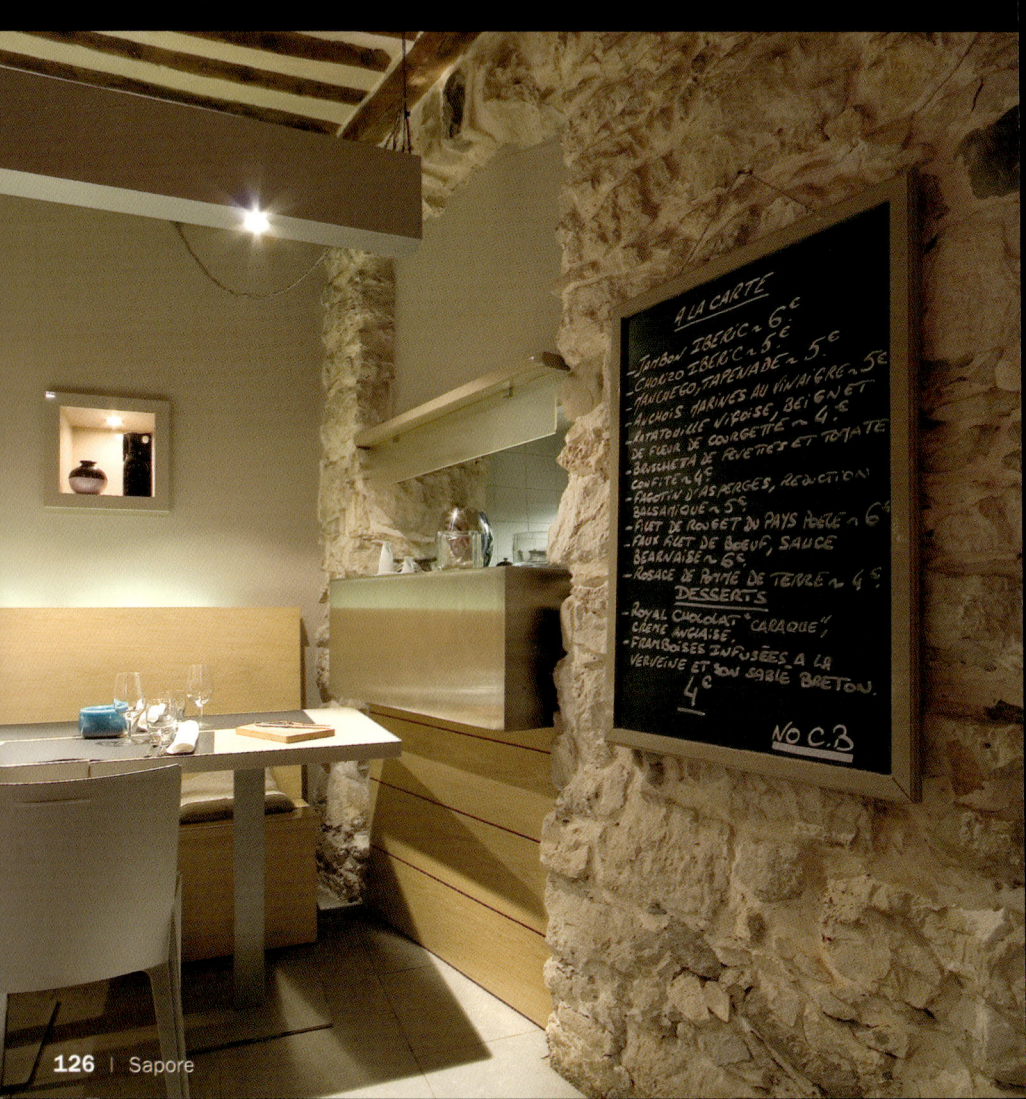

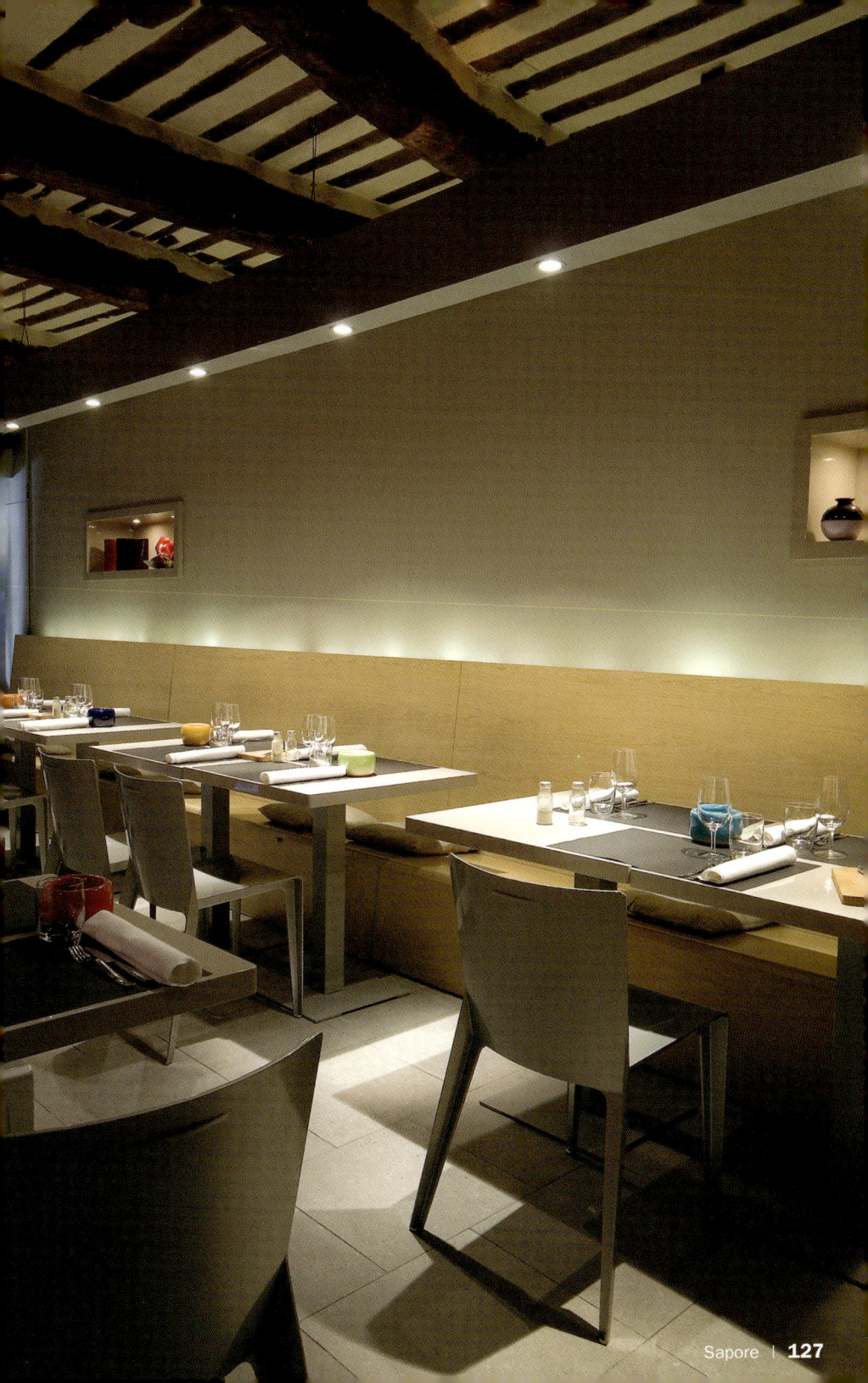

Spoon Byblos

Design: Patrick Jouin

Avenue du Maréchal Foch | 83990 Saint-Tropez
Phone: +33 4 94 56 68 20
www.spoonbyblos.com
Opening hours: From 8 pm to 12:30 pm
Special features: Music and cuisine meet at this Alain Ducasse location, where the sound designers Jean-Yves Leloup and Eric Pajot have created a special musical environment which ranges from slow tempo, Hip Hop to seventies music. The style and intensity of the sound system blend into the rhythm of the evening

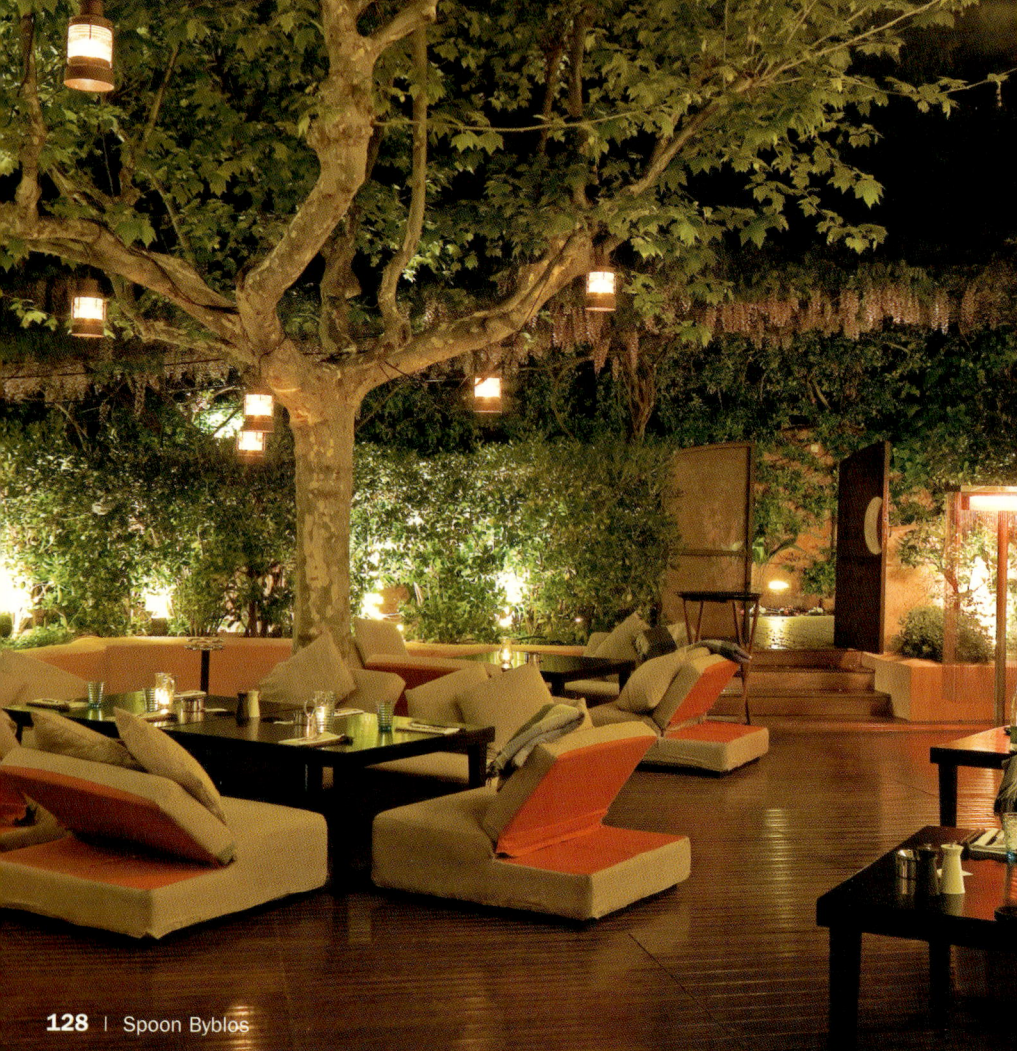

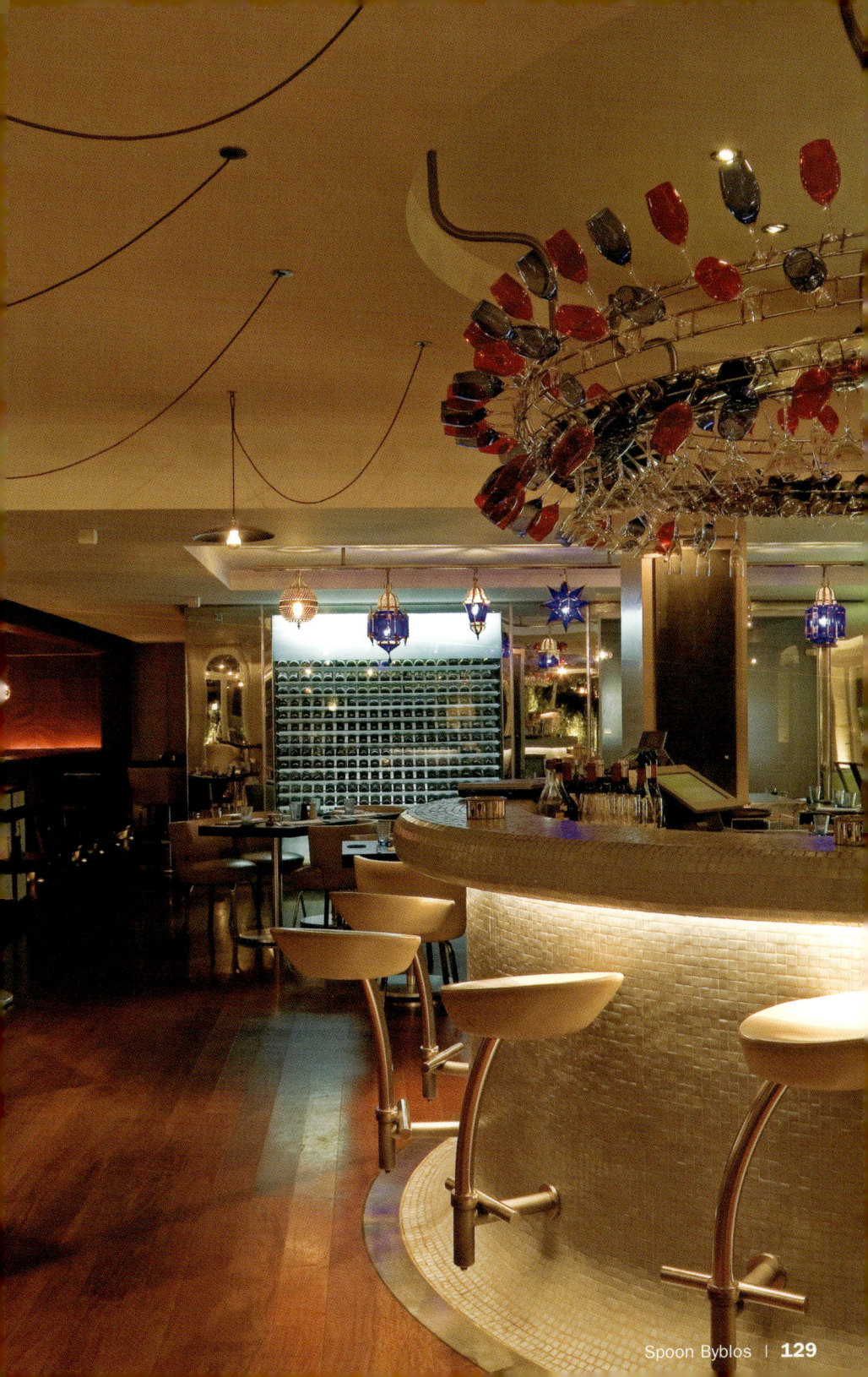

V.I.P. Room

Design: Ora Ito

Résidence du Nouveau Port | 83990 Saint-Tropez
Phone: +33 4 94 97 14 70
www.viproom.fr
Opening hours: Every day from noon to 7 pm
Special features: A touch of New York glamour in Saint-Tropez, and many celebrities
just having fun at Jean Roch's temple of parties

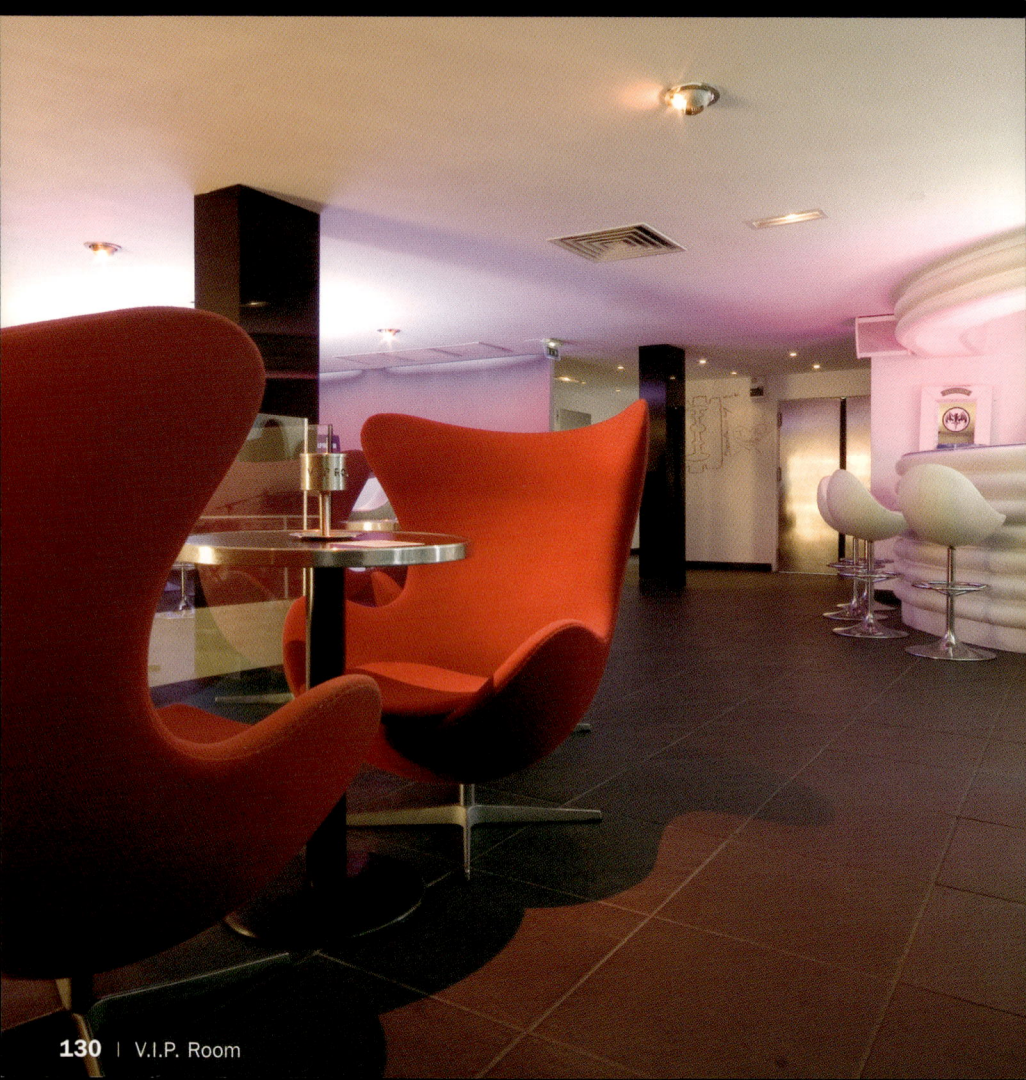

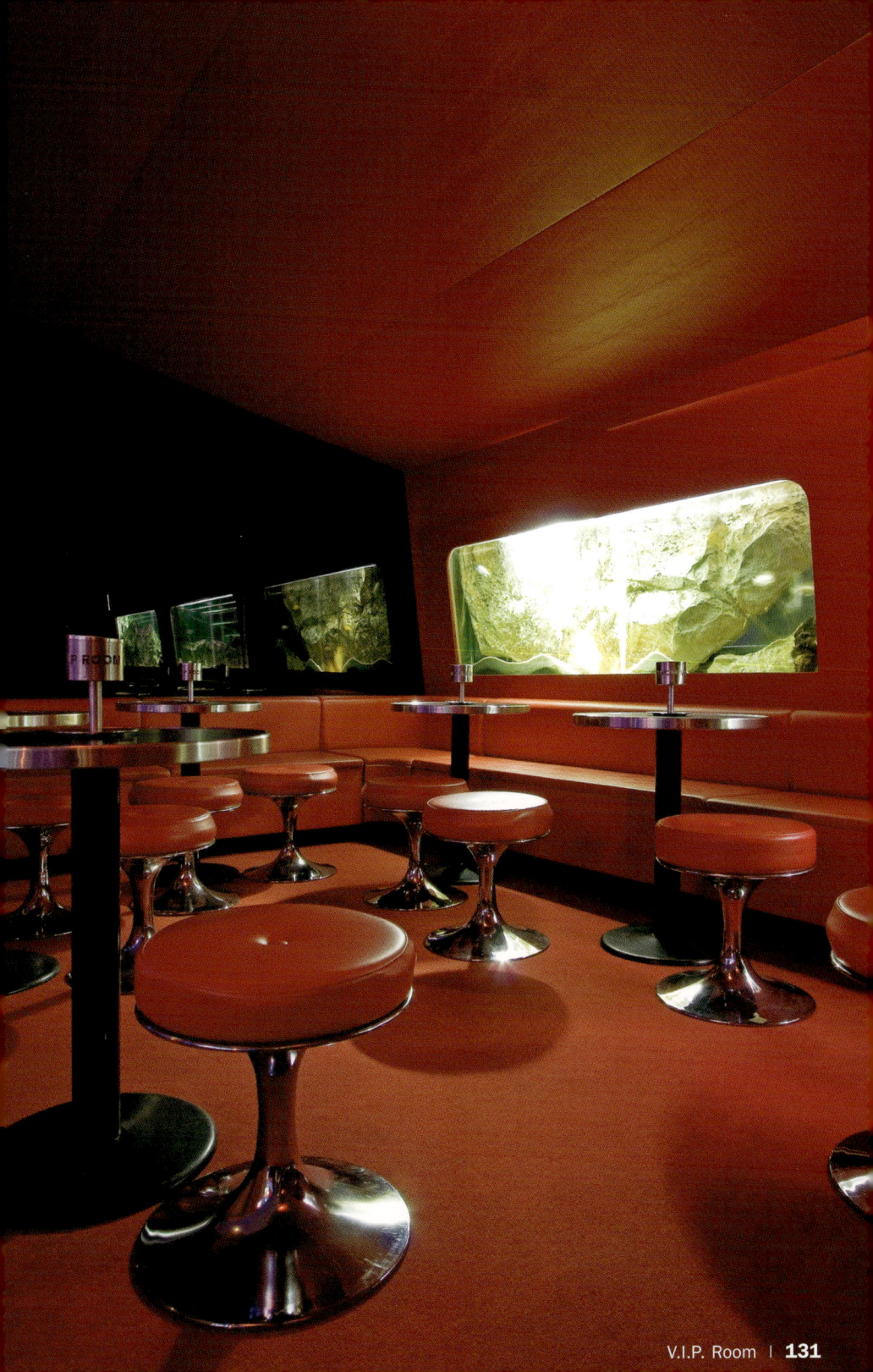

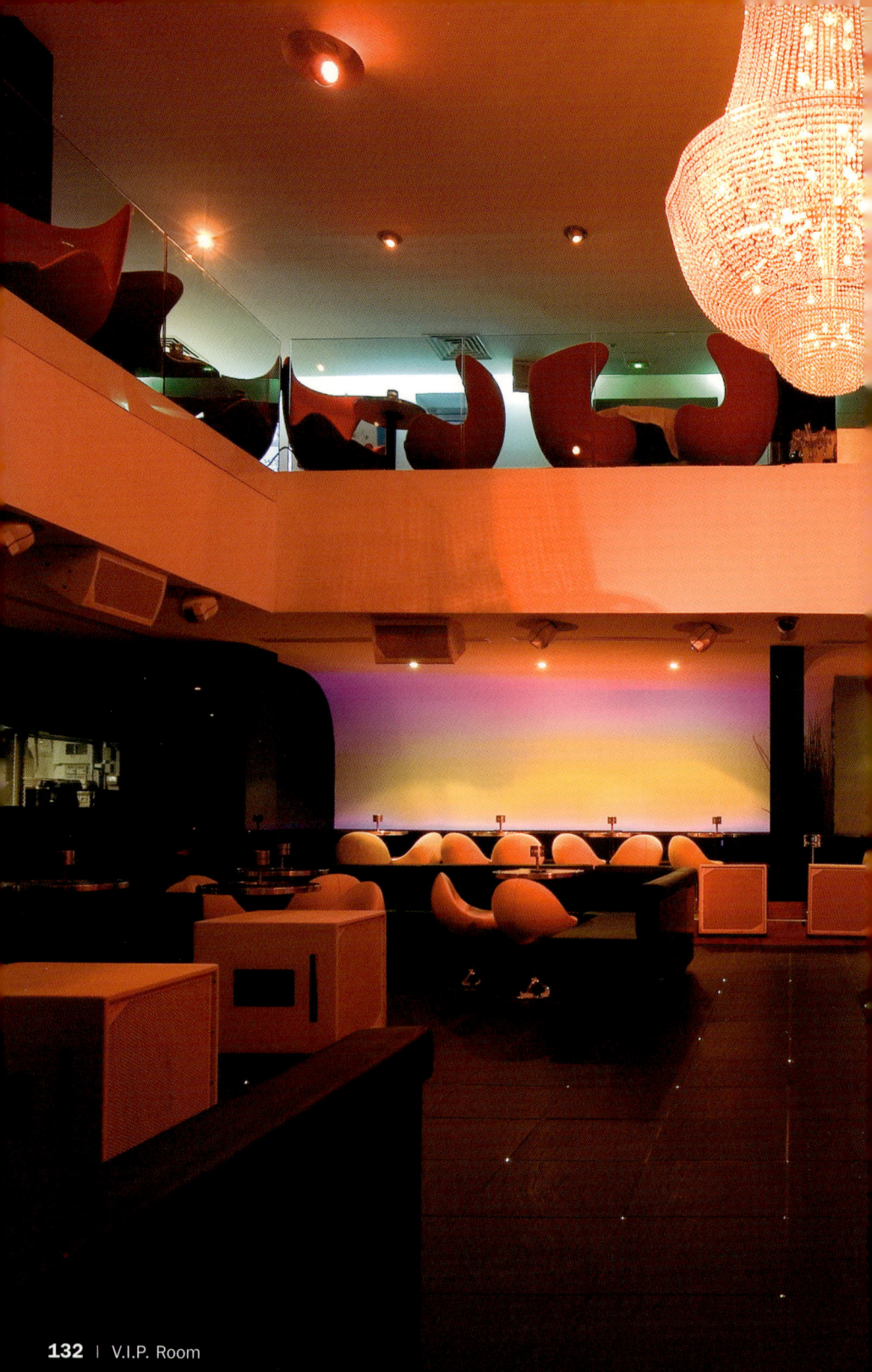

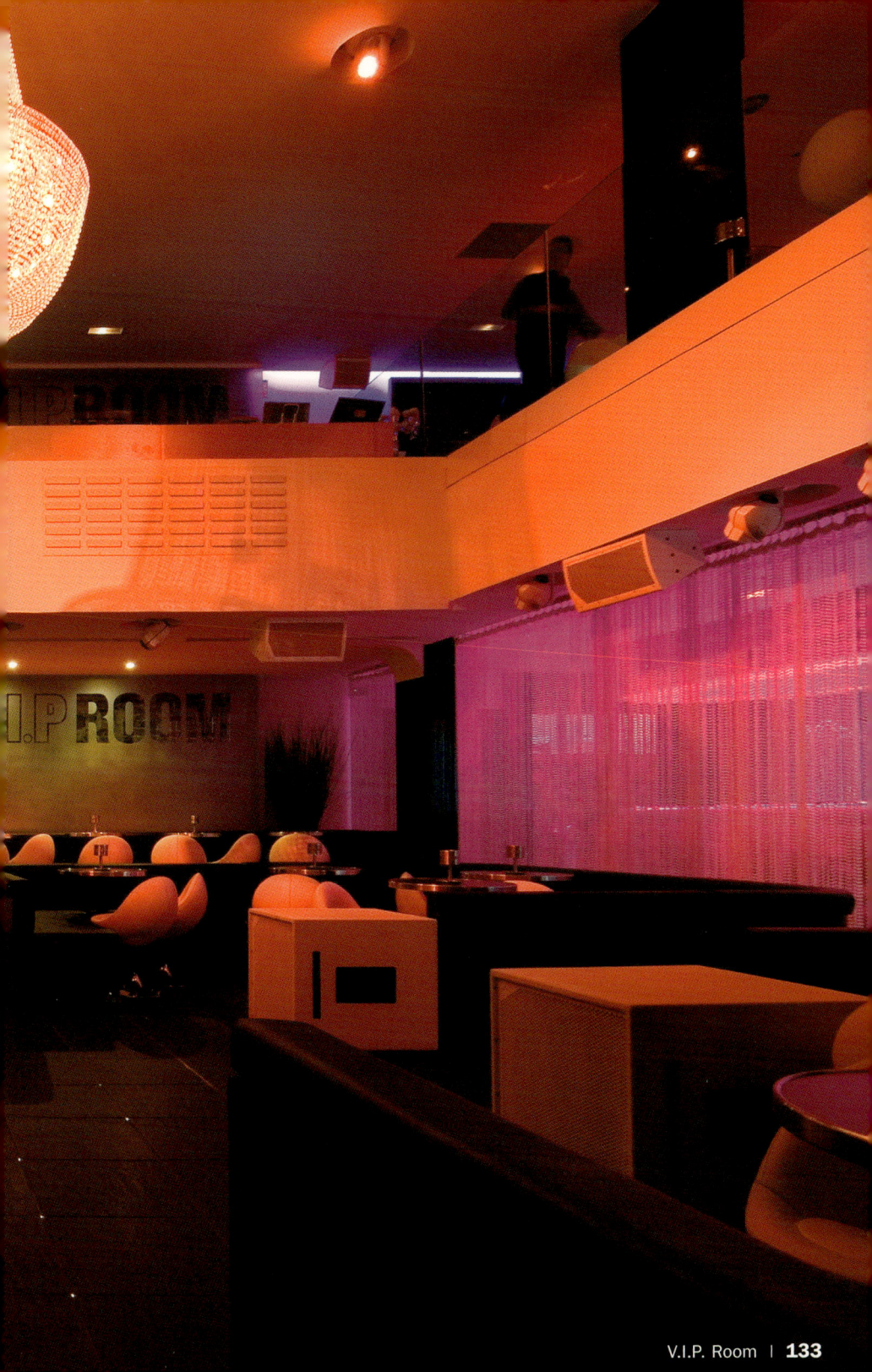

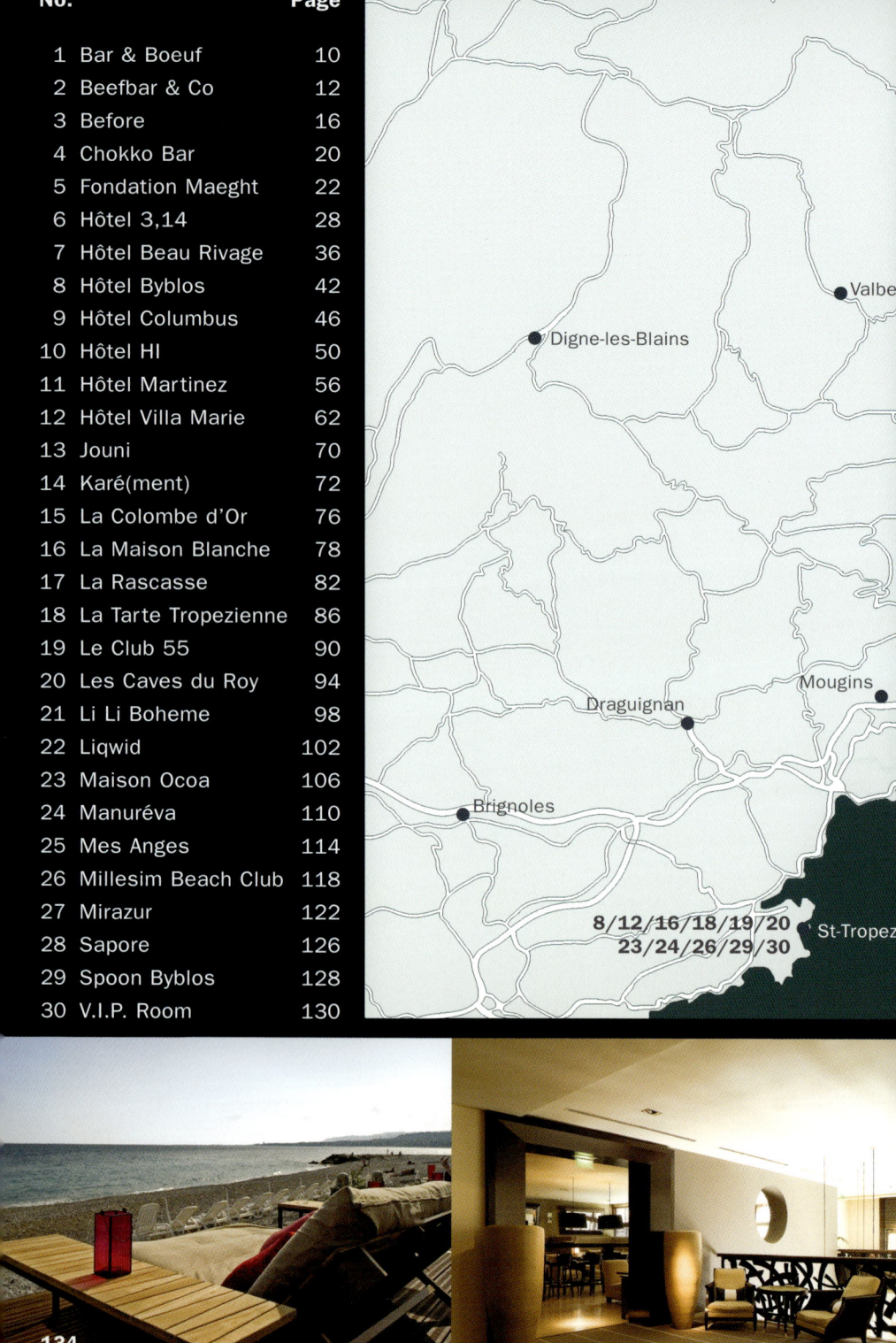

Valbe

Digne-les-Blains

Mougins

Draguignan

Brignoles

8/12/16/18/19/20
23/24/26/29/30

St-Tropez

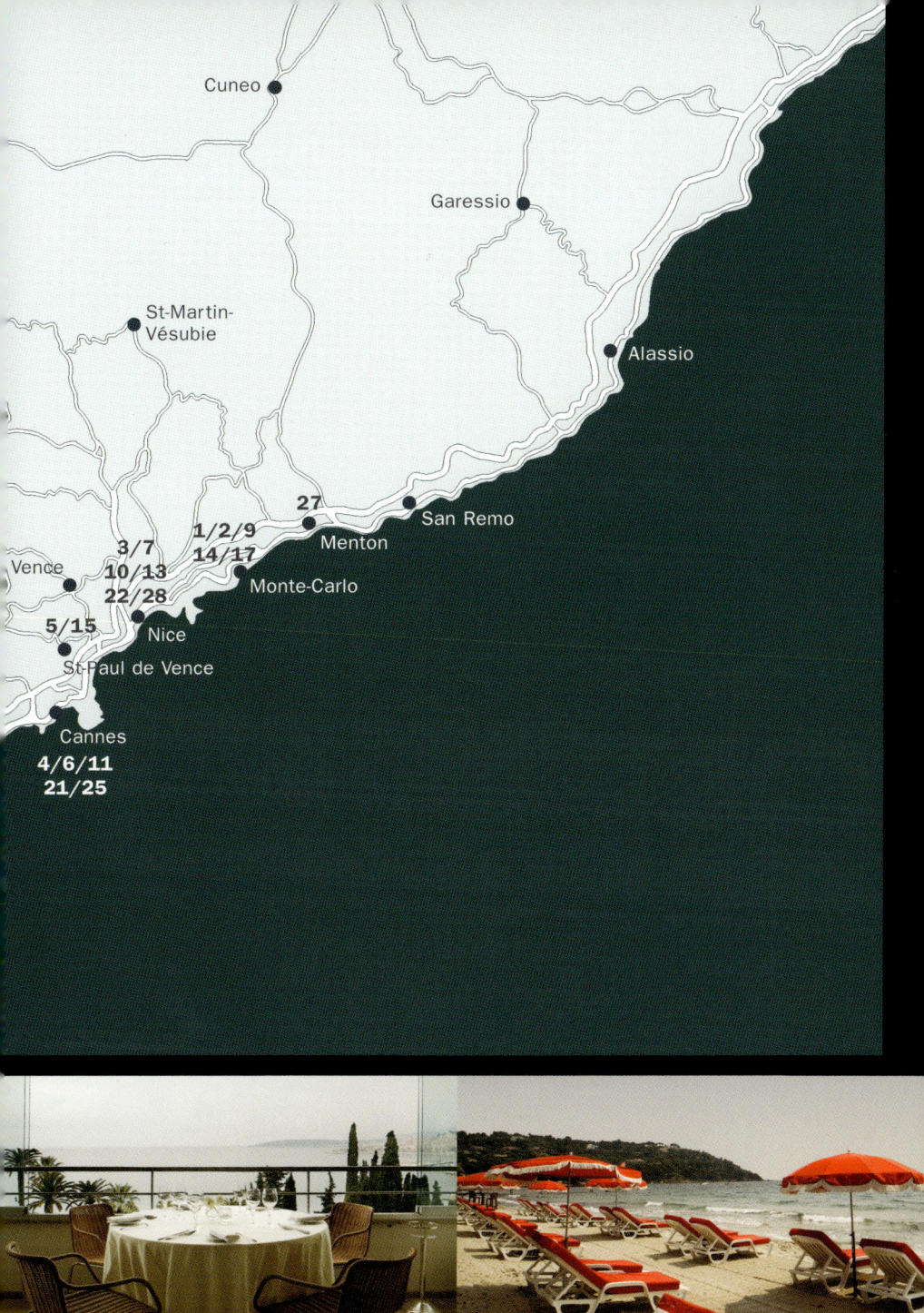

Cuneo

Garessio

St-Martin-
Vésubie

Alassio

27

1/2/9
14/17

3/7
10/13
22/28

San Remo

Menton

Vence

Monte-Carlo

5/15

Nice

St-Paul de Vence

Cannes
4/6/11
21/25

Cool Restaurants

Amsterdam
978-3-8238-4588-1

Barcelona
978-3-8238-4586-7

Berlin
978-3-8238-4585-0

Brussels (*)
978-3-8327-9065-3

Cape Town
978-3-8327-9103-2

Chicago
978-3-8327-9018-9

Cologne
978-3-8327-9117-9

Copenhagen
978-3-8327-9146-9

Côte d'Azur
978-3-8327-9040-0

Dubai
978-3-8327-9149-0

Frankfurt
978-3-8327-9118-6

Hamburg
978-3-8238-4599-7

Hong Kong
978-3-8327-9111-7

Istanbul
978-3-8327-9115-5

Las Vegas
978-3-8327-9116-2

London 2nd edition
978-3-8327-9131-5

Los Angeles
978-3-8238-4589-8

Madrid
978-3-8327-9029-5

Mallorca / Ibiza
978-3-8327-9113-1

Miami
978-3-8327-9066-0

Milan
978-3-8238-4587-4

Moscow
978-3-8327-9147-6

Munich
978-3-8327-9019-6

New York 2nd edition
978-3-8327-9130-8

Paris 2nd edition
978-3-8327-9129-2

Prague
978-3-8327-9068-4

Rome
978-3-8327-0028-8

San Francisco
978-3-8327-9067-7

Shanghai
978-3-8327-9050-9

Sydney
978-3-8327-9027-1

Tokyo
978-3-8238-4590-4

Toscana
978-3-8327-9102-5

Vienna
978-3-8327-9020-2

Zurich
978-3-8327-9069-1

COOL SHOPS

BARCELONA
978-3-8327-9073-8

BERLIN
978-3-8327-9070-7

HAMBURG
978-3-8327-9120-9

HONG KONG
978-3-8327-9121-6

LONDON
978-3-8327-9038-7

LOS ANGELES
978-3-8327-9071-4

MILAN
978-3-8327-9022-6

MUNICH
978-3-8327-9072-1

NEW YORK
978-3-8327-9021-9

PARIS
978-3-8327-9037-0

TOKYO
978-3-8327-9122-3

COOL SPOTS

CÔTE D'AZUR
978-3-8327-9154-4

LAS VEGAS
978-3-8327-9152-0

MALLORCA / IBIZA
978-3-8327-9123-0

MIAMI / SOUTH BEACH
978-3-8327-9153-7

**To be published in the
same series:**
Salzburg / Kitzbühel

Size: 14 x 21.5 cm
5 1/2 x 8 1/2 in.
136 pp, Flexicover
c. 130 color photographs
Text in English, German, French,
Spanish, Italian or (*) Dutch

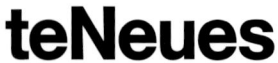